EARLY CHILDHOOD EDUCATION SERIES

Leslie R. Williams, Editor Millie Almy, Senior Advisor

ADVISORY BOARD: Barbara T. Bowman, Harriet K. Cuffaro, Stephanie Feeney, Doris Pronin Fromberg, Celia Genishi, Stacie G. Goffin, Dominic F. Gullo, Alice Sterling Honig, Elizabeth Jones, Gwen Morgan, David Weikart

(Continued)

MAJOR TRENDS AND ISSUES IN EARLY CHILDHOOD EDUCATION
Challenges, Controversies, and Insights

JOAN P. ISENBERG
MARY RENCK JALONGO
EDITORS

Foreword by Sue Bredekamp

Teachers College, Columbia University
New York and London

Published by Teachers College Press, 1234 Amsterdam Avenue, New York, NY 10027

Library of Congress Cataloging-in-Publication Data

Major trends and issues in early childhood education : challenges,
  controversies, and insights / Joan P. Isenberg, Mary Renck Jalongo,
  editors ; foreward by Sue Bredekamp.
     p. cm.—(Early childhood education series)
  Includes bibliographical references and index.
  ISBN 0-8077-3623-6 (cloth).—ISBN 0-8077-3622-8 (paper)
  1. Early childhood education—United States. 2. Child
development—United States. 3. Curriculum planning—United States.
4. Early childhood educators—Training of—United States.
I. Isenberg, Joan P., 1941–   . II. Jalongo, Mary Renck.
III. Series.
LB1139.25.M353 1997
372.21'0973—dc21   96-50440

ISBN 0-8077-3622-8 (paper)
ISBN 0-8077-3623-6 (cloth)

Printed on acid-free paper

Manufactured in the United States of America

04 03 02 01 00 99 98 97   8 7 6 5 4 3 2 1

For all the early childhood educators who have dedicated their professional lives to the care and education of the very young.

J.P.I.

M.R.J.*

Contents

Foreword

This book is an important part of what has become a long tradition in the field of early childhood education—the thoughtful and critical examination of issues and controversies surrounding our practices, policies, and professional development. In my work at National Association for the Education of Young Children (NAEYC) over the last 15 years, I have had the unique opportunity to observe and participate in the ongoing discussions about many of these issues at the national level, especially in the areas of developmentally appropriate practice, curriculum and assessment, and teacher preparation and development. Although much of this work remains controversial, what has been exhilarating for me as a professional has been the opportunity to engage in dialogue (sometimes heated, always challenging) about the most fundamental concerns facing those who work with young children today. Such dialogue with individuals from all the diverse perspectives represented in our field has given me the most wonderful opportunity for an early childhood professional—to continually learn more about children and teaching. What excites me about this book is that it offers those opportunities to new generations of professional leaders who will carry on the dialogues in the future.

Three important themes provide the conceptual organizers for this volume: context, continuity, and controversy. Just as development and learning occur in and are influenced by social and cultural contexts, so too do all the major questions confronting our field demand examination in relation to various contextual factors. The first section of this book explores these contextual issues in depth, especially the political and cultural contexts, while every chapter in the book also contextualizes the issues for the reader. Contextual influences are always present, but usually implicit. However, any thoughtful analysis of critical issues must explicate the context within which beliefs, values, or even specific practices are deemed appropriate.

Of course, the "burning" issues of our day are not really new. Some of these debates—such as what and how to teach very young children— began in the last century and continue today in much the same form as they did when the Committee of Nineteen of the International Kindergarten Union was forced to issue three reports because it could not come to consensus on the kindergarten curriculum in the early 1900s. Too often, however, early childhood educators are ahistorical and present ideas or concepts as though they are being discovered for the first time. For example, Polly Greenberg, editor of *Young Children,* reports that she rarely reviews a submitted journal article that even acknowledges the historical roots of the topic, much less explores them in any depth. This book attempts to correct this often repeated error by focusing on the theme of continuity in examining each issue.

Finally, as they should, the authors of this book confront the controversies that continue to challenge our field. Because our work is so underfunded and undervalued, early childhood educators sometimes fear that if we do not present a united front about what is good for children, we will lose the little public support that we have been able to obtain. We have worked hard to promote the importance of high-quality care and education for young children and to set some standards to guide our professional practice. At times, we fear that any internal disagreement, especially if it becomes too public, will undermine our meager achievements. And yet, professions have multiple responsibilities; they must be the standard-setters for their own members while, at the same time, they must continually question their own practices and beliefs so as to ensure that the knowledge base continues to grow and develop. Just as young children must experience some disequilibrium to learn more complex cognitive concepts, so too early childhood professionals' understanding can be increased through exploration of disagreements or differences of opinions within the field. Such open discussion of controversy serves the important function of helping professionals socially construct solutions to problems or alternatives for ineffective practices or policies.

Understanding the contexts, continuities, and controversies of early childhood education is a particularly challenging task because of the diversity of our field. The number and types of settings in which early childhood educators work (far beyond the traditional public school kindergarten), the range and levels of professional preparation, and the crises of low salaries and high turnover make all the issues more complex. But future leaders of early childhood education must recognize that we are one profession and be aware of the ways in which the issues connect with and influence each other. Perhaps the most important aspect of continuity is between and among the many issues dissected in this book; making those connections is partially the responsibility of the reader.

Recently, NAEYC developed a recruitment videotape as part of the *Career Encounters* series broadcast on cable and public television. The producers have a long history of producing such programs for career fields as diverse as podiatry, psychiatry, and engineering. To develop the script, they surveyed hundreds of early childhood educators for their views about their jobs. They were struck by something very different in the way early childhood educators describe their work compared with people in other careers. While all survey respondents cited the challenges of inadequate salaries and low status, all the respondents also expressed optimism about their chosen field. The potentials of young children tend to make early childhood educators view their work as vitally important and themselves as capable of making a difference. One hopes that current and future leaders of the early childhood profession who read this book will also share that optimism about the future of our profession. The dialogue that will result as readers explore the issues and controversies of the past, present, and future will surely serve to make the world better for young children and families.

> —Sue Bredekamp
> Director of Professional Development
> National Association for the Education of Young Children

Acknowledgments

We would like to acknowledge the many people who worked on this book to fill a critical need in the field. Thanks to all of the authors for their insightful chapters and for working under very tight time constraints. Our appreciation also goes to Sue Bredekamp, Director of Professional Development for NAEYC, who recognized the timeliness of this collection and whose foreword offers a powerful statement about our profession and shared vision for the future of the field. Without the skillful guidance of Susan Liddicoat of Teachers College Press, who supported our idea on the pressing changes in the field, *Major Trends and Issues in Early Childhood Education: Challenges, Controversies, and Insights* would not have become a reality. We wish to acknowledge the keen insights of the Early Childhood Series Editor, Leslie Williams, as she reflected on what our authors had written and our ways of framing their ideas. Our production editor, Lori Tate, provided detailed and consistent editing. We also want to thank our graduate students, who struggled long and hard with us over these issues in our graduate classes, and the children, families, and teachers with whom we have worked over the years. It is those people who have enabled us to gain a broad perspective on these issues and who keep us grounded in the realities of our daily practice.

Because writing a book places such heavy demands on many people, we would like to thank our families, friends, and colleagues for their unfailing support as we conceived, developed, and completed this book. To them, we extend our heartfelt appreciation. And to the teachers, children, and families living and learning in contemporary society, we hope that *Major Trends and Issues in Early Childhood Education: Challenges, Controversies, and Insights* plays a small but significant role in providing more optimal learning environments for America's children.

Introduction

What enables an early childhood educator to attain the highest standards of practice as a caregiver, classroom teacher, or teacher educator? The National Association for the Education of Young Children's (1994) published standards for advanced programs identified a constellation of traits. Among the abilities noted were such things as understanding the sociocultural, historical, and political forces that influence early childhood, critically examining alternative perspectives on issues in the field, applying theoretical and research knowledge to practice, and engaging in reflective inquiry that leads to deeper professional understandings of the early childhood educator's role and code of ethics.

The advanced study of early childhood education ordinarily includes experiences and courses that are designed to offer a broad perspective on the field. Usually, these courses and seminars include the words *issues* or *trends* in their titles. In the past, undertaking this formal study of the field often has been approached as a survey, a quick overview that was admittedly superficial and sometimes overwhelming for the early childhood educator due to the complex nature of our profession. The implicit assumption of this approach is what Mary Belenky and her colleagues (1986) would refer to as "received knowing," the view that there are experts who "own" the knowledge and graciously bestow it upon others.

When we conceived of this book, we wanted to take a different stance on early childhood trends and issues, one that would welcome and embrace practitioners from diverse early childhood settings. We knew that while the vast majority of our readers would be able, quite literally, to put a face on each trend and issue by reflecting on their immediate or previous experiences with young children, some readers would be new to the field and need specific examples to better understand the underlying principles. Our book, we agreed, was intended to support both relative newcomers to advanced study of early childhood education and more seasoned scholars in examining key dimensions of the field from multiple, collected perspectives. Additionally, we wanted our diverse readership to

1

recognize that their individual enlightenment and collective power as early childhood educators was predicated not merely on how much information they could absorb, but on their efforts to arrive at personally constructed meaning and participate in thoughtful lines of inquiry that would offer keen insights into their multifaceted roles. It was anticipated that our readers' ideas, experiences, theoretical orientations, and ethical principles would interact with those of their colleagues, and that our book might play a role in stimulating thinking as readers engaged in "thinking along" with our authors and critically evaluating what each one of them had to say. Fostering this transactional process is the essential purpose of our work on this book.

This volume has no pretensions about being an exhaustive review of the field even though it is replete with useful information. Rather, we asked our authors to draw on their experiences, to communicate their deeply felt commitment, and by so doing to enfranchise our readers in the larger community of early childhood professionals. We wanted to raise our readers' level of awareness that, taken as a field, early childhood education has highly revered traditions, is profoundly significant for society at large, poses perpetually challenging situations, and is undergoing a period of dynamic growth and change. We also wanted to celebrate the fact that, as a profession, we can lay claim to a certain clarity of focus because most early childhood educators are firmly grounded in the concept of the "whole child"—education that affirms and balances the child's physical, social, emotional, cognitive, and aesthetic needs in learning experiences. As a result, early childhood educators have, generally speaking, resisted pressure to encourage them to become one-dimensional, to consider, for example, only basic skills or scores on tests. It is interesting to see other fields suddenly awaken to something that outstanding early childhood professionals have always emphasized—a learner-centered orientation that takes children's developmental needs and uniquenesses as individuals into account. We hear educators from other areas of specialization advocate such things as whole language, hands-on science, math manipulatives, or middle schools founded on developmental characteristics, and we cannot help feeling some pride that such insights about the dynamic qualities of the learning process have been a part of our profession and early childhood programs for decades. This is not to suggest, however, that we can as a profession afford to maintain the status quo. As this volume will suggest, there is always much more that can and should be done to ensure that every young child is afforded the best possible educational opportunities, opportunities that will nurture his or her capacity to participate in a democratic society.

GOALS FOR THE BOOK

To further clarify and elaborate on our goals for this book, we turn to the metaphor of a lens. There are lenses that offer a sharper focus, lenses that expand our range of vision, and lenses that magnify details. Metaphorically speaking, the authors represented in this volume supply such lenses on the field of early childhood education by sharing the depth and breadth of their professional perspectives on various aspects of early childhood education as well as striving to give an overall "state of the art" in their particular areas of specialization. As editors, we are confident that these leaders in the field are sufficiently knowledgeable and insightful to expand and enlarge the vision of our readership. Like a young child on a sunshine-bright day who is hoisted onto an adult's shoulders to gain a better look at things and outfitted with small plastic sunglasses to reduce the glare, *Major Trends and Issues in Early Childhood Education: Challenges, Controversies, and Insights* is designed to offer our readers the multiple vantage points and clarity of vision represented by our authors. The substance of this volume is not intended to be prescriptive. Rather, our overarching goal was to invite a diverse group of early childhood educators into the ongoing conversation about what we can do as a profession to meet the needs of all young children. If our book has succeeded in attaining the goals we originally set for it, then it will stimulate further interest, encourage readers to try out new lenses, and serve as an impetus to delve deeper into those aspects of the field that have the greatest personal and professional significance for each reader.

FRAMEWORK FOR THE BOOK

In order to provide a framework for this volume, we return to the key words in the book's title. Each author has identified *trends:* the general direction, course, or tendency of events, data, or ideas. If we return to the metaphor of the lens, trends can be likened to a wide-angle lens, for they give a simultaneous sense of where we have been, where we are now, and where we may be headed in the future. As part of reviewing these directions in the field, our authors typically find themselves revisiting the long-standing traditions within the field and referring to our historical roots as a profession. The trends in early childhood education influence future policies and practices, thereby setting directions for the way we live, learn, teach, and work. When considered in this way, trends represent the social, philosophical, political, technological, and economic realities of the new millennium.

Additionally, each author has addressed key *issues:* significant points and matters of consequence that are worthy of discussion and resolution. As a lens, issues are comparable to a powerful set of binoculars, for although there are many possible things that we can look at, binoculars are used primarily for the purpose of focusing on something that rivets our attention and merits more careful scrutiny. Issues often provide the forum for public debate that has profound significance for policies, funding, and educational outcomes affecting young children, their families, and their teachers.

Because there are different perspectives on trends and issues, *challenges* and *controversies* emerge. By a challenge, we mean a difficult and complex task that taxes the resources and problem-solving abilities of those who hope to accomplish a worthwhile goal that serves the best interests of children and families. Challenges are comparable to the view through a kaleidoscope—there are such intricate and rapidly shifting patterns that it is exceedingly difficult to discern exactly what has happened even though it is right before our eyes. Ways of counteracting neglect and violence in children's lives are good examples of challenges. These things are pervasive in society, yet they are difficult to fully comprehend and resistant to our best problem-solving strategies. Each author in this volume explicitly states many of the challenges before us as a profession in the implications section of the chapter.

When professionals in the field are pulled in different directions, *controversies* inevitably emerge. By a controversy, we mean an area of disagreement that occurs between groups who hold opposing viewpoints. When we return to the analogy of the lens, we see that controversies are like distributing a professional camera operator's assortment of lenses to various groups and asking them to film the same reality. Some will be zooming in on small details while others will pan the entire scene; some will see a smaller picture within a larger one, others will use various filters that soften harsh lines or cast things in a completely different light. When these individuals compare what they see, they may become convinced that the perceptions held by others are wrong. Seeing the same reality in a decidedly different way leads to comparable disputes within the field of early childhood education and often leads to divisiveness among various factions. Such controversies have undeniable implications for children, families, and teachers of young children as they work to achieve some shared vision of who we are as a profession, where we are headed, and why.

As early childhood educators examine trends, explore issues, meet challenges, and reflect on controversies, the best possible outcome would be the final key word of our title: *insight*. By insight we mean a brilliant flash of understanding, an "aha!" that illuminates our thinking and enables us to see, in the full sense of that word, more clearly. This capacity to discern the true nature of a situation enables practicing educators to figure out new and better ways of how best to teach young children in rapidly changing times.

We suggest that our readers think about those five key words—trends, issues, challenges, controversies, and insights—as a superstructure that encompasses all of the work herein and unifies the entire volume. Although each author's voice is unique and each chapter is distinctive, readers will be able to recognize that the specific content of every chapter has been built on some combination of these five elements. Several specific questions that the authors used to "frame" their chapters can also be used by readers to guide their inquiry into other areas of the early childhood education field. Our framework for the chapter readings is in Table 1 on page 6.

PHILOSOPHICAL STANCE OF THE BOOK

Three themes run across the chapters in this volume. First of all, the authors represented here are scholar-practitioners. These are the voices of professionals who know early childhood education "from the inside out," individuals who are intimately acquainted with the realities of caring for and educating the very young. We hope that some aspects of the authors' collective commitment to educational equity, the clarity of their language, and their struggle to translate theory and research into practice will resonate within each one of our readers. Although some readers may see this scholar-practitioner stance as a limitation, we consider the fact that our authors speak clearly and directly to practitioners to be an important strength of this work.

Second, because our authors know young children and understand child development, they hold all young learners in high esteem and recognize that every child plays an active role in her or his own learning. Thus, in the Piagetian sense of the word, the authors for this volume are constructivists who underscore the importance of child-centered learning and who regard learning as a complex set of interactions instead of an easily quantifiable product. Out of their commitment to the very young, our authors offer their best thinking about how to design practices, policies, and programs that actualize the goal of the Children's Defense Fund (1995) to "leave no child behind."

TABLE 1. Questioning Framework for Early Childhood Trends & Issues.

Introduction to the trends and issues
- Why are these trends significant?
- Why are these issues of concern?

Exploration of the trends and issues
- What are the different trends and key struggles associated with this challenge or controversy?
- Why does this aspect of early childhood education generate discussion, debate, and controversy?
- How realistic are the proposed solutions?

Theoretical/historical social context
- How is this contemporary problem rooted in social/historical traditions?
- How do these traditions influence its current interpretations?

Exploration of the trends and issues
- How do these trends and issues affect the individual early childhood practitioner? The profession as a whole?
- How do these trends and issues affect children and families?
- What do these trends and issues mean for the future of teaching and learning?
- What other questions does this controversial issue generate?
- What obstacles will we have to overcome in the future?
- What are the consequences of these trends, issues, challenges, and controversies for you, the reader, in your current professional role and setting?

Third, and finally, our authors share an appreciation for the Vygot-skian notion that learning is fundamentally social in nature, that all of us—children, families, caregivers, classroom teachers, and teacher educators—learn from one another. This statement might seem obvious until our readers consider the full meaning of that assertion. Everyone knows that children learn from their teachers, but it literally turns education on its head to consider the other direction—the many ways that teachers can and must learn from children and families. Likewise, most people assume that scholars have something of value to share with practitioners, but it is a fairly recent development for faculty to study alongside practitioners as equal partners. Collectively speaking, our authors stress the importance of human relationships as well as the social contexts in which learning occurs and, in light of that recognition, all the authors call in their unique voices for meaningful collaboration, establishing a sense of community, promoting educational equity, and reforming early childhood education in ways that put children's needs first. Furthermore, each author "lets readers in" on his or her efforts to arrive at shared meaning and common purposes about the field while simultaneously acknowledging that other meanings and purposes exist (Wein, 1995). We identify these theoretical underpinnings at the outset so that readers can determine for themselves how much of their own thinking is attributable to these influences and decide for themselves which of these lenses on the field are worth using or are sufficiently powerful to warrant modifying their customary point of view.

OVERVIEW OF THE CONTENTS

This book is divided into three parts, each with its own brief introduction to the inclusive chapters. The three questions that undergird inquiry for their respective parts of the book are

- Part I: What forces have influenced and shaped early childhood education and the settings and contexts in which it occurs?
- Part II: What are the best ways of optimizing every young child's growth, development, and learning?
- Part III: How can practitioners in the field of early childhood education be best prepared to meet challenges both now and in the future?

Part I contains four chapters and deals with the social, political, and historical trends and issues affecting the field of early childhood today. Chapters 1–4 provide the foundation for the rest of the book by chronicling the connection between the field of early childhood education and the major social and political issues, child development challenges, diversity imperatives, and collaboration with families.

In Part II, the authors explore curricular trends and issues affecting practice. Chapters 5–8 illuminate the curricular struggles with developmentally appropriate practice, technology use with young children, performance assessment, and play-based curriculum. These chapters raise the issues, delineate the challenges, and make strong statements about the curricular directions needed for 21st-century teaching and learning.

Part III focuses on the challenges affecting early childhood teacher preparation and professional development. Chapters 9–11 address the trends and issues of inclusive education, international perspectives on early childhood programs, and early childhood caregivers' and teachers' professional development. The volume concludes with issues of professionalism within the field and the factors that have contributed to its continuing low status in the public's eye.

Throughout these eleven chapters, the authors raise more questions than they answer and challenge readers to revisit our past traditions as we seek solutions to today's and tomorrow's dilemmas. The tough questions raised and the difficult challenges presented provide a significant forum for powerful discussions that are foundational to changing practice.

Everyone associated with this project has worked to present a well-reasoned and carefully documented perspective on some of the major trends and significant issues facing the field of early childhood education. Yet we know that in a book such as this, we risk omitting an issue that some of our readers may think important, and if this is the case, we urge readers to make these issues part of their inquiry into the field. As co-editors, as co-authors, and as early childhood educators, it is our fervent hope that this work will encourage practitioners and teacher educators to enter into the dialogue in knowledgeable, skillful, and insightful ways as we work together in a profession that dedicates itself to the care and education of the very young.

REFERENCES

Belenky, M. F., Clinchy, B. M., Goldberger, N. R., & Tarule, J. M. (1986). *Women's ways of knowing: The development of self, voice, and mind.* New York: Basic Books.

Children's Defense Fund. (1995). *The state of the child: 1995.* Washington, DC: Author.

National Association for the Education of Young Children. (1994). *Guidelines for preparation of early childhood professionals: Associate, baccalaureate, and advanced levels.* Washington, DC: Author.

Wein, C. A. (1995). *Developmentally appropriate practice in "real life": Stories of teachers' practical knowledge.* New York: Teachers College Press.

Social, Political, and Historical Trends and Issues Affecting Young Children

We begin Part I with a case that illustrates how social, political, and historical forces interact and exert an influence on young children's lives.

In contrast to several of his classmates, Jason cried, not at the beginning of kindergarten and the start of the school day, but in October at the end of the school day. His teacher was sympathetic at first but eventually lost patience and complained that Jason's crying was "driving her crazy." In desperation, she resorted to the behavioristic approach recommended by a more experienced teacher, convinced that if she ignored the crying it would eventually disappear. Clues to the puzzling pattern of Jason's behavior began to emerge after a concerned neighbor reported the child's situation to Children and Youth Services. Jason's mother had abandoned the family during the summer, and his father, who had a demanding job and a long commute, suddenly had sole responsibility for the boy. Monday through Friday, 5-year-old Jason was getting off of the school bus, unlocking the front door, and staying home alone until his father arrived around 7:00 P.M. When the social worker spoke with Jason, the kindergartner confided that he had been frightened by a television commercial and was terrified to stay by himself when it was dark outside. Reflecting on Jason's situation illustrates that growth and learning cannot be separated from the social, political, and historical contexts in which education occurs.

Some of the social ramifications of Jason's experiences include his difficult family situation, his relationship with teacher and peers, the influence of the media, and the role of social services. Additionally, there is a political side to Jason's situation. Some political questions to consider include: Why has the United States lagged behind other nations in providing a federally supported system of child care that would provide the high-quality after-school programming this child and family so desperately need? Why did the teacher defer so readily to the recommendation of another teacher, and why did she persist with it long after it proved to be unsuccessful? The history of early childhood education is another key influence that can be used to shed light on this particular situation. Child development theory, Maria Montessori's *Casi de Bambini,* the first American kindergartens, and the Head Start pro-

9

gram have all contributed in some way to early childhood educators' collective wisdom of practice. As readers begin to consider the particular cases of children they know, these reflections lead to the question that undergirds Part I: *What forces have influenced and shaped early childhood education and the settings and contexts in which it occurs?*

In Chapter 1, Stacie Goffin, Catherine Wilson, Jennifer Hill, and Stuart McAninch portray the critical role of public policy in the field of early childhood care and education. The authors chronicle the growth of the field during the past 30 years, as they describe struggles external to the field such as public policy and the federal government's role in early care and education. Also delineated are internal struggles among early childhood educators as they debate the best way to create a system of early education that is responsive to the diversity of the children and families in America. Throughout Chapter 1 the authors stretch readers' thinking about the role of government in early childhood care and education as well as the political and pedagogical challenges to building coalitions within our own profession. The chapter concludes with an annotated bibliography that lays the groundwork for policy formation prior to the twentieth century.

In Chapter 2, by Joan Isenberg (with David L. Brown), the focus is on teachers' concerns with meeting the needs of every child regardless of the conditions each child confronts. The authors describe five major factors that jeopardize children's development. Chapter 2 also critically examines the concept of resiliency and concludes by making a strong case for providing children with the educational opportunities, challenges, and knowledge they need to function successfully in the workplace of the future.

In the third chapter of Part I, Marilyn Chipman provides insight into how education and society at large can, in effect, ignore children, invite them to pursue pathways of growth, development, and learning, or prevent them from doing so. Chipman charts the mandate for multicultural education, raises questions about the failed "melting pot" philosophy, and explores multicultural pedagogy as a means of meeting the needs of youngsters in a pluralistic society. The author makes a strong case for reexamining our values and beliefs and challenges readers to confront their own biases as they struggle to become more culturally sensitive teachers. Chapter 3 concludes with a look to the future and describes responses from educators that celebrate diversity.

Chapter 4, by Nancy Briggs, Mary Renck Jalongo, and Lisbeth Brown, examines the roles of child, family, and educator in the traditional, modern, and postmodern culture. The authors call for a redefinition of the word *family* and provide a rationale for authentic collaboration, meaningful communication, and high-quality programming that provides resources and support to contemporary American families. Chapter 4 concludes with a strong statement about the prerequisites for actualizing and implementing a new paradigm for the home/school/community dynamic.

Together these four chapters in Part I remind us that early childhood education can never be decontextualized or occur in isolation. Rather, our work on behalf of young children is deeply woven into the social, political, and historical fabric of our lives, children's lives, and their families' lives both in and out of school.

Chapter 1

Policies of the Early Childhood Field and Its Public: Seeking to Support Young Children and Their Families

Stacie G. Goffin
Catherine Wilson
Jennifer Hill
Stuart McAninch

As the 20th century draws to a close, the field of early childhood care and education faces both internal and external challenges. Externally, the field is confronted with the federal government's shifting provision of early care and education programs and services. Internally, the field is grappling with how best to create a coherent system from its multiple histories, philosophies, and delivery systems—and to do so in a way that remains responsive to the diversity that characterizes the field and the children and families it serves.

The early care and education field has experienced tremendous growth during the past 30 years. With the advent of Head Start in 1965 and dramatic expansion since the fifties in the use of child care by women entering the labor force, the growth of early care and education programs has skyrocketed. Serving children from birth to age 5, the array of new programs is sponsored by state and federal governments, religious organizations, and for-profit and nonprofit agencies and organizations. A review of the past 30 years—though they were not free of challenge, frustration, and backsliding—portrays both a growing demand for early care and education programs and an escalating public awareness of its importance.

Increasing numbers of mothers with young children in the work force, the national spotlight on education reform, concern with anticipated labor shortages along with the country's accompanying need for skilled labor, and continued concern with the unequal school success of children from economically disadvantaged circumstances have propelled the nation's growing appreciation for the need and importance of early childhood care and education. Changing attitudes, in turn, set the stage for significant advances in public policy.

Since 1988, Congress has created four new child care programs for low-income families. After 4 years of intense lobbying by early childhood advocates, the Child Care and Development Block Grant passed in 1990 and represents the nation's first federal legislation to address the quality, as well as availability, of child care. In 1991, President Bush and the National Governors Association launched Goals 2000 and pronounced early childhood education a national priority. The first education goal "that by the year 2000 every child should enter school ready to learn" spurred activity throughout the nation, including state policymaking (see Kagan, Goffin, Golub, & Pritchard, 1995).

These legislative activities, however, have maintained the federal government's traditional focus on children from low-income families, ignored universal needs of young children and their families, and denied sufficient financial resources to serve children well. Still, these new policies advanced public supports for children and provided a foundation for further progress. This fragile foundation is being placed under severe stress by results of the 1994 congressional election, however, and the resultant mandate to fulfill the tenets of the Contract with America.

As a result of a changing political landscape, the federal government's mounting involvement in early care and education issues during the past 30 years has been stalled, if not revoked. Early childhood care and education is thus confronted with the likelihood of a dramatic decrease in public financing, even as demands and expectations for programs accelerate. With the advent of block grants[1] to the states, many early childhood advocates also will find themselves championing anew the value of quality early care and education programs—in effect programs that act on the inseparability of children's early care and education—and the importance of public support. To help frame issues now confronting the field, this chapter describes the origins of current views of childhood and the history of the federal government's involvement with young children and their families. It concludes by juxtaposing these frames of reference with the field's attempt to serve children well and to provide more culturally responsive early care and education programs.

THE ROMANTICIZED CHILD AND PUBLIC POLICY

Occupied with the pressing challenges facing public support of children and families in the political arena, it is easy to lose sight of the social, economic, and intellectual experiences that influence current thinking about the relationships of child to family and family to community. Outside the disciplinary boundaries that form the perimeter of the early childhood profession, inquiry into the stories we create as a culture about childhood and families reveals powerful social narratives underlying present and past efforts to create early care and education policies. Too often, as early childhood teachers, we follow these narratives as we interact with children and respond to their behaviors—viewing their actions as examples of either childish naiveté or intentional disruptiveness.

A romantic vision of the child, in particular, as pure yet vulnerable has served as a powerful force in shaping the cultural construction of childhood and in guiding social policies on behalf of children. Inspired by Rousseau's (1911) image of the child as a "sapling chance sown in the midst of the highway" (p. 5), the literary and social sensibilities of the 19th century cultivated a revolutionary appreciation for the early years of human life and influenced the direction of new social responses to childhood—well before the advent of the field of child development.

With insistent and eloquent voices, literary children kindled the imaginations of readers and furthered the purposes of social activists promoting policies for child welfare, labor, health, and education. From Oliver Twist's sufferings in Victorian England to Little Eva's indictment of slavery in the United States, literary children have served as victims of exploitation, as well as voices of compassion and morality.

Two dimensions informed the romantic vision of the poet and reformer: the "child to be saved" and the "child as savior." The child to be saved was to be protected from abuse in a rapidly changing social and economic order, not simply because children were fragile and inexperienced, but because childhood was a moment of extraordinary significance. For the poet, childhood symbolized the innocence lost in the passage to the adult world. For the reformer, childhood became the crucial point for shaping the future of the social order. Children were to be saved, but more important, children were to become saviors. Childhood would be a unique moment for intervention—a time period in which social reform (or preservation) could be set in motion, and (by the 20th century), a time when reform could be exacted through "optimum" practices of child development.

These dimensions of the romanticized child have shaped a vision for the institutions and policies initiated on children's behalf. From the establishment of public schools to the creation of juvenile courts, the idea of childhood as a critical period for the development of the individual—and of society—has dominated the rhetoric of social policy (Hawes, 1991). Noteworthy, however, is the fact that non-European children, until recently, have fallen outside the conversation of policymakers.

Romanticized dimensions of the child link in significant ways with a more recent acceptance of children as human capital. Closely aligned to capitalist values and undergirded by economic theory, the human capital model assesses the cost benefits of investing time and money in children in terms of return to society relative to other possible investments (Haveman & Wolfe, 1993). This rationale has been particularly powerful in securing ongoing public support for Head Start and for procuring state support for early intervention programs for children deemed at-risk for school success. By arguing the future returns to society earned from public investments during early childhood, the human capital model has provided an economic rationale for the romanticized child; at the same time, perhaps, acceptance of the romanticized child has provided a benevolent veneer for an economic framework that calculates public resources based on a cost-benefit rationale. These multiple versions of childhood, despite their seemingly disparate views of the child, mutually reinforce ideas that have helped contour American social policy for children and families.

Dual Views of Childhood

When the two dimensions of childhood—the child who must be saved and the child who will act as savior—are expressed in public policy, public investment becomes differentiated by the anticipated future value of the child. The rationale for child-saving, as Grubb and Lazerson (1982) contend, is to "control the child so that he or she does not disrupt social stability" (p. 119). Investment made in Head Start, for example, represents the child who will be saved from dropping out of high school, early pregnancy, or prison (Berrueta-Clement, Schweinhart, Barnett, Epstein, & Weikart, 1984). In a variation of the child-as-savior motif, public investment in programs for children "in need of saving" protects society from social disruptions.

Given our nation's categorical approach to children's programs, belief in the privacy of families, and professed concern with intrusion into family life (see below), the child as savior has accrued a deficit orientation. Current rhetoric categorizes the child to be saved as "at-risk." The human capital model has been particularly successful in securing public support for children so identified. Economic evaluation of the Perry Preschool Project (Berrueta-Clement et al., 1984), the preschool precursor to the High/Scope curriculum model, has served as a particularly powerful tool for early childhood advocates because it has enabled policymakers to contemplate the worth of early childhood programs in economic terms.

A different, more opportunistic, rendering of child as savior, however, emerges from children who are white and middle class. They are more likely to be an idealized circle of children whose access to public resources is based on a rationale of positive worth. The child who benefits from public policies as a "right," rather than as a "need," transposes the image of the child who must be saved—and a society that must be protected—from the disruptive possibilities of being unprepared to take a role in productive social and economic life (Gordon, 1994). Too often, our nation's history of public responses to the double vision of childhood has been based on differences in the race and socioeconomic status of the child.

The Relationship of Child and Family

"Subtly but pervasively," Anne MacLeod (1994) observes, "romanticism altered relations between children and adults in every aspect of life" (p. 156). From compulsory education to prohibitions against child labor, the years of childhood became protected, prolonged, and separated from the daily commerce and social life of the community (Suransky, 1982). While the romantic view of children inspired care and attention to the early years of life, it also increased the stakes for safeguarding childhood. And, as the assumption of public responsibility for children increased, concern for children, as expressed in social policy, was promulgated as a "failure in child rearing"; public intervention was justified through constructing a view of families as deficient in providing for the child (Grubb & Lazerson, 1982, p. 5).

Romanticizing the child as an innocent and worthy recipient of public funds justifies investment in programs created for the child, rather than in larger social and economic dimensions effecting childhood. Gordon (1994) traces the separation of child from family in the design of Aid to Dependent Children (AFDC, enacted in 1961), citing the political need to frame the program as assistance for the child, and to a lesser extent the mother, rather than as a support for families in the process of raising children. AFDC provides financial support to low-income families, including provisions for child care. It is interesting to note that in its first iteration as the Mother's Pension Act, enacted in 1921, the support was focused on widowed, divorced, or abandoned mothers so they could attend to parenting. The shift in focus from parents to children was enabled, in part, because of a psychological shift that focused on children as individuals distinct from their families (Cravens, 1993).

Similarly, Head Start, while more broadly conceived to include the family, was promoted as a way of rescuing preschoolers from "cultural deprivation," not as a concerted effort to address the conditions that kept families in poverty (deLone, 1979). Narrowing attention to the child, rather than the context of childrearing, limits public investment, displaces attention from the broader economic inequities confronting families, and enables government to view its policies as nonintrusive. It also projects the benefits of public policy for the next generation, rather than focusing on the present (Lazerson, 1970), thus perpetuating a deficit orientation of the child as savior.

Romanticizing childhood, however, does not provide the same script for all families. While some parents are blamed for their inadequacies, others are cast as hard-working providers, caring for their own and increasingly hostile toward families who are not "sacrificing" for their children (Grubb & Lazerson, 1982). Just as childhood has flourished as an idealized entity, a parallel narrative has romanticized families, from the cult of domesticity to present idealized versions of the "traditional" family. Thus, a double image exists for children as well as their families.

Families with economic resources to manage and select experiences for their children are viewed much differently from those who must rely on public resources. Families who appear to be raising children as a self-sufficient endeavor sustain our idealized notions of parenting, while the "needs" of other families require public intervention and bear the stigma of failure (Goffin, 1988; Gordon, 1994; Wrigley, 1991).

The advent of the family support movement in the sixties and seventies attempted to redirect public discourse regarding families and to reconnect children with their families in the realm of public policy. Premised on such beliefs as the need of all families for support, regardless of economic status, the family support movement altered the nation's deficit orientation toward families in "need" and began to move the public discourse beyond a deficit model (Kagan & Weissbourd, 1994). Unfortunately, current discussions in Congress and state legislatures suggest that early childhood advocates will have to argue in terms of both "the child in need of saving" *and* "the child as savior" to ensure public involvement on behalf of children and their families.

CONFRONTING EXTERNAL CHALLENGES

Government Involvement in Early Childhood Care and Education

The current swirl of debate around welfare reform and full funding of Head Start underscores society's uncertainty regarding the role of government—especially the federal government—in supporting the provision of early care and education programs. Determining whether government's involvement as a societal partner in childrearing exemplifies a role of support or represents unnecessary public intrusion into private, family matters has been an enduring question of public policy. How best to justify government involvement, whether in terms of education, family support, or some as yet undetermined way, remains a subject of considerable contention.

Policies of early childhood care and education have been a response to social, economic, and political issues. Debates on child care, parent education, and preschool education have been—and continue to be—embroiled in other public policy issues such as women's rights, welfare, employment, teenage pregnancy, and high school dropouts. As a nation, we have yet to affirm an appropriate role for government in the area of early childhood and family support (Goffin, 1988, 1990). And governments at the federal and state levels have yet to define a legitimate function for their involvement or the proper policy tools for its enactment (Fuller & Holloway, 1992; O'Connor, 1990, 1992). Most often, early childhood programs have been used to facilitate achievement of other policy initiatives, but without concurrently considering the needs of children and families.

In terms of the nation's first education goal, this issue takes on particular urgency because of increasing numbers of impoverished children. Quality early childhood programs confer especially positive contributions on their development ("Forging the Link," 1995). An equal sense of urgency derives from the ongoing increase in mothers' employment outside the home. Only 10% of children lived with a mother who was in the labor force in 1940. By 1990, nearly 60% of children had a working mother, a sixfold increase in 50 years (Hernandez, 1994). The resultant impact on the daily lives of children has been monumental. As noted by Hernandez (1994),

> Just as children in an earlier era experienced a massive movement by fathers out of the family home to work at jobs in the urban-industrial economy, children since the Great Depression have experienced a massive movement by mothers into the paid labor force. Both of these revolutions in parents' work brought enormous changes in the day-to-day lives of children. As fathers entered the urban labor force, children aged 6 and over entered schools and spent increasing proportions of their lives in formal education settings. Now as mothers are entering the labor force, children under age 6 are spending increasing amounts of time in the care of someone other than their parents. (p. 6)[2]

Policy in Early Care and Education: A History of Fragmentation

Government, whether at the local, state, or federal level, becomes involved when convinced that an issue presents a problem needing its involvement to be resolved. When implemented, proposed solutions become public policies that frame a particular solution or course of action to deal with the matter of concern.

Public policies represent a broad-based consensus about government's responsibility in helping to solve an issue and the kinds of solutions that will help resolve it (Kelman, 1987). Policies made by decision makers in Washington, in state capitals, and in city halls respond to the problems we are living. The solutions devised become the programs and practices early educators attempt to implement. Hence, public policies for children and families are solutions/plans that influence the circumstances of children's lives; they are part of the environment influencing children's development (Bronfenbrenner, 1974; Bronfenbrenner & Weiss, 1983). They also help promote or hinder the ways in which early childhood educators can educate and care for young children.

Public policies are more than just decisions in favor of particular programs or services for children, however. They also are reflections of the kinds of relationships policymakers believe should exist among families, various levels of government, and the needs of children (Goffin, 1988, 1990). It is in this way that public policies reflect generally held beliefs and the consensual values of the nation and its policymakers.

Not surprisingly, therefore, the history of early childhood policy reflects the impact of changing social and economic contexts, as well as changing perceptions of childhood. It is also a story about the constancy and tension among assumptions and beliefs about the kinds of relationships that should exist among families, children, and various levels of government (Goffin, 1990). This historical tradition, furthermore, has persisted throughout the final quarter of the 20th century.

During the mid-1960s, the civil rights movement, our nation's concern with the economically disadvantaged, a determination to regain the competitive edge with our Soviet competitors, and the then revolutionary notion that children's intellectual development was malleable catalyzed the federal government to launch Head Start. The federal government's involvement with early childhood issues continued to escalate during the succeeding 30 years, with only a brief pause after the election of President Ronald Reagan. After the 1994 congressional elections and the transfer of power from Democrats to Republicans, however, the devolution of power from the federal government to the states begun by President Reagan escalated.

Early childhood care and education, however, has a long and rich history dating back to the late 1800s. This history, at the level of both practice and policy, has been marked by the distinction between care and education. The distinction between the care (family support) and education of young children has been most evident in expectations associated with child care versus preschool education.

Child care has traditionally been a response to mothers who need to work in order to be self-sufficient; child care policy, therefore, has tended to focus on the needs of working parents—not on the development needs of children. In contrast, preschool education has always had as its focus the promotion of children's social, emotional, and intellectual development (Cahan, 1989; Wrigley, 1991). The distinctive history and purpose of kindergartens, whose presence has become a mainstay in public schools since the mid-1980s, have further contributed to the policy (and practice) fragmentation in early childhood care and education.

Of course, it is possible for early childhood programs to serve the needs of children for stimulating learning experiences, prepare them for formal learning, *and* respond to the needs of their working parents. Yet these differentiations remain resistant to change, especially at the level of federal and state policy. Early childhood policies continue to serve only certain categories of children (e.g., children at-risk; children with special needs) as policymakers wrestle with whether the care and education of young children is an issue of public or private responsibility.

Current government involvement in early childhood education and child care, therefore, is characterized by an absence of coherent purpose and universality. Public support for early care and education programs during the past 30 years has been garnered by focusing on the importance of preschool programs for disadvantaged children and the need for child care by low-income families. In contrast, between 1933 and the end of World War II, public support for early childhood programs was tied to the nation's defense efforts and to job creation during the Depression. With the notable exception of public response to World Wars I and II and the Depression (responses that had finite life spans), federal involvement in early education has targeted a narrow range of children (Takanishi, 1977). Public involvement at the state level, a relatively recent development, follows a similar pattern (Adams & Sandfort, 1994).

Consequently, federal- and state-funded child care and preschool programs do not operate as an integrated system (General Accounting Office [GAO], 1994; Kagan et al., 1995). At the federal level, for example, over 90 early childhood programs in 11 federal agencies and 20 offices were funded in fiscal years 1992 and 1993 (GAO, 1994). Although the majority of these programs permit funding for early childhood programs rather than target child care and early education as a primary focus, these statistics highlight the fragmentation that characterizes the nation's policy approach to children's early care and education. They also spotlight the extent to which categorical programming and funding thwarts a recognition of the multiple policy agendas served by individual early childhood programs.

As exemplified by public support for the Contract with America, we continue, as a nation, to respond most comfortably to children's needs as the sole—and private—responsibility of families. Families, in turn, are perceived as self-sufficient, capable of independently caring for their own needs and those of their children, and in control of their personal futures. As a result, families seeking help tend to be viewed as incompetent and accessing public support is considered, at best, a sign of weakness. Significantly, parental inadequacies and designations of need have been largely defined in terms of race and class. Too often, discussion of this fact is bypassed in the literature that speaks to early care and education issues.

DIFFERENT CHILDHOODS IN POLICY AND PRACTICE: THE INTERNAL CHALLENGE

Views on the nature of childhood and our nation's views on public responsibility for its youngest citizens provide critical context for how we fulfill our roles as early childhood educators. They help determine the choices we make regarding appropriate curricula and guidance strategies, the nature of our relationships with families, and the resources made available for program support.

In the absence of coherent and well-funded public policies for children and families, the field of early childhood care and education has struggled to respond to dramatic increases in the number of children attending early childhood programs, as well as growing expectations for the outcomes of early care and education for children and for society. Driven by false distinctions between care and education, early childhood programs have had different clients and purposes, based on whether the program was conceived as child care, kindergarten, preschool, or Head Start. Created to redress economic inequities, early childhood programs have been charged with producing measurable improvements in a child's social and academic functioning. And, shaped by ambivalent views of the interplay of governments and childrearing, early childhood programs have been given different resources and agendas for creating relationships with families.

In an effort to mend the fractures created by public policies and to mobilize support for quality early childhood programs, the field conceptualized a more elaborate and less fragmented interpretation of early childhood education, one that recognizes the commonalities of children's needs and potentials and encompasses the programmatic diversity that characterizes the field.

Kagan (1989) has attributed the success of coalition building among early childhood education's various strands to the position statement on developmentally appropriate practice (DAP) of the National Association for the Education of Young Children (Bredekamp, 1987). This document, which identifies pedagogical characteristics of developmentally appropriate early childhood programs, regardless of sponsorship, has functioned as a consensus document, presenting a description of early childhood care and education practices around which the field can coalesce. Not only has this document helped to unify the early childhood profession, it has become familiar rhetoric in business reports seeking high-quality early childhood programs to assure the competence of the future labor force and educational associations committed to education reform.

While the position statement has served to draw together the programmatic variations serving children and families, and to inform decision makers outside the field of early childhood care and education, it has provoked significant controversy within the field. Led by early childhood academics, critics have questioned prevailing assumptions regarding the universality of its tenets (Kessler, 1991; Lubeck, 1993; Swadener & Kessler, 1991), arguing that too often early childhood programming has acted on assumptions that an enriched curriculum could compensate for a child's economic disadvantages and parental inadequacies, rather than recognizing the richness of a child's cultural experiences and the contributions of familial and community relationships.

Derived from a normative knowledge base of scientific theorizing on child development, DAP is being challenged for promoting the belief that all children, regardless of culture, gender, race, or class, benefit from a similar pedagogy. Often this is reflected in curricula that presume that all children are the same and that differences—if they exist in any important ways—should be minimized. Critics bring cultural, critical, and feminist perspectives to their analyses of early childhood pedagogy and argue that the perspective presented by DAP does not address the ways in which social forces prevent poor and minority children from achieving success; nor does it value divergent beliefs about the purposes of education and the relationships among children, teachers, and families (Bloch, 1991; Delpit, 1988). Once secure in the universality of its knowledge base and pedagogy, the early care and education field now finds itself struggling to define the meaning of cultural diversity for early childhood practice.

Thus the profession of early childhood care and education faces internal challenges from its own constituency regarding the validity of its pedagogical underpinning, even as it confronts the possibility of having to cope with a significant reduction in public funding and renewed polarization between the care and education of young children. In the arena of policy, the field of early childhood care and education struggles to reverse the nation's fragmented and categorical response to the needs of young children and their families and to build the public and policy support that will enable all of America's children to have a better quality of life and to actualize their potential. Children's maximum development depends on their opportunities to be supported by a nurturing family, and all families, in turn, depend on an array of societal supports to enable them to fulfill their childrearing responsibilities. Government policies have the potential to either enable or hinder the well-being of young children. Needed is a willingness to transcend the nation's historical focus on children deemed "in need" because their families are considered inadequate to the task of childrearing. Early childhood advocates must renew their efforts to demonstrate to policymakers the ways in which government policies (including their absence) help to structure children's childrearing environments.

In contrast to the need to create more universal policy supports for children and families, in the arena of practice, the field of early childhood care and education is challenged to examine its assumptions regarding the universality of child development principles and to devise a pedagogy more responsive to the diversity that children bring to early childhood classrooms. Similarly, it is being asked to be more responsive to the cultural values and practices of families served by early childhood programs. In an ironic turn of fate, the very issues of cultural difference and economic disparity that have undermined the development of cohesive and comprehensive policies of public support are the same issues believed too long ignored in practice. As the field of early childhood care and education advocates for policymakers to build supportive contexts for raising children, we too, as teachers, must recognize the ways in which our day-to-day interactions have the potential to create relationships and shape environments that are informed and enriched by the contributions of all children and families.

NOTES

1. Block grants collapse an array of categorical federal programs into a single funding stream. As of this writing, Congress is negotiating the collapse of federal child care programs into block grants. Consistent with the intent to devolve decision making to the states, block grants contain few federal guidelines.

2. A closer look at African-American mothers clearly shows that they always have worked outside the home in significantly higher numbers (Jones, 1985), a reality that might also be representative of other ethnic groups. As a result, for many women, the dilemma of child care is hardly new; neither is the problem of inadequate child care. What is new is the type of parents needing access to child care—white, middle-class parents—thus making the need a problem "worthy" of response by policymakers.

ANNOTATED BIBLIOGRAPHY

This chapter focuses on 20th-century public policy. An array of sociohist-orical and economic precedents, however, laid the groundwork for policy formation for children and families during the 1900s. The four references listed below provide an introduction to this area of study.

Giddings, P. (1984). *When and where I enter: The impact of black women on race and sex in America.* New York: Bantam Books.

    Giddings examines the interlocking grid of race and sex and its impact on America's view of African-American women from slavery through the 1980s. She also explores the implications of this view and how African-American women of every decade have fought against negative views of themselves and their children, families, and communities.

Hiner, N. Ray, & Hawes, J. M. (Eds.). (1985). *Growing up in America: Children in historical perspective.* Urbana, IL: University of Illinois Press.

    This volume includes 17 essays that collectively explore the changing nature and conceptions of childhood in the United States from the colonial era to the 20th century. The essays also provide some sense of social class, racial, and regional variations historically in patterns of family organization and childrearing practices, as well as insights into the development of public policy regarding children.

Jones, J. (1985) *Labor of love, labor of sorrow: Black women, work and the family from slavery to the present.* New York: Basic Books.

    This seminal work within the relatively new field of African-American women's history gives an excellent treatment of how the lived experience of African-American women differed from that of white women, even when of the same socioeconomic class. Jones traces the world of work of African-American women from indentured servitude, slavery, Reconstruction, pre- and post–World Wars I and II to the present. Highlighted in particular is the impact of African-American women's work patterns on family and childrearing practices.

Tyack, D. and Hansot, E. (1982). *Managers of virtue: Public school leadership in America, 1820–1980.* New York: Basic Books.

    This volume provides a useful general context for the historical development of public policy in early care and education. While not directly empha-sizing care and education of young children, the authors nevertheless me-thodically describe the political processes through which networks of influential social reformers and education officials were able to shape poli-cymaking in education during the 19th and 20th centuries.

REFERENCES

Adams, G., & Sandfort, J. (1994). *State prekindergarten initiatives in the early 1990s*. Washington, DC: Children's Defense Fund.

Berrueta-Clement, J. R., Schweinhart, L. J., Barnett, W. S., Epstein, A. S., & Wei-kart, D. P. (1984). *Changed lives: The effects of the Perry Preschool Program on youth through age 19*. Ypsilanti, MI: High/Scope Press.

Bloch, M. N. (1991). Critical science and the history of child development's in-fluence on early education research. *Early Education and Development, 2,* 95–108.

Bredekamp, S. (Ed.). (1987). *Developmentally appropriate practice in early childhood programs serving children from birth through age 8*. Washing-ton, DC: National Association for the Education of Young Children.

Bronfenbrenner, U. (1974). Developmental research, public policy and the ecol-ogy of childhood. *Child Development, 45*(1), 1–5.

Bronfenbrenner, U., & Weiss, H. (1983). Beyond policies without people: An eco-logical perspective on child and family policy. In E. F. Zigler, S. L. Kagan, & E. Klugman (Eds.), *Children, families, and government: Perspectives on American social policy* (pp. 393–414). Cambridge: Cambridge University Press.

Cahan, E. D. (1989). *Past caring: A history of U.S. preschool care and education for the poor, 1820–1965*. New York: National Center for Children in Poverty.

Cravens, H. (1993). *Before Head Start: The Iowa Station & America's children*. Chapel Hill: The University of North Carolina Press.

deLone, R. H. (1979). *Small futures: Children, inequality, and the limits of lib-eral reform*. New York: Harcourt Brace Jovanovich.

Delpit, L. D. (1988). The silenced dialogue: Power and pedagogy in educating other people's children. *Harvard Educational Review, 58,* 280–298.

Forging the link between child care and education (1995). Washington, DC: Coun-cil of State School Officers.

Fuller, B., & Holloway, S. D. (1992). *When the state innovates: Institutions and interests construct the child care sector*. Cambridge, MA: Child Care Organi-zation and Family Choice Project.

General Accounting Office. (1994). *Early childhood programs: Multiple pro-grams and overlapping target groups*. Washington, DC: Author.

Goffin, S. G. (1988). Putting our advocacy efforts in a new context. *Young Chil-dren, 43*(3), 52–56.

Goffin, S. G. (1990). Government's responsibility in early childhood care and education: Renewing the debate. In C. Seefeldt (Ed.), *Continuing issues in early childhood education* (pp. 9–26). Columbus, OH: Merrill.

Gordon, L. (1994). *Pitied but not entitled: Single mothers and the history of welfare, 1890–1935.* New York: Free Press.

Grubb, W. N., & Lazerson, M. (1982). *Broken promises: How Americans fail their children.* New York: Basic Books.

Haveman, R., & Wolfe, B. (1993). Well-being, entitlement, and investment in children: An economic perspective. In M. Jensen & S. Goffin (Eds.), *Visions of entitlement: The care and education of America's children* (pp. 31–84). Albany: SUNY Press.

Hawes, J. M. (1991). *The children's rights movement: A history of advocacy and protection.* Boston: Twayne Publishers.

Hernandez, D. J. (1994, Spring). Children's changing access to resources: A historical perspective. *Social Policy Report, Society for Research in Child Development, 8*(1).

Jones, J. (1985). *Labor of love, labor of sorrow: Black women, work and the family from slavery to the present.* New York: Basic Books.

Kagan, S. L. (1989). Early care and education: Tackling the tough issues. *Phi Delta Kappan, 70,* 433–439.

Kagan, S. L., Goffin, S. G., Golub, S., & Pritchard, L. (1995). *Toward systemic reform: Service integration for young children and their families.* Washington, DC: National Center for Service Integration.

Kagan, S. L., & Weissbourd, B. (1994). Toward a new normative system of family support. In S. L. Kagan & B. Weissbourd (Eds.), *Putting families first: America's family support movement and the challenge of change* (pp. 473–490). San Francisco: Jossey-Bass.

Kelman, S. (1987). *Making public policy: A hopeful view of American government.* New York: Basic Books.

Kessler, S. A. (1991). Alternative perspectives on early childhood education. *Early Childhood Research Quarterly, 6,* 183–197.

Lazerson, M. (1970). Social reform and early childhood education: Some historical perspectives. *Urban Education, 5,* 83–102.

Lubeck, S. (1993). The politics of developmentally appropriate practice: Exploring issues of culture, class, and curriculum. In B. Mallory & R. New (Eds.), *Diversity and developmentally appropriate practices: Challenges for early childhood education* (pp. 17–43). New York: Teachers College Press.

MacLeod, A. S. (1994). *American childhood: Essays of children's literature on the nineteenth and twentieth centuries.* Athens: University of Georgia Press.

O'Connor, S. M. (1990). Rationales for the institutionalization of programs for young children. *American Journal of Education, 98,* 114–146.

O'Connor, S. M. (1992). Legitimating the state's involvement in early childhood programs. In B. Fuller & R. Rubinson (Eds.), *The political construction of education* (pp. 89–98). New York: Praeger.

Rousseau, J. J. (1911). *The minor educational writings of Jean Jacques Rousseau* (W. Boyd, Trans.). London: Blackie and Son.

Suransky, V. (1982). *The erosion of childhood*. Chicago: University of Chicago Press.

Swadener, B. B., & Kessler, S. (Eds.). (1991). Reconceptualizing early childhood education [Special issue]. *Early Education and Development, 2*(2).

Takanishi, R. (1977). Federal involvement in early education (1933-1973): The need for historical perspective. In L. G. Katz (Ed.), *Current topics in early childhood education* (Vol. 1, pp. 139–164). Norwood, NJ: Ablex.

Wrigley, J. (1991). Different care for different kids: Social class and child care policy. In L. Weis, P. G. Altbach, G. P. Kelly, & H. Petrie (Eds.), *Critical perspectives on early childhood education* (pp. 189–209). Albany: SUNY Press.

Chapter 2

Development Issues Affecting Children

JOAN P. ISENBERG
WITH DAVID L. BROWN

Lynette is a first-grader who lives with her single-parent mother. She generally arrives at school unclean, hungry, and with her hair hanging in her eyes. Although she is quite capable of handling intellectual tasks, Lynette has difficulty establishing positive peer relationships. Consequently, she plays alone on the playground, is often the last to be selected for group work, and is sometimes the object of ridicule from her peers. Nonetheless, Lynette works hard to please her teachers and her peers. Although she reads above grade level, Lynette rarely is recognized for her intellectual capabilities. It seems that in school, Lynette can do little to create a favorable impression among teacher or her peers.

Many children like Lynette arrive at school tired, unhealthy, or unduly stressed, yet they have the same developmental needs all children must have met in order to thrive. Developmental needs are essential requirements that affect the "long-term implications of childhood events, not just their immediate consequences" (Garbarino, 1995, p. 156). Now, consider the following frightening statistics about America's children:

- 15.7 million children live in poverty, a sharp increase since 1970 (Children's Defense Fund, 1995).
- 9 million children lack health care, including needed vaccinations (Children's Defense Fund, 1995).
- 20% of children ages 3–17 have one or more developmental, learning, or behavioral disorders (Zill& Schoenborn, 1990).
- Reported rates of child abuse have tripled since the 1970s (Fuchs & Reklis, 1992).

These data and Lynette's case clearly portray conditions that affect more children today than at any other time since the Great Depression (Danziger, Sandefur, & Weinberg, 1995; Garbarino, 1995). Even though some progress has been made on behalf of children, such as decreased infant mortality, early education programs for children born into poverty, and a national vaccination program for preschool children, trend data continue to document an increase in the physical, behavioral, social, and learning problems of America's children and youth (Garbarino, 1995). Such conditions pose serious threats to children's growth and development. Thus, teachers and caregivers must reexamine their roles and responsibilities to address the realities children bring to early childhood settings. Simultaneously, broad societal changes must be institutionalized to foster children's well-being both in the United States and throughout the world.

This chapter first identifies children's developmental needs and defintional debates related to child development, and examines the historical traditions of the field of early childhood. Next, it addresses selected adverse and positive influences on children's development. The chapter concludes with suggestions to educators of young children about ways to meet these developmental challenges. The topics selected for this chapter, while not exhaustive, have relevance for the entire field of early childhood.

CHILDREN'S DEVELOPMENTAL NEEDS

What exactly do children need in order to develop optimally? At a minimum, all children have physical, social and emotional, and cognitive needs. Physical needs include food, clothing, shelter, and medical care. Basic social and emotional needs include a consistent and predictable relationship with an attentive and caring adult who has high social and moral expectations, strong peer acceptance, and "freedom from exploitation and discrimination in their communities" (Weissbourd, 1996, p. 8). Minimal cognitive needs include the ability to communicate thoughts and feelings, to process information in a meaningful way, to engage in constructive problem solving, and to experience success both at school and in the community (Dodge, Jablon, & Bickart, 1994; Garbarino, 1995; Weissbourd, 1996). Many children also need "special health, social, and educational services to deal with inherited and acquired ailments and disabilities" (Weissbourd, 1996, p.8). How well early childhood professionals meet children's essential needs strongly influences how successful children will be as learners and as future citizens (Garbarino, 1995).

Children who grow up with their basic physical and material needs met are likely to trust themselves and their community, possess a vitality for life, and rely on inner resourcefulness for particpating in society regardless of the obstacles they face. They are also more likely to develop a sense of confidence and competence in family, school, and community endeavors as a result of repeated, successful coping experiences (Anthony & Cohler, 1987; Bronfenbrenner, 1979; Erikson, 1963; Vygotsky, 1978; Weissbourd, 1996).

On the other hand, children who grow up without having basic needs met are at a clear disadvantage for a healthy start in life (Anthony & Cohler, 1987; Carnegie Corporation, 1994; Children's Defense Fund, 1995). Many of these children exhibit particular behavioral and developmental characteristics (e.g., developmental disabilities, medical fragility, poor school performance) making them vulnerable to being unable to function effectively as learners (Bradley et al., 1994).

DEFINING TERMS

Professionals across disciplines—social workers, teachers, parents, and policymakers—rely on their understandings of children's development to determine responsible policies and practices. Most agree that child development issues, while complex and fluid, are foundational and interdisciplinary. Beyond that, however, there is little agreement about what child development goals entail, how best to optimize development in varying circumstances, or how to prepare children developmentally for an unpredictable future (Katz, 1996).

Development is often defined as a dynamic change over time (Katz, 1996). Implicit in this definition are two controversial issues. The first concerns an "end state" or an assumption that early experiences affect later learning and behavior. The second implies that development is facilitated or hindered by psychological characteristics, behavioral capabilities, cultural context, and individual life circumstances. Both issues generate debate and contoversy over definitions and implications.

Additionally, recent child development theory and research have called into question three long-standing notions associated with development. They have challenged the assumptions about (1) developmental universals, making us increasingly aware of cultural influences on development; (2) the simplistic use of ages and stages to explain behavioral norms; and (3) theoretical dichotomies such as nature versus nurture to describe development (Damon, 1989). These new data have reopened the definitional debate and are providing the context that is challenging and changing old views and assumptions that influence early childhood educators' beliefs and actions. This is a more difficult challenge than it was in the past, for not only is there more information about every aspect of development, but it is increasingly difficult to integrate the information.

Similarly, notions of resiliency have challenged early childhood educators' thinking. Resiliency is defined as the ability to adapt to disappointment, setbacks, or obstacles in one's life—taking "an active stance towards an obstacle or difficulty" (Dugan & Coles, 1989, p. 4).

The study of resiliency may be the most important research in child development in postmodern times, for it represents a shift in viewing children's development from one of remediation to primary prevention and from deficit to strength. While few dispute the resiliency paradigm, Weissbourd (1996) questions its unilateral acceptance. His assumption that everyone is vulnerable under the right set of conditions portrays resilient children as those "who have not yet encountered an environment that triggers their vulnerabilities" (p. 43). While this perspective challenges the prevailing resiliency paradigm, it neglects to account for those children who have already succeeded in spite of adversity.

Thus, the explosion of new child development knowledge has prompted new insights into the complexity of development. Both past and present child development theory and research have deep roots in the traditions and history of early childhood as a distinct field.

HISTORICAL VIEWS OF DEVELOPMENT IN EARLY CHILDHOOD

Early leaders in the field have provided a strong tradition of care and education that has consistently guided the profession's thinking. The centrality of positive interaction experiences and nurturing environments to children's healthy development suggests one example of this long-standing tradition. Our roots begin in the 1800s with Rousseau's (1947) empowering paradigmatic change from a utilitarian and adult view of children to one that affirmed their goodness and their need for supportive adults in their lives and for humane treatment. Later in history, Dewey's (1916) work centered on the belief that education is an integral part of life, and the school community offers children an opportunity to practice democratic principles in group living. While Dewey's principles are still advocated, they often conflict with current views of education for children and provide a possible reason for the tensions between schools and families and the school reform movement.

From the field of psychology, child development theorists (Ainsworth, Bell, & Stayton, 1974; Bowlby, 1969; Spitz, 1949) also found human relationships central to the care and education of children. Later, Piaget (1951) focused his theory on the inseparability of cognitive and affective development, while Erikson (1963) explained that the early years are critical for healthy psychosocial development, establishing the traits of trust, autonomy, initiative, and industry. The current view of development as occurring in a highly influential sociocultural context is exemplified by renewed interest in Vygotsky's (1978) work. For Vygotsky, the social context—individuals, family, school, and societal expectations—shapes the child's thinking and development. The scope of psychological theory and research continuously provokes reexamination of the assumptions early childhood edcuators hold regarding children's development.

From anthropology, Bronfenbrenner's (1979) ecological model of child development reminds us of the crucial relationship between the child and the immediate and surrounding environments. Moreover, Bronfenbrenner's belief in the bidirectionality of responses between adults and children gives children an equal role in shaping adults' behaviors.

Like their forebears in the field, contemporary early childhood professionals recognize and reinforce the early antecedents of healthy development and model the conviction that children are good and worthwhile, competent rather than helpless, and survivors rather than victims. Thus, child care, school, and family settings must be safe havens for children where life is organized and predictable, and every adult holds realistic but high expectations for all children regardless of their backgrounds.

ADVERSE INFLUENCES ON CHILDREN'S DEVELOPMENT

Even as we approach the 21st century, many professionals still tend to blame children for their plight rather than finding solutions to their problems (Kozol, 1995). Adversities, often termed *risk factors,* place children "at high risk of adverse outcomes when they become adolescents" (Schorr, 1988, p. xix). A 1994 report by the Carnegie Corporation has warned that "poor quality child care, inadequate health care, and increasing poverty are creating a quiet crisis among children younger than three" (p. 4), while Kozol (1995) has advocated systemic change to public education.

Consider the case of the Clark family, a middle-class, dual-parent, suburban family with no apparent problems. When Jennifer Clark, a housewife for many years, suddenly found herself faced with a divorce and little financial support for her two young children, she was forced to sell her home, move to a less costly area, and find employment. Now her children are living in a single-parent household, with a working mother, and in a neighborhood that is less safe and protected. As a result of their changing circumstances, the Clark children have more challenges to meet in their daily lives.

Such changes have profound consequences for children, yet there is much that teachers can do to enable children to become successful learners and citizens and "partially immunize" them against the stresses and strains of their lives when multiple adverse influences interact (McMillan & Reed, 1993).

Five major adversities—poverty, inadequate health and safety protection, violence, prenatal drug exposure, and substandard child care—and their influences on children's development will be delineated next.

Poverty

The risks from child poverty—including poor health, inadequate child care, developmental delays, and insufficient nutrition—pose serious threats to children's well-being. While poverty is defined as insufficent income, two pervasive myths abound about low-income families (Weissbourd, 1996).

The myth that all poor children are alike does not account for the diverse conditions children in poverty can experience "in the length of time they are poor, in the circumstances and quality of their families' lives, in the work patterns of their parents, in the circumstances of their communities, in the nature of their problem" (Weissbourd, 1996, p. 10).

The second myth, that poverty is more common among children of color than among white children, overlooks the fact that white childen comprise the largest group of poor in America even though a higher percentage of African-American children are poor and are likely to remain so longer.

Moreover, the costs of child poverty are both economic and social. Children who live in poverty, taken as a group, will cost billions of additional dollars in services to support special education, foster care, programs for teenage parents, and the criminal justice system (Children's Defense Fund, 1995). Almost all the adversities that lead to devastating outcomes are out of proportion among poor children who are denied access to many products and services available to most advantaged Americans (Schorr, 1988).

Inadequate Health and Safety Protection

Access to health care for all children is also an issue affecting children's development. In spite of this country's advanced health systems, there are still 9.4 million American children without the care necessary for a healthy start in life. Whereas immunization rates have increased dramatically since 1990, one-third of American children still are not immunized before their second birthday, leaving more than one million 2-year-olds vulnerable to a host of preventable diseases such as measles, tetanus, polio, and hepatitis B. Additionally, recent statistics in America reveal that 7 infants out of 100 are low-birthweight babies (less than 5.5 pounds), placing them at greater risk of infant death and disability, and 500,000 pregnant women are uninsured, risking inadequate prenatal care (Carnegie Corporation, 1994; Children's Defense Fund, 1995). These conditions seriously jeopardize children's physical growth, brain development, and abililty to learn.

Despite increased societal attention to providing safe environments for children, efforts to protect children from harmful influences do not reach enough children in the early years, particularly infants and toddlers. Unprotected children may reside in unsafe neighborhoods and be supervised by babysitters who are unqualified, or adults who abuse or neglect them in the home (Lewit, 1992). These conditions are known antecedents to later unhealthy development and must be addressed at the policy level by communities and comprehensive school efforts to ensure young children's health and safety. Clearly, healthy children have a greater chance of growing into productive learners and citizens.

Violence

A third threat to children's healthy development, violence, has reached epidemic proportions in America (Children's Defense Fund, 1995; Garbarino, 1995; NAEYC, 1994). Senseless killings cause not only personal grief and tragedy but also an enormous financial public burden in the form of emergency services, law enforcement, and prison maintenance. As the following bleak figures detail, the toll is great:

- The average cost of treating a child wounded by gunfire equals that of a year of college education (Garbarino, 1995).
- Gun-related violence kills at least 50 children each week and injures another 30 children each day (NAEYC, 1994).
- More than half of fifth graders in New Orleans reported they had been victims of some type of violence; 70% had witnessed weapons being used (NAEYC, 1994).

There are prevention measures that lessen the effect of all forms of violence on children's development. Because violence is often interconnected with other adverse factors that collectively inhibit children's development, it must be viewed as a broad social problem. Experts agree that violence prevention must not only include efforts to control violent behavior but also address its root causes (poverty, repression, absence of individual responsibility and family support) and risk factors (guns, media, drugs, incarceration, witnessing violent acts, community deterioration) (Carnegie Corporation, 1994; Children's Defense Fund, 1995; Garbarino, 1995; NAEYC, 1994). Curbing violence requires a systemic approach that includes changes in families, neighborhoods, and schools and requires a critical mass of people willing to work together to change the structure and policies that frame children's lives.

Prenatal Drug Exposure

Prenatal drug exposure has contributed to a new and rapidly growing population of prenatally drug-exposed or "crack" children who are entering the public schools at a rapid rate. Because crack is seldom used exclusively, a developing fetus may be exposed to a variety of substances. The profile of drug-exposed children is clear in the literature (Greer, 1990; Lewit, 1992). These children often suffer from cognitive defects such as poor abstract reasoning and memory, poor judgment, and an inability to concentrate or process information, or they experience physical abnormalities—brain damage, deformed hearts, missing limbs. Drug-exposed children may also exhibit behavioral problems such as hyperactivity, frequent tantrums, and the inability to cope with stressful events in their lives (Greer, 1990). Those with profound to moderate effects from prenatal drug exposure are usually identified by age 6. However, most of these children do not receive preschool education; thus developmental difficulties are not professionally diagnosed until first grade.

Societal conditions often associated with crack children—poverty, substandard education, violence—also influence children's development. The interaction of these social and physical factors may cause dysfunctions and social stigmas. Meeting the unique needs of prenatally drug-exposed children is particularly challenging to teachers in self-contained classrooms, for they often lack specialized training in instructional strategies. Consequently, they rely heavily on referrals for assessment and placement in special education settings.

Substandard Child Care

Because young children represent society's future, how they are cared for and educated and who cares for them clearly affect their development.

According to the 1995 study by Helburn and her associates, of the 5 million children in child care, most are receiving "poor to mediocre" care and one in eight is in a setting so poor that children's basic health and safety needs are jeopardized. In this study of over 400 child care centers in four states, only one in seven centers was rated good based on NAEYC accreditation criteria (e.g., enjoying close relationships with caring adults who focus on individual needs). Even worse, the children receiving the poorest quality care were typically the very youngest—the infants and toddlers. These findings parallel similar findings related to quality child care (Galinsky, Bond, & Friedman, 1993; Kontos, Howes, Shinn, & Galinsky, 1995) and are integral to the current political debate requiring welfare mothers to work.

Related to quality is the issue of cost. Within the political debate over putting mothers on welfare to work, little thought has been given to its outcome—a dramatic increase in the need for more child care at the very time when federal funding is being reduced. The connection of cost of child care to its quality and outcomes serves as a potent reminder that high-quality child care programs are indispensable in preparing children for better school performance and developing stronger self-esteem (Boyer, 1991; Helburn, 1995) and reducing later juvenile crime and delinquency (National Center for Youth Law, 1995). What are these positive influences and how can they be achieved?

POSITIVE INFLUENCES ON CHILDREN'S DEVELOPMENT

Children who grow up in environments with positive influences are likely to succeed even "against the odds." Often termed *protective factors,* positive conditions include a combination of sustenance; significant relationships with available and caring adults; consistency and predictability in relationships, expectations, and limits; strong emotional ties within the family; regular acceptance and affirmation of actions; and a variety of stimulating materials in family and school settings (Bradley et al., 1994; Dugan & Coles, 1989; Schorr, 1988; Werner, 1990). These psychological influences are likely to develop traits of self-efficacy, personal responsibility, optimism, and coping ability (Bradley et al., 1994; Coles, 1995).

Early childhood professionals are well positioned to provide positive conditions for all children. Most researchers agree that reaching children through quality early education programs is a proven strategy to help children achieve success in school and lead healthier, more productive lives. Many successful intervention programs for children at all ages levels (e.g., Accelerated Schools, Comer Schools, the Coalition of Essential

Schools, Reading Recovery, and Success for All) are dispelling the myth "that race, socio-economic status, or family background is a reason to assume failure for any child" (Children's Defense Fund, 1995, p. 98; Weissbourd, 1996).

Why are children succeeding in these programs despite the many threats to their development? These programs incorporate the multiple variables that we know interact to influence development in a positive direction. They employ certified and caring adults who are knowledgeable and trained in best practice, who view themselves as facilitators, who are skilled in their ability to establish relationships built on mutual trust and care, and who approach children with an "open eye" to their needs (Haberman, 1994; Schorr, 1988). These programs also involve parents, community agencies, and educators in a collaborative endeavor for children's education and development.

Looking broadly at the effects of both adverse and positive influences on children's development gives insight into why some children succeed in school while others do not. It also illuminates the many challenges early childhood professionals face in reeducating themselves to understand and take a proactive stance on the critical issues affecting children's development.

IMPLICATIONS AND RECOMMENDATIONS FOR CHILD DEVELOPMENT

What is essential to recognize about the conditions affecting all children's development is their implications. Adults who strive to build children's adaptability view children as resources, not problems, and create environments that protect them from adverse risks rather than attempting to "fix" them. The following five suggestions provide a starting point for meeting these developmental challenges.

1. *Teach coping skills to children.* Early childhood professionals can help all children maximize their potential by fostering self-esteem and a sense of efficacy. Developing nurturing relationships and focusing on children's strengths rather than labeling, blaming, and criticizing children's behavior fosters children's belief in their abilities and rests on the core principles and traditions of early childhood education. Early childhood curricula must enable children, despite disadvantages, to develop social competence, problem-solving skills, autonomy, adaptability, and a sense of purpose or future to maximize their healthy development. Conflict resolution, characterized by community building and social and moral problem solving, can be taught to teachers, parents, and children

from diverse backgrounds through its inclusion in early childhood education programs and training (Wheeler, 1994). Strong early childhood programs also provide children with predictable environments so they can develop the "language skills, social competence, self-confidence, and ways of thinking that would help them discover how the world works . . . the attributes that help in the mastery of school tasks" (Schorr, 1988, p. 182).

2. *Institute reform in schools and programs that serve poor children.* According to Haberman (1994), current educational settings for children in poverty are hostile, prisonlike environments that differ dramatically from those experienced by advantaged children. Proponents of school reform have taken the position that all children can learn and that children's learning is more alike than different. Yet, just as in the past, schools continue to label poor children as special learners who need "direct instruction" and reinforce the myth that poor children cannot be expected to learn very much. This kind of labeling perpetuates a self-fulfilling prophecy for poor children (Weissbourd, 1996). Instead, early childhood professionals must teach to all children's strengths. Educators who ask the question "How do I make this child part of the curriculum?" rather than "How can I be expected to teach this child?" are beginning to reduce the barriers that are created for poor children by assuming a more holistic approach to teaching.

3. *Provide teachers and caregivers with access to resources that protect children's health and safety.* There is strong evidence that timely and appropriate environmental interventions by an interdisciplinary team of professionals including health care professionals, teachers, social workers, and other caring adults can minimize children's personal pain and distress (Carnegie Corporation, 1994; Children's Defense Fund, 1995). Teachers must be open to actively participating on these teams to develop better methods and strategies to identify children's special needs. Moreover, because schools and other early childhood programs are the settings in which most children spend their days, teachers and caregivers must be knowledgeable about the community resources and help families access those resources for children. Early childhood educators must work with other professionals dedicated to serving young children in order to ensure children's health and safety.

4. *Prepare future and practicing teachers with the dispositions to work with children abused by violence and poverty.* Early childhood educators can help children deal with the effects of violence and poverty in their lives through the development of strong programs and curricula and establishing strong partnerships with parents (NAEYC, 1994). Cooperative, respectful, and egalitarian teachers and caregivers are generally

the most successful in working with children facing multiple threats to development. Additionally, these successful teachers tend to be nonjudgmental in their interactions with children; take a problem-solving approach to children's life events; believe in their ability to influence children's development rather than fantasizing about rescuing children from their hostile environments; and try to accept the views of all stakeholders in children's lives (e.g., parents, children, community members) as potential sources of important information. Perhaps most important, these teachers and caregivers have high expectations and efficacy beliefs for all children. Teacher preparation and staff development programs must revisit the portrait of successful teachers and align coursework, experiences, and training toward the development of these dispositions (Coles, 1995; Kagan, 1994).

5. *Develop nonauthoritarian teachers and administrators.* Adults who regularly interact with children can not only establish trust but also serve as role models for other kinds of social interaction. A gentle, nonthreatening, supportive approach to guiding children's behavior is important for highly stressed children. Equally important is the avoidance of public humiliation, which is so damaging to already stressed children. Valuing children for who they are helps them understand that the classroom is a predictable, caring environment where individuals assume responsibility for their own actions (Kagan, 1994).

CONCLUSION

The controversial and challenging issues in child development require all early childhood educators to think differently about those conditions that are known to optimize children's healthy development. The ideas presented in this chapter are intended to stimulate thought, provoke discussion, and lead to better solutions to breaking the barriers to children's optimal development. Even though many children continue to experience seemingly unabated adverse influences, early childhood educators must move beyond shocking statistics and appalling acounts of children's circumstances. Early childhood teachers and caregivers can provide all children with the positive influences that will enable them to thrive both academically and socially. Perhaps children like Lynette, in the opening case of this chapter, would have benefitted if her teacher had adopted a model of learning that emphasized comprehensive and coordinated services, provided an environment that encouraged adaptability and affirmation, embraced an attitude that Lynette could be successful in school despite her vulnerability, and utilized a nonthreatening, supportive teaching style. Early childhood professionals, regardless of roles, must find ways to accept and nurture all children and provide the conditions necessary to their healthy growth and development.

REFERENCES

Ainsworth, M., Bell, S., & Stayton, D. (1974). Infant and mother attachment and social development: Socialization as a product of reciprocal responsiveness and stigmas. In M. P. Richards (Ed.), *The integration of a child into a social world* (pp. 99–135). New York: Cambridge University Press.

Anthony, E. J., & Cohler, B. (Eds.). (1987). *The invulnerable child.* New York: Guilford.

Bowlby, J. (1969). *Attachment and loss* (Vol. 1). New York: Basic Books.

Boyer, E. L. (1991). *Ready to learn: A mandate for the nation.* New York: Carnegie Foundation for the Advancement of Learning.

Bradley, R. H., Whiteside, L., Mundfrom, D. J., Casey, P. H., Kelliher, K. J., & Pope, S. K. (1994). Early indications of resilience and their relation of experiences of low birthweight, premature children living in poverty. *Child Development,* 65(2), 346–360.

Bronfenbrenner, U. (1979). *The ecology of human development.* Cambridge, MA: Harvard University Press.

Carnegie Corporation of New York. (1994). *Starting points: Meeting the needs of our youngest children.* New York: Author.

Children's Defense Fund. (1995). *The state of America's children yearbook.* Washington, DC: Author.

Coles, R. (1995). *Educating everybody's children.* Alexandria, VA: Association for Supervision and Curriculum Development.

Damon, W. (1989). Introduction: Advances in developmental research. In W. Damon (Ed.), *Child development today and tomorrow* (pp. 1–13). San Francisco, CA: Jossey-Bass.

Danziger S., Sandefur, G. D., & Weinberg, D. H. (Eds.). (1995). *Confronting poverty: Prescriptions for change.* Cambridge, MA: Harvard University Press.

Dewey, J. (1916). *Democracy and education.* New York: Macmillan.

Dodge, D., Jablon, J., & Bickart, T. (1994). *Constructing curriculum for the primary grades.* Washington, DC: Teaching Strategies.

Dugan, T., & Coles, R. (Eds.). (1989). *The child in our times: Studies in the development of resiliency.* New York: Guilford Press.

Erikson, E. H. (1963). *Childhood and society.* New York: W. W. Norton.

Fuchs, V., & Reklis, D. (1992). America's children: Economic perspectives and policy options. *Science,* 255, 41–46.

Galinsky, E., Bond, J. T., & Friedman, D. E. (1993). *The changing American workforce: Highlights of the national study.* New York: Families and Work Institute.

Garbarino, J. (1995). *Raising children in a socially toxic environment.* San Francisco: Jossey-Bass.

Greer, J. (1990). The drug babies. *Exceptional Children,* 56(5), 382–384.

Haberman, M. (1994). Can teachers be educated to save students in a violent society? In D. R. Walling (Ed.), *Teachers as leaders: Perspectives on the professional development of teachers* (pp. 153–177). Bloomington, IN: Phi Delta Kappa.

Helburn, S. (Ed.). (1995). *Cost, quality, and child outcomes in child care centers.* Denver: University of Colorado, Economics Department.

Kagan, S. L. (1994). Leadership: Rethinking it—making it happen. *Young Children, 49* (5), 50–54.

Katz, L. G. (1996). Child development knowledge and teacher preparation: Confronting assumptions. *Early Childhood Research Quarterly, 11*(2), 135–146.

Kontos, S., Howes, C., Shinn, M., & Galinsky, E. (1995). *Quality in family child care and relative care.* New York: Teachers College Press.

Kozol, J. (1995). *Amazing grace: The lives of children and the conscience of a nation.* New York: Crown.

Lewit, E. M. (1992). *U.S. health care for children. 2(2)*, Los Altos, CA: Center for the Future of Children.

McMillan, J. H., & Reed, D. R. (1993). *Defying the odds: A study of resilient at-risk students.* Richmond, VA: Metropolitan Educational Research Consortium.

National Association for the Education of Young Children [NAEYC]. (1994). NAEYC position statement on violence in the lives of children. *Young Children, 48*(6), 80–84.

National Center for Youth Law. (1995, January-February). Links between early childhood services and juvenile justice. *Youth Law News*, 4–8.

Piaget, J. (1951). *The child's conception of the world.* Savage, MD: Littlefield Adams.

Rousseau, J. (1947). L'Emile ou l'education. In O. E. Tellows and N. R. Tarrey (Eds.), *The age of enlightenment.* New York: F. S. Croft.

Schorr, L. (1988). *Within our reach: Breaking the cycle of the disadvantaged.* New York: Anchor Books.

Spitz, R. (1949). The role of ecological factors in emotional development in infancy. *Child Development, 20*, 145–156.

Vygotsky, L. (1978). *Mind in society: The development of higher psychological processes.* Cambridge, MA: Harvard University Press.

Weissbourd, (1996). *The myth of the vulnerable child.* Reading, MA: Addison-Wesley.

Werner, E. E. (1990). Protective factors and individual resilience. In S. J. Meisels & J. P. Shonkoff (Eds.), *Handbook of early childhood education* (pp. 97–116). Cambridge: Cambridge University Press.

Wheeler, E. J. (1994). Peer conflict in the classroom: Drawing implications from research. *Childhood Education, 70*(5), 296–299.

Zill, N., & Schoenborn, C. A. (1990). Developmental learning and emotional problems: Health of our nation's children, United States, 1988. In U.S. Department of Health and Human Services, *Advance data,* No. 190.

Chapter 3

Valuing Cultural Diversity in the Early Years: Social Imperatives and Pedagogical Insights

Marilyn Chipman

Desiree glanced upward at the clock on the wall. It was 10:40 P. M., almost time for her shift to end. Desiree loved her position as a delivery room nurse at Grace Covenant Community Hospital. This had been a particularly busy evening on the obstetrics ward. She smiled as she thought of the six new babies who had begun the journey of life. Looking at each tiny sleeping head, she said softly, "Being born is hard work, and you have earned your rest. I'll see you tomorrow. Good night."

Six infants, born in the United States in the same city on the same date—LaShaniqua, Feliciano, Christopher, Chung Li, Amy, and Jonas. Each one entered the world without any "past," and yet their "futures" will be affected by factors beyond their control. All six infants are citizens of the United States by virtue of birth. Yet, because of the group into which each was born, society's *view of* and *treatment of* these infants will be different as each life unfolds.

Ethnicity, gender, social class, religion, and the challenge of disability are but a few of the factors that may determine the paths along which each child will be *permitted* or *forbidden* to travel. The innocent newborn, sleeping peacefully, does not know anything about his or her cultural group. If the infant is from an underrepresented culture, then in 3 or 4 short years the child may become acquainted with the sharp sting of discrimination (King, Chipman, & Cruz-Jansen, 1994). By merely being born, these children enter a battle that was already engaged before their births.

As the forces of socialization come into play, each infant will be influenced differently. Some, like Euro-Americans Christopher and Amy, will be the beneficiaries of societal systems that historically have been

43

weighted in their favor. Others, like African-American LaShaniqua or Mexican-American Feliciano, will encounter centuries-old prejudices that may derail their progress in life. Chung Li, whose parents are newly arrived from the Pacific Rim, also will be exposed to struggle. Little Jonas, of Jewish descent, will alternately be accepted and rejected, depending on the situational context in which he finds himself at the time. As a whole, the females will have more difficulty than the males in most arenas, but the ethnic-minority girls will experience the hardest time of all (O'Callaghan, Bryant, & Price, 1989; Wiley, 1989). Regardless of ethnicity, if one of these infants becomes physically or cognitively challenged, the disability may subject that child to discrimination and cultural bias.

THE MANDATE FOR MULTICULTURAL EDUCATION

Understanding multicultural education must begin with an undestanding of the pluralistic nature of our population; the role of American schools in educating children from different cultures; and the philosophical framework of educating children from diverse backgrounds. Whether and how early childhood educators value the diverse language, cultural, and learning abilities of children is pivotal to the success or failure in school settings.

A History of Pluralism

This land of America always has been characterized by pluralism. The very fabric of our nation was woven with threads of diversity. The Native Americans were the first inhabitants of what is now the United States. (While other groups "came to this country," the fact is that for the Native Americans, this nation "came to them.") Immigrants from Europe chose to cross the Atlantic seeking a new life. Workers from the Pacific Rim were invited to come and help build the transcontinental railroad. Although Mexicans coming northward found barbed-wire fences rather than a welcoming Statue of Liberty at their point of entry, they were able to persevere against all odds. The African Americans were not given the original choice of coming, and once here, they were forced to stay against their will. Brought to this land as slaves beginning in 1619, they actually were here some 350 years before the government itself was established on July 4, 1776. Once freed, most elected to remain and forge a new life for their children.

Thus it is not difficult to see that diverse groups—Native Americans,

Europeans, African Americans, Asians, and Hispanics—all have had an integral part in the shaping of our nation. Contributions to its greatness have been made by all, even under harsh conditions. Yet for generations the school system magnified the story of one group and ignored or marginalized the contributions of the rest. In children's storybooks, in classroom films, in textbooks, on posters, and even in the playhouse, the white was beautified while the black, brown, red, and yellow were ridiculed or not represented at all.

The School as Power

The school's subtle assent to its curricular treatment and maltreatment of ethnic groups was all the more insidious because of its power. Society is comprised of various institutions that are the "power-brokers" for the socialization of its members. The family, the church, and the government are among the prime examples of such. Yet it is evident that the school must be included on this list, for its powerful impact on the lives of citizens cannot be overlooked (Asante, 1987; Grant & Sleeter, 1986).

One reason for the school's power is that attendance is compulsory in all 50 states. Not sending one's child to school is tantamount to neglect, and is punishable by law. Preschool-age children can scarcely wait for the big day to come when they can "go to school." Once they reach the ripe old age of 5, they are privileged to enter that "real" building inhabited by their older siblings or friends. They are admonished to study hard, to pay attention, to obey their teachers. On returning home each evening, usually they are asked, "What did you learn today?" Therefore, early in life little children tend to internalize the notion that those things taught by the teacher in a place called school are important and true.

Early childhood has been defined as the years from birth through age 8. Brewer (1992) asserts that these years are more important than any other 8-year span in life in terms of human cognitive and physical development and social learning. A century ago, when our nation was more agrarian, the young were kept close to their mothers and fathers, and socialized in a pattern of extended families. The young grew up in a safe, supportive, intergenerational environment, and the first years of life were more nurturing. Roles and expectations were established and clearly set forth for each member of the family. The individuals the young child saw in the town marketplace, the church, and the one-room schoolhouse basically were homogeneous in appearance as well as in life-style.

Such is not always the case as America faces the year 2000. More than ever, young children are socialized in urban settings (Webb & Sherman, 1989). There are various family configurations. Neighbors and friends come from many backgrounds, and classmates may be bussed from sections of the city that are unlike their own. The school becomes a microcosm of the world.

Diversity in the schoolroom may be related to ethnicity, gender, religion, social class, or physical challenges. The effective teacher finds ways to make each child feel accepted and valued by all other children in the class. The earlier in life that the lesson of self-worth and the equal worth of others is imparted, the more beneficial it will be.

All too often, however, diversity is treated negatively by the teacher. What subliminal messages of *inferiority* are sent to youngsters from other cultures when only the dominant Euro-American culture is magnified? Likewise, what subliminal messages of *superiority* are sent to the children who are of European descent when they see only their own culture positively reflected? King and colleagues (1994) said that the curriculum must be a *mirror* for young children, in which they can see images of themselves and of those like them. Yet for too many of our children, the curriculum is a *wall,* blocking all likenesses of themselves and their heritage from view, or portraying them negatively. At some point in the school experience, each child should see himself or herself "centered" on the stage of history as well as within the current context. In this way the child can be empowered to learn (Asante, 1987).

A Failed Philosophy

A century ago, the "melting pot" philosophy was espoused, wherein all ethnic groups were encouraged to assimilate. Cultural assimilation is the process that takes place when an individual or group acquires traits and habits that are inherent within another group. Banks (1991) asserts, however, that although some members of ethnic groups may take on all the characteristics of Euro-Americans, they still will experience discrimination because of their different physical appearance. In other words, some groups cannot ever "melt in."

Thus, the melting pot analogy has been replaced by that of a stew pot. In preparing a delicious stew, the cook uses a variety of ingredients. Yet the meat, potatoes, and vegetables all retain their identities. Further, the stew is more than just delicious, it is life-sustaining. All cultural groups are integral to the life of America. Therefore, children of diversity should not be asked to negate or deny their cultural heritage by "melting" in order to participate in and excel in school. To ask this of any young child is unfair, and expressly so since the characteristics that cause the difference are outside of the child's ability to alter.

It becomes incumbent on caregiving adults to set in place effective and qualitative measures to ensure that little children are not emotionally destroyed due to "being different." Attitude formation begins early in life. A disdain for differences, especially those that are physically evident, can manifest itself in a child as young as the age of 3. Sadly, self-hatred based on physical attributes that are different also has been documented in the very young (U.S. Supreme Court, 1954).

Adults who are responsible for educating young children in a diverse society are beginning to recognize the importance of helping them to learn, at an early age, that *difference is not deficiency.* Such awareness is vital for *all* children and can take the form of something as simple as learning to pronounce a child's "different-sounding" name correctly (and ensuring that all the other children in the room do so, too).

As adults shape young lives, they will send a message of worth or nonworth to the children. A youngster who is a member of the dominant Euro-American population should not be allowed to grow up feeling that he or she is inherently worthy of good things, nor should a child from a different culture be allowed to grow up feeling that he or she is inherently *un*worthy of good things.

Textbook Reform

The school system has come to grips with the realization that pluralism in America is a *fact,* not merely a topic of debate. In order to have an informed discussion about the school, one must look at the curriculum. To do this, one must consider the most instantly recognizable icon of the curriculum—the textbook.

Initially, when textbook publishers began to recognize the acts of commission (untrue depictions) and omission (total exclusion) that had been performed against culturally diverse groups, they attempted to rectify the problem by "adding on" to the existing curriculum. Storybooks with "Dick and Jane"–type families began to add one black neighbor to the picture. Other scenes and storylines added a Hispanic worker, an Asian friend, or someone who was confined to a wheelchair. However, the *basic core* remained unchanged.

Later, as awareness grew, the publishers began to *feature* culturally diverse families and heroes in their books. In time, they recognized the very real need to deal with cultural *values* and with societal *issues* relative to various types of diversity. As a result, many educators began to conduct their classes using a multicultural framework.

Educators now know that at the very youngest age, children under the instructive care of a sensitive adult can begin to understand and appreciate the values and symbols of various cultural groups. This cannot be done by the old method of merely "adding on" heroes and holidays to a curriculum that glorifies one dominant group. Rather, multicultural theorists (Banks, 1991; Grant & Sleeter 1986; King et al., 1994) have proposed a curriculum "transformation" in which all content areas are taught from a perspective that includes women as well as men, people who are disabled as well as those who are not, individuals from different social classes, and those from various religious and racial groups.

It became clear that a paradigm shift was necessary in order to challenge the existing canon and correct errors in content and methodology (Banks, 1991). This metamorphosis benefitted not only the children but also the teachers. Why? Teachers tend to believe the material they teach, especially when holding the Instructor's Manual in hand. Planning lessons from a guide that presents the true story of all groups of people indeed has helped to sensitize the best teachers of young children to the needs of their students.

Dissent and Rationale

As with all issues, the pluralistic curriculum is not without its opponents. Some schoolteachers hope that it is simply another passing educational trend or fad that will disappear in time and be forgotten. Other critics decry multicultural education as divisive (Bloom, 1987; Ravitz, 1992; Schlesinger, 1992).

Such persons fail to acknowledge that, in all of history, a primary tool of subjugation has been the dissemination of misinformation. Hilliard (1992) found that groups in power will "defame, stigmatize, stereotype, and distort" the history, influence, and contributions of the people they are oppressing (p. 12). Thus, multicultural education came about in response to the social and pedagogical mandate to provide a full and truthful rendering of our nation's past and present record, for "*human* culture is the product of the struggles of *all* humanity, not the possession of a single racial or ethnic group" (p. 12; emphasis added).

Dr. James Banks (1991) has set forth the typology of "The Emerging Stages of Ethnicity" through which individuals may pass. He theorizes that "*ethnic psychological captivity*" is the stage in which a person is ashamed of his or her group and experiences self-rejection and low self-esteem. All too often those who are locked in this stage are children of color. "*Ethnic encapsulation*" refers to a stage in which one participates primarily within one's own community and believes that his or her group is superior to all others. Miel (1967), in her discourse on suburbia, describes the many members of the dominant culture who are in this stage.

Banks (1991) posits that, through the pluralistic curriculum, teachers can and should help their students move toward the stage of *"multiethnicity,"* where they can accept themselves and others as members of a culturally diverse society.

It is important to understand that what is described by Hilliard (1992), Banks (1991), and others as ethnic-related phenomena also is experienced by children whose diversity is occasioned by disability, social class, gender, or other factors.

INSIGHT INTO MULTICULTURAL PEDAGOGY

Those involved in the educational process are well aware that the term *curriculum* does not refer solely to textbooks and manuals. The curriculum encompasses the entire classroom learning environment, including the affective tone (Chipman, 1990). In planning to meet the needs of youngsters in a pluralistic society, the early childhood educator must look into all aspects of the educational experience. Certain pedagogical strategies are necessary for the good of the children.

Cooperative Learning

In addressing the matter of cultural diversity, the teacher must ensure that cultural learning styles are considered. For instance, at home and in their communities, most children of color are socialized in cooperative rather than competitive environments. Yet the typical classroom in the American school is geared to emphasize the dominant notion that one child's success is contingent on another's failure. The teacher who is culturally sensitive will plan activities that enable the young child to compete only against his or her own prior level of learning. Piaget & Inhelder (1969) emphasized peer interaction and extensive verbalization as basic tenets of his theory relative to cognitive development in the early years; these are important components of the culturally sensitive classroom as well.

Assessment

It also is important that today's early childhood educator utilize a wide range of assessment techniques to determine a child's ability (McAfee & Leong, 1994). The effective teacher will focus on *potential* rather than merely on *performance,* believing that every child can learn, regardless of ethnicity, gender, disability, or social class. Rather than relying on standardized tests and paper/pencil tasks, the teacher will use developmentally appropriate tools such as portfolios, time samples, self-assessments, and narratives. Often, children from diverse backgrounds may express themselves more accurately in authentic situations (Hilliard, 1991).

Multiple Intelligences. Today's effective teacher will be aware of the fact that there is more than one arena in which a child can excel. Gardner (1993) has theorized that there are seven identifiable areas of intelligence that can be considered valid. Typically teachers value logical-mathematical thinking and exclude the other six types of ability: linguistic, musical, spatial, kinesthetic, interpersonal, and intrapersonal. Yet children may manifest intelligence in any of these ways. Since children also are capable of growth in combinations of these areas, they should be valued for excellence wherever it surfaces (Armstrong, 1994).

The inability of teachers to acknowledge this fact has led to a grossly disproportionate underrepresentation of children of color, particularly boys, in classes for the gifted and talented. There are vast numbers of underachievers among ethnic children (Ford, 1993).

Discipline

The area of discipline and guidance must be addressed in the multicultural classroom. Ethnic boys are overrepresented in special education classes because their actions often are misinterpreted by the teacher. A misunderstanding of body language or cultural interactions with peers (Hale-Benson, 1982) may cause anger or frustration in the teacher. A lack of cultural sensitivity can prevent an objective evaluation of situations that call for discipline.

Special Needs

Across the nation, the movement toward "inclusion" is helping to meet the needs of children with disabilities (Martinez, 1995). Young children are curious by nature, and their questions or fears relative to someone's disability are not to be disregarded. The teacher must *openly* and *consciously* model acceptance of the child with special needs in the inclusive classroom. In this way, the other youngsters will follow suit and become more accepting, realizing again that *difference is not deficiency.* King and colleagues (1994) posit that young children with disabilities can be given the opportunity to become leaders and to excel in their areas of strength. In this way their classmates can be helped to understand that, regardless of physical or cognitive challenges, the child is still a valued member of the classroom and quite capable of succeeding.

Gender

Research by Sadker and Sadker (1986) has documented the fact that teachers use different approaches when teaching boys than when teaching girls. If a task is difficult, the male child may be instructed how to perform it, while the female child may have the task performed for her. Longer wait time is given to boys than to girls, and boys are asked more open-ended questions in order to stimulate critical-thinking skills. Teachers must be aware of subtle messages sent to young children by these strategies, and make efforts to correct them.

SCHOOL/HOME RELATIONS

Berger (1995) strongly sets forth the premise that the teacher must create an environment in which parents are perceived as partners in the educational process, not as adversaries. The valuing of the mother as teacher is set forth by Harris (1995), who discusses the important role that can be played in the life of her children even by a mother who is uneducated and economically deprived.

It is not uncommon to hear teachers voice the opinion that ethnic or poor parents "don't care about their children." The reason usually given for having reached this conclusion is because "they never *come*" to conferences, programs, or field trips, or "they never *send*" items for the classroom or money for fund-raisers. In making such comments, these teachers assume the role of judge. Usually such judgment is based on a comparison between poorer parents and themselves: These teachers feel that they themselves are the standard by which parents should be measured.

The culturally sensitive teacher will realize that there may be mitigating factors that preclude such participation. For instance, a lack of transportation, a second job, or the lack of funds for a baby-sitter for younger siblings during the time of the school event all are hindrances. Moore (1995) found that "married Black mothers are more likely than are their White counterparts to be employed," with some 73% of married black mothers in the labor force as compared with only 59% of whites (p. 47). Parents may feel intimidated by teachers or administrators, especially if language is a barrier.

Many teachers will interact with a young child in a negative way due to this perceived "lack of concern" on the part of the parents. Others openly make derogatory remarks to the child regarding their parents or their home. Still others call into play the "Pygmalion Effect," whereby they initially assume that the child cannot learn (because of the home situation), and then fail to teach the child. When the child does not learn, the teacher smugly feels that the initial prediction was correct. Yet it is the child who suffers from this travesty. The effective teacher will acknowledge that parents from all cultures are a valuable resource in the education of their own children.

INTROSPECTION FOR THE TEACHER

It is important that teachers of the very young examine their inner feelings relative to diversity. Little children imitate the behavior of those adults whom they wish to please, and in a place called school, there is no one whom the child wishes to please more than the teacher. Thus children will emulate their teachers as much as possible.

Unconscious Strategies

If personal prejudices are not dealt with, they will manifest themselves in the classroom. The young student may notice and subconsciously internalize three distinct types of teacher behavior directed toward the child who is "different." The teacher may *ignore* the child, consistently calling on others while refusing to respond to or offer help to her or him. The teacher may treat the child as *infantile,* talking down to her or him in a condescending manner or gushing with feigned praise over the slightest task completed. The teacher may interact with the child by showing *ridicule or open repulsion,* displaying exasperation when he or she seeks even small attentions or favors.

In all of these unfortunate instances, the other students will imitate what is being modeled by the teacher. These types of interaction will carry over into the cafeteria, onto the playground, and onto the schoolbus as well. Even if the teacher is unaware of reacting in such a negative manner, the impact on *both* the individual child and the other youngsters in the room will be the same. Whether or not the actions were intentional, one child will be hurt by feeling inferior and unworthy, while others will be harmed by being given false feelings of superiority.

The teacher must also realize that "silence means consent." A teacher who does not act immediately to stop hurtful words or actions directed toward a child gives tacit approval to them.

Becoming Aware

Educators can learn much about diversity by venturing outside their own cultural enclave. For instance, on Sunday mornings at 11:00 A.M., many Euro-American teachers and their families enter a quiet sanctuary for a worship service characterized by meditation and soft organ music. At that very same hour, many African-American families enter a sanctuary for a worship service where "loudness" and "movement" permeate everything from the singing of the choir, to the percussionist's beat, to the cadence of the preacher, to the deafening shouts of affirmation from the congregation. Experiencing cultural differences of this sort can help teachers understand that their own method is not the "only way" or the "right way," but rather "one way" of doing things. They also may see how their students' culture outside the classroom may impact what transpires inside it.

Cultivating acquaintances among people from diverse walks of life will enrich the educator as well. Reading cultural publications and attending celebrations and other events also will lead to becoming more sensitive to the beauty of diversity in American life.

LOOKING AHEAD

Where will we go from here? The social imperative is clear. Our nation still stands as a utopia for many from around the world, inviting an international populace to find safety and promise on these shores. Demographically, our nation is increasing in numbers of women, of people of color, of poor. In most major urban centers, children of color cannot be termed "minority" any longer, for they comprise far more than 51% of the whole (Chipman & Martinez, 1992; Kuykendall, 1992). Our playgrounds and classrooms reflect the changes taking place each year. Youngsters from *all* groups comprise the school population.

CONCLUSION

At the beginning of the chapter we met Desiree and six infants. Born in America on one date, they will grow up to become members of the adult community of the 21st century, charged with the responsibility of leading the nation. They will serve at the helm of the family, the church, the government, business and commerce, the military, and, of course, the school. The pedagogical implications are too monumental to be ignored.

Cultural diversity was part of our nation's past. It is perhaps one of the most prominent and distinguishing characteristics of our present. It is the essence of our future. In a diverse society, pluralism takes many forms. Early childhood educators who are dedicated, sensitive, and aware will meet the challenge of preparing the next generation to live in harmony.

REFERENCES

Armstrong, T. (1994). *Multiple intelligences in the classroom.* Alexandria, VA: Association for Supervision and Curriculum Development.

Asante, M. (1987). *The Afrocentric idea.* Philadelphia: Temple University Press.

Banks, J. A. (1991). *Teaching strategies for ethnic studies* (5th ed.) Boston: Allyn and Bacon.

Berger, E. H. (1995). *Parents as partners in education* (4th ed.). New York: Merrill/Prentice-Hall.

Bloom, A. (1987). *The closing of the American mind.* New York: Simon and Schuster.

Brewer, J. (1992). *Introduction to early childhood education: Preschool through primary grades.* Boston: Allyn and Bacon.

Chipman, M. (1990, September 22). *Curriculum decision in the '90s: The Impact upon the African American Child.* Paper presented at the annual conference of the National Black Child Development Institute, Washington, DC.

Chipman, M., & Martinez, L. M. (1992). Multicultural education: A foundation for critical thinking and creative teaching. In *Scholarship Reconsidered: The Collected Papers of the Colorado Exchange Faculty Conference* (pp. 23–30). Gunnison, CO: Western State College.

Ford, D. Y. (1993). An investigation of the paradox of underachievers among gifted Black students. *Roeper Review, 16,* 78–84.

Gardner, H. (1993). *Multiple intelligences: The theory in practice.* New York: Basic Books.

Grant, C., & Sleeter, C. (1986). *After the school bell rings.* London: Falmer Press.

Hale-Benson, J. (1982). *Black children: Their roots, culture and learning styles.* Provo, UT: Brigham Young University.

Harris, W. J. (1995, August). Mothers and education. *The Proclaimer, 1,* 6–7.

Hilliard, A. G. (1991). *Testing African American students.* Morristown, NJ: Aaron Press.

Hilliard, A. G. (1992, January). Why we must pluralize the curriculum, *Educational Leadership, 49*(4), 12–14.

King, E. W., Chipman, M., and Cruz-Jansen, M. (1994). *Educating young children in a diverse society.* Boston: Allyn and Bacon.

Kuykendall, C. (1992). *From rage to hope.* Bloomington, IN: National Educational Service.

Martinez, T. (1995, July/August). Building a bridge with special students. *Instructor,* 105(7), 44–46.

McAfee, O., & Leong, D. (1994). *Assessing and guiding young children's development and learning.* Boston: Allyn and Bacon.

Miel, A. (1967). *The shortchanged children of suburbia.* New York: Institute of Human Relations Press.

Moore, E. K. (1995, May). Mediocre care: Double jeopardy for black children. *Young Children,* 50(4), 47.

O'Callaghan, K., Bryant, C., and Price, B. (1989, March 1). *Black women, double jeopardy.* Paper presented at the annual conference of the National Convention of the American College Personnel Association, Washington, DC.

Piaget, J., & Inhelder, J. B. (1969). *The psychology of the child.* New York: Basic Books.

Ravitz, D. (1992, January). A culture in common. *Educational Leadership,* pp. 8–11.

Sadker, M. & Sadker, D. (1986, March). Sexism in the classroom: From grade school to graduate school. *Phi Delta Kappan,* pp. 512–515.

Schlesinger, A. (1992). *The disuniting of America.* New York: Norton.

U.S. Supreme Court. (1954). *Brown v. Board of Education of Topeka.* 347 U.S. 483.

Webb, R. B., & Sherman, R. (1989). *Schooling and society* (2nd ed.). New York: Macmillan.

Wiley, E. (1989, May 25). SAT takes its harshest toll of black females, study finds. *Black Issues in Higher Education,* 6(6), 1,6.

Chapter 4

Working with Families of Young Children: Our History and Our Future Goals

Nancy Briggs

Mary Renck Jalongo

Lisbeth Brown

Families, schools, and communities represent the various contexts in which children grow and develop; they are inextricably connected by the roles and functions they share in facilitating the development and education of children. The quality of connections among them has a profound influence on the quality of life the children will have. As contemporary early childhood educators, our task is an exceptionally challenging one as we strive to forge stronger connections between and among families, schools, and communities.

Early childhood educators need to identify with and respect families despite the fact that perspectives on childhood may differ drastically; we need to collaborate with families in ways that place children's needs uppermost and optimize growth and learning socially, physically, emotionally, cognitively, and artistically; and we need to build mutual trust and respect, particularly for those families who have had negative experiences with the educational system. To accomplish these goals, we must confront our own biases, embrace diversity, respect the knowledge that families have about children, and willingly share power. In every situation early childhood educators face, the overarching purpose is how to respond in ways that serve children's best interests.

Today, more than ever, families need help in ensuring that their children develop the values, attitudes, and behaviors that will help them succeed in school and beyond. Communities, schools, and programs must all recognize and accept that "yesterday's strategies will not be able to address tomorrow's realities or meet the needs of tomorrow's children" (Kagan, 1990, p. 272). Therefore, one of the most persistent themes in the current school reform movement has been the strengthening of the connections among families, schools, programs, and communities—the issue of parental involvement in children's care and education.

Parental involvement in children's education is not a new strategy, however. On the contrary, since the beginning of civilization, parents have been the first teachers and socializers of their children, passing on the skills, customs, and laws of their culture, intentionally or otherwise, so that their children could not only meet their own basic needs but be productive citizens and carry on their cultural traditions (Berger, 1995).

In this chapter, we will address the changing structures and functions of families and societal institutions, provide a rationale for collaboration, address major controversies in home/institution collaboration, and conclude with implications and recommendations. We begin with several fundamental considerations: What is a family? How have families and their role as educators of their children changed? What is the appropriate relationship among families, schools, and the community?

CHANGING RELATIONSHIPS BETWEEN FAMILY AND SCHOOL

American society, the American educational system, and the American family are mirror reflections of one another; as one changes, the others change as well, although not necessarily at the same rate. The fundamental paradigmatic shift that has occurred in American society, especially within the past half century, has been rapid, bringing about a reconfiguration of the family that has resulted in a dramatic change in its relationship with the school (Elkind, 1995).

This social revolution has created major changes in both the structure and function of families in recent decades, making it exceedingly difficult for early childhood and other professionals to define "family" (Kagan, Powell, Weissbourd, & Zigler, 1987). Elkind (1995) incorporates both biological and social influences, defining the family as "a social system characterized by a kinship system and by certain sentiments, values, and perceptions" (p. 10). Elkind (1994) also points out that another major function the family has historically performed is that of "preparing its members for life in a larger society" (p. 209). Madeleine Grumet (1988) captured the powerful and, at times, conflicting emotional influences that families exert on children when she wrote that home is "the place where we were most thrilled, most afraid, most ashamed, most proud" (p. xvii).

The American family has already undergone two major transformations in the past 200 years, resulting in both liberation and stress. In each case, the educational system has been altered by the changes occurring in society at the time. For instance, the typical early-modern family was an extended family that lived together on a farm, sharing the responsibility for and the products of their labor. The industrial revolution brought many of these families to urban areas, permanently altering the structure of the family unit. The result was what Elkind (1994) refers to as the modern nuclear family. This family structure provides clear boundaries between the roles and responsibilities of parents and children, between private and public lives, and between home and work lives. These distinctions can provide security and allow children to be children, although they can also be confining for both adults and children (Elkind, 1994, 1995).

The nuclear family structure is, in reality, primarily a white middle-class fantasy, never realized by the majority of American families; nonetheless, it has been proffered as the ideal family structure (Weissbourd, 1996). Traditionally, the family's function was to serve as "nurturer and protector of the next generation" (Kagan et al., 1987, p. 4). In concert with this perspective, therefore, American society has taken a "fortification" approach and provided services to children and families that maintain and sustain this protective function.

The American free public education system is a prime example of society's efforts to equalize opportunity in achieving the "American Dream" by supporting family efforts to ensure children a better future through education. The early American schools reflected the values of the "ideal" nuclear family structure at that time. However, recent changes in society have focused attention on the growing diversity in family structure, creating the need for social service and educational institutions to adapt to contemporary American families (Elkind, 1994, 1995; Kagan et al., 1987).

Elkind (1994) labels today's postmodern family structure as "permeable." The divisions between parent and child, public and private lives, work and home lives, have "become blurred and difficult to discern" (p. 1). Of particular importance for early childhood professionals is the shift of the permeable family's focus—away from the children's needs and toward the needs of the adults—as life-style options that were not available during earlier times are exercised. Divorce, single-parent families, blended families, women working full-time outside the home, adults returning to higher education and training programs, out-of-home child care, and movement away from extended families have all provided adults relief from family function and structure constraints of the past, but such changes have been unsettling and often detrimental to the children (Elkind, 1994).

Contemporary society is faced with broadening its perspective of family structure and function, recognizing changes in family dynamics, realistically acknowledging the contemporary family's influence on children, and determining the impact these changes have on the school. Increasingly, early childhood programs in diverse settings will have to assume responsibility for children in ways once thought to be the exclusive province of parents and families.

CURRENT TRENDS IN PARENT INVOLVEMENT

The "parent-involvement movement" actually began soon after the invention of the printing press, in the mid-fifteenth century, when authors were first able to give advice directly to parents. By the seventeenth and eighteenth centuries, when new thoughts about education and the importance of the family in the education of children were emerging, a new profession—parent educator—began to flourish (Berger, 1995). The parent-education movement was resurrected most recently in the 1960s because parents were being blamed for the failures and shortcomings of their children. As part of the war on poverty, schools and community programs reached out into the community again, to educate parents not only in child development and behavior management, as had been the earlier emphasis, but also about their role in helping their children succeed in school (Berger, 1995; Powell, 1991). This was the beginning of the "transmission of school practices model," which seeks to involve parents as partners in the education of their children by transferring the school culture and practices to parents so that they can reinforce them at home with their children (Auerbach, 1995, p. 14).

It is important to note that the traditional parent-education and contemporary parent-involvement movements originated because of different needs, and differ in their goals as well as in the information provided to parents. Nonetheless they are both based on the same questionable assumptions: (1) learning occurs only in a unidirectional relationship—from school to parent to child; (2) learning occurs only in school-like contexts; and (3) learning is valid only if it is representative of mainstream values. Auerbach (1995) points out that these assumptions simply represent an updated version of the outdated deficit hypothesis, still placing the responsibility for school problems on families rather than on the social conditions that contribute to the problems.

Sarason (1995) agrees, stating that for all of the well-intentioned sloganeering and justification of past parent education and involvement efforts, the rhetoric has missed the scope of what is at stake in terms of control over educational programs. In fact, Sarason thinks that the continued push for parental involvement is actually "an explicit challenge to the *status quo* in regard to the use and distribution of power in the formulation of educational policy and in educational practice" (p. 40). It is generally understood that parent involvement does not, in and of itself, ensure improved educational outcomes, but the opportunity to participate in the decision-making process regarding policy and practice does ensure more accountability for those outcomes. In other words, "what is at stake is not power in and of itself but the concrete ways by which alterations of power will in turn alter the ecology of the classrooms, school, and their surrounding communities" (p. 12). With this in mind, what is the next step?

FUTURE TRENDS AND IMPLICATIONS

Both the historical traditions and contemporary circumstances of early childhood education have led to widespread agreement concerning the importance of families' interest in and commitment to their children's academic achievement, as well as the need for school and community support for these efforts. There is, however, far less agreement on current programmatic approaches that are beneficial—rather than intrusive—for families. According to Epstein (1995), such questions "have challenged research and practice, creating an interdisciplinary field of inquiry into school, family, and community partnerships with 'caring' as a core concept" (p. 701). Indeed, a subtle shift has begun to take place in the way policymakers and educators view the relationship between the family and the school (Morrow, 1995; Powell, 1991). As a result, educational researchers have not only made a case for improved home–school relationships that offer support, collaboration, and open communication between family and school, but they have also provided a foundation for a new model of family–school–community partnerships that will serve to empower the family, rather than merely serve as another unproductive, sporadic intervention (Berger, 1995; Epstein, 1995; Williams, 1992).

According to Epstein (1995), family, school, and community partnerships have the potential to improve educational programs, provide families with support services, encourage family connections with community resources and other families, and assist teachers in meeting the needs of children. However, two underlying issues still must be addressed if the goal of home–school–community partnerships is going to be realized for the 21st century:

1. In what ways must the school's role change in order to meet the increasingly complex needs of diverse families?

2. In what ways must the interaction and communication between and among families, early childhood programs, and communities change in order for them to lend authentic support to one another?

The Changing Role of the School

Edwards and Young (1992) raise the question of the role the school should play in the lives of children, families, and the communities they serve. They point out that the boundaries separating responsibilities for children are blurring, with schools expected to meet far more than just the academic needs of today's students. Schools, in general, confront daily changes in society, changes in family demographics, a shifting value terrain, and new perceptions of social responsibility. Therefore, the mission of America's schools has been seriously broadened. This is particularly true for early childhood programs because young children require special care and nurturing (Epstein, 1995; Kagan, 1994; Powell, 1991).

Widespread agreement exists, however, that early childhood education has limited resources and cannot by itself respond to all of the elements of family functions (Chavkin, 1990; Coleman, 1991; Edwards & Young, 1992). Powell (1991) firmly believes that early childhood education's response to the needs of today's families must be governed, first of all, by a traditional interest in the children's learning. At the same time, early childhood programs must align themselves with other social institutions that have complementary expertise and function as "multiple-service brokers for children" (Edwards & Young, 1992, p. 78).

Kagan (1994) suggested that education should be viewed as a shared responsibility within an ecological context, and that to improve the educational outcomes for today's children, schools should reach out to families, the community as a whole, and community institutions that serve families. In fact, such efforts to restructure schools closely resemble the rich traditions of early childhood education to expand services for young children in Susan Blow's kindergartens, Maria Montessori's *Casi de Bambini,* and Head Start. The family resource and support movement and collaborative community services are a continuation of early childhood education's leadership role in the field of education.

Family Resource and Support Programs. Family resource and support programs recognize the value of early childhood programs in promoting services that will enhance family life, thereby improving the personal, social, and academic development of children. In response to the ongoing changes affecting today's families, family resource and support programs originally emerged as a result of research that recognizes the importance of the family's influence on children's development. The parent-education and self-help movements have also contributed to the growth of family resource and support programs, by recognizing and promoting the importance of empowering individuals to help themselves (Davies, 1991; Kagan et al., 1987). However, family resource and support programs differ significantly from the earlier parent programs in that they recognize and respect the fact that while all families share many of the same needs, they do not all need the same type of information or service at the same time. As a result, family resource and support programs are capable of offering a myriad of services for families, but focus on those most needed in any one community or neighborhood at any one time (Kagan, 1994; National Task Force on School Readiness, 1991).

Community Collaborations. Early childhood educators, whether in a school or in an early childhood program setting, are in a critical position to lead the way in restructuring efforts to work with families because they are in contact with families at a time when parents are most receptive to becoming involved in their children's educational experiences. Additionally, they are the community professionals who see children and their families on the most consistent basis throughout the year (Chavkin, 1990). The early childhood educator can also serve as an advocate for families, referring them to appropriate agencies to satisfy their family needs, or lobbying to put the services where the parents are—in the neighborhood (Allen, Brown, & Finlay, 1992).

When early childhood programs and community agencies recognize their distinct, but related, roles in the lives of children and families, and collaborate to enrich the services each offers, they eliminate the fragmentation of services that prevents professionals from seeing the cumulative impact of their interventions. When parents, educators, and social service agencies form community collaborations, everyone benefits (Kagan & Rivera, 1991; Kirst, 1991; Stone, 1995). Advantages of such collaborations include the assurance of equitable distribution of goods and services, improved access to and continuity of services for families, minimization of expenses, the elimination of the duplication of services, and the improvement of training opportunties for agency and school staff (Epstein, 1995; Rutherford & Billig, 1995; Stone, 1995). To this end, Kirst (1991) states that a complete overhaul of children's services—educational, social, and medical—is necessary to bring together public and private services to meet the comprehensive needs of children and families.

As Kagan (1994) indicated, if children's education is to be a responsibility shared by the family, the community, and the school, both family resource and support programs and community collaborations have the potential to shape the direction a community moves in when restructuring its educational programs for the future. Furthermore, such alliances allow all parties involved to focus on their own area of expertise, which for early childhood educators is children's learning needs (Edwards & Young, 1992).

Authentic Home–School Communication

Early childhood personnel and family members will have to develop new attitudes, communication strategies, and skills in order to ensure that their new relationship builds trust and respect, and opens doors for problem-solving dialogue. Some early childhood educators just seem to know how to effectively communicate and work with parents, making home-school communication and involvement an important part of day-to-day operations. What makes this difference in teachers and schools?

Isenberg and Jalongo (1997) suggest that to effectively communicate with families, teachers must understand and overcome the obstacles that block effective communication. They cited four roadblocks to effective communication that can occur in any communication with families: teachers' lack of knowledge of how to work with families; priorities other than children's families; failure of families to respond to invitations to collaborate; and adversarial, uncooperative, or defensive parents.

The literature is replete with suggested strategies for building effective partnership communication strategies between teachers and families. These strategies are usually categorized by the types of communication process involved, which are based on models derived from the development of modern communication theory (Fenwick, 1993; Stone, 1993).

Communication Models. In many educational settings, one-way communication predominates, flowing from program to home with an information focus. Newsletters, handbooks, and written notes are examples of one-way communication (Adler & Rodman, 1988). However, research has indicated that this model is an inadequate strategy for interpersonal communication.

Interpersonal communication is a two-way process that entails some type of relationship and responsiveness. Telephone calls, informal conversations, and scheduled conferences are examples of two-way interpersonal communication. Yet even in these two-way communication strategies, little true interaction occurs.

True interactive communication differs from previous models in that all participants are considered equal participants. Further, when all participants—family, community, and school—are mutually and simultaneously involved in the process of communicating, the relationship among them begins to build and can be maintained more readily (Katz, 1993).

Communication Styles. In addition to the relationship among the participants, the communication process is comprised of two other components: *what is said* and *the way it is said.* The way something is said is referred to as communicator style and has 10 variables related to the way a person communicates: friendly, impression-leaving, relaxed, contentious, attentive, precise, animated, dramatic, open, or dominant (Norton, 1983). Thus, the research clearly indicates that in addition to what is communicated, teachers and schools also should be concerned with the way they communicate. A transactional model of communication that lets families know they are respected, that their input is valued, and that they are considered true partners in the education of their children is an important aspect of home–school–community collaboration (Blatt & Benz, 1993; Brown, 1989; Sallinen-Kuparinen, 1992).

RECOMMENDATIONS

The following three recommendations regarding national comprehensive policies, national teacher preparation standards, and national program accreditation standards are suggested as ways to create colloborative relationships that support families, schools, and communities:

1. *Early childhood educators should advocate a coordinated national policy on family support systems and collaborations.* Families, schools, and administrators should work with professional organizations such as Parent Teacher Association/Parent Teacher Organization (PTA/PTO), the National Association for the Education of Young Children (NAEYC), the Association for Childhood Education International (ACEI), the National Coalition for Campus Child Care (NCCC), and the National Association of Elementary School Principals (NAESP) to advocate comprehensive family support systems. No one organization can manage the complex issue of meaningful family–school–community collaboration alone. Therefore, professional organizations such as these and others should form alliances that will make families an integral part of teacher education preparation and in-service teacher professional development; provide parent education in collaboration and communication practices; prioritize support for families; begin family support systems early; and evaluate programs and schools to assess family involvement (Lombardi, 1992).

Even though the American public is well aware that large numbers of children are without even the basic necessities of life, citizens often balk at the suggestion of increased funding for health care, a school breakfast program, or Head Start. The public would rather embrace the fantasy of the white, middle-class American nuclear family than confront today's reality. Thus, part of our responsibility as early childhood educators is to keep these issues in the forefront until they can no longer be ignored, something that groups like the Children's Defense Fund have been working tirelessly to do.

The issue of family support should be addressed as a national public policy issue so that a coordinated effort can be put into action (Galinsky, Shubilla, Willer, Levine, & Daniel, 1994). If comprehensive family support programs such as these are to continue "to move into the forefront of the nation's conscience" (p. 136), a great deal of political action must be carried out.

2. *Early childhood educators should advocate teacher preparation standards that support family–school–community educational partnerships and community collaborations.* Demonstrating a commitment to families must begin with teacher preparation institutions; however, a recent national study reported that teachers and administrators were poorly prepared for their role in working with families (Radcliffe, Malone, & Nathan, 1994). Few states require teachers to study parent-involvement strategies or to develop abilities to enhance communications with parents; only seven states require administrators to take a course or demonstrate competence in promoting home–school relationships (Trawick-Smith & Lambert, 1995; Williams, 1992).

Where necessary, teacher education programs ought to be restructured, not only in terms of the content but also in terms of the experiences they provide to orient preservice teachers to family-centered approaches (Berger, 1995; Greenberg, 1989; Swick, 1991; Williams, 1992). Additionally, workshops, courses, and seminars that highlight techniques, strategies, and ways to reach out to families must be an integral part of professional development for in-service teachers and administrators (Davies, 1991; Swick, 1991).

As Madeline Grumet (1988) points out, there can be no real sense of community in schools and no real authentic parent involvement until educators begin to do the hard work of helping families and communities feel a sense of responsibility for "other people's children" as well as their own. It is only when families, educators, and other community members will accept nothing less for every child in the program than they would for their own children that the democratic ideal of education for all will be realized.

To accomplish this, early childhood educators at all levels must

- use their knowledge of child development and problem solving when interacting with families;
- acknowledge and respect the parent's feelings; and
- remain focused on both the individual child's and the group's needs (Newman, 1995)

These skills are part of developing a professional demeanor when working with families and community agencies (Bredekamp & Willer, 1993; Katz, 1993). Dynamic, supportive interrelationships with programs, schools, and community agencies must begin as early as possible in the family's life and continue throughout the early childhood years (Gage & Workman, 1994; Swick, 1991).

3. *Early childhood educators should advocate coordinated national accreditation standards for family–school–community educational partnerships and community collaborations.* There are many "shining examples" of people, schools, and programs that are making a difference in families, schools, and communities (Berger, 1995). As educators we must critically examine programs reputed to be successful in order to differentiate between those that capitalize on good public relations and programs that genuinely collaborate with and support families. Any meaningful evaluation of these programs cannot rely exclusively on administrator's self-report data or on the level of satisfaction expressed exclusively by families who traditionally have been enthusiastic supporters of the school.

Greenberg (1989) suggests the development of acceptable minimum levels and standards for family involvement. Failure of schools, programs, and institutions to comply with these standards would result in loss of funding and/or accreditation. It is a truism that "you get what you measure," so linking family–school involvement to teacher and administrator evaluation is another way of emphasizing the importance of this role for educators.

CONCLUSION

Three things are needed for social reform: a knowledge base, a public will, and a social strategy (Richmond & Kotelchuck, 1984). Where family support is concerned, American society certainly has a knowledge base and research support for greater home, school, and community collaboration (Roberts, Wasik, Casto, & Ramey, 1991). The thing that is lacking is public will to act on that knowledge (Lewis, 1991).

As this chapter has suggested, we have, in the field of early childhood education, an emerging social strategy—one that recognizes how families have changed and how the school's role has expanded; one that appreciates the need for family resources and support, community collaboration, authentic communication, effective teacher preparation, and exemplary parent involvement programs.

Early childhood educators will know that they have made significant progress toward the new paradigm of home, school, and community collaboration when their programs reflect an increasingly clear conception of how culture, power, and knowledge interrelate (Giroux, 1992). Unless we embrace family diversity, share power with families in meaningful ways, and strive for consensus on what knowledge is of most value, the new support services will be a new label rather than the sweeping reform that the field of early childhood education has begun and American education in general so desperately needs.

REFERENCES

Adler, R., & Rodman, G. (1988). *Understanding human communication.* New York: Holt, Rinehart & Winston.

Allen, M., Brown, P., & Finlay, B. (1992). *Helping children by strengthening families.* Washington, DC: Children's Defense Fund.

Auerbach, R. (1995). Which way for family literacy: Intervention or empowerment? In L. Morrow (Ed.), *Family literacy: Connections in schools and communities* (pp. 11–27). New Brunswick, NJ: International Reading Association.

Berger, E. (1995). *Parents as partners in education: The school and home working together* (4th ed.). New York: Prentice Hall.

Blatt, S., & Benz, C. (1993, April). *The relationship of communication competency to perceived teacher effectiveness.* Paper presented at the Joint Meeting of the Southern States Communication Association and Central States Communication Association, Lexington, KY.

Bredekamp, S., & Willer, B. (1993). Professionalizing the field of early childhood education: Pros and cons. *Young Children, 48*(3), 82–84.

Brown, L. (1989). The relationship between communicator style and the perceived outcomes of rural elementary children's parent-teacher conferences. *Dissertation Abstracts* ACC 9010777.

Chavkin, N. (1990). Joining forces: Education for a changing population. *Educational Horizons, 68*(4), 190–196.

Coleman, M. (1991). Planning for the changing nature of family life in schools for young children. *Young Children, 46*(4), 15–20.

Davies, D. (1991). Schools reaching out: Family, school, and community partnerships for student success. *Phi Delta Kappan, 72*(5), 376–382.

Edwards, P., & Young, L. (1992). Beyond parents: Family, community and school involvement. *Phi Delta Kappan, 74*(1), 72–80.

Elkind, D. (1994). *Ties that stress: The new family imbalance.* Cambridge, MA: Harvard University Press.

Elkind, D. (1995). School and family in the postmodern world. *Phi Delta Kappan, 77*(1), 8–14.

Epstein, J. (1995). School/family/community partnerships: Caring for the children we share. *Phi Delta Kappan, 76*(9), 701–712.

Fenwick, K. (1993). Diffusing conflict with parents: A model for communication. *Child Care Information Exchange, 93,* 59–60.

Gage, J., & Workman, S. (1994). Creating family support systems: In Head Start and beyond. *Young Children, 50*(1), 74–80.

Galinsky, E., Shubilla, L., Willer, B., Levine, J., & Daniel, J. (1994). State and community planning for early childhood systems. *Young Children, 49*(2), 54–57.

Giroux, H. (1992). *Border crossings: Schools and the politics of education.* New York: Routledge.

Greenberg, P. (1989). Parents as partners in young children's development and education: A new American fad? Why does it matter? *Young Children, 44*(4), 61–75.

Grumet, M. (1988). *Bitter milk: Women and teaching.* Amherst, MA: University of Massachusetts Press.

Isenberg, J. P., & Jalongo, M. R. (1997). *Creative expression and play in early childhood* (2nd ed.). Englewood Cliffs, NJ: Merrill/Prentice-Hall.

Kagan, S. (1990). Readiness 2000: Rethinking rhetoric and responsibility. *Phi Delta Kappan, 72*(4), 272–279.

Kagan, S. (1994). Families and children: Who is responsible? *Childhood Education, 71*(1), 4–8.

Kagan, S., Powell, D., Weissbourd, B., & Zigler, E. (1987). *America's family support programs: Perspectives and prospects.* New Haven, CT: Yale University Press.

Kagan, S., & Rivera, A. (1991). Collaboration in early care and education: What can and should we expect? *Young Children, 47*(1), 51–56.

Katz, L. (1993, June). School-parent relations: General principles. Distributed at a presentation in Brussels, Belgium (mimeographed copy).

Kirst, M. (1991). Improving children's services: Overcoming barriers, creating new opportunities. *Phi Delta Kappan, 72*(8), 615–618.

Lewis, A. (1991). Coordinating services: Do we have the will? *Phi Delta Kappan, 72*(5), 340–341.

Lombardi, J. (1992). Early childhood 2001: Advocating for comprehensive services. *Young Children, 47*(4), 24–25.

Morrow, L. (1995). Family literacy: New perspectives, new practices. In L. Morrow (Ed.), *Family literacy: Connections in schools and communities* (pp. 5–10). New Brunswick, NJ: International Reading Association.

National Task Force on School Readiness. (1991). *Caring communities: Support-*

ing young children and families. Alexandria, VA: National Association of State Boards of Education.

Newman, R. (1995). The home-school connection. *Childhood Education, 71*(5), 296–297.

Norton, R. (1983). *Communicator style: Theory, applications, and measures*. Beverly Hills, CA: Sage.

Powell, D. (1991). How schools support families: Critical policy tensions. *The Elementary School Journal, 91*(3), 307–319.

Radcliffe, B., Malone, M., & Nathan, J. (1994). *Training for parent partnerships: Much more should be done*. Minneapolis: University of Minnesota, Hubert H. Humphrey Institute of Public Affairs.

Richmond, J., & Kotelchuck, M. (1984). Commentary on changed lives. In J. Berrueta-Clement, L. Schweinhart, S. Barnett, A. Epstein, & D. Weikart (Eds.), *Changed lives: The effect of the Perry Preschool Program on youths through age 19* (pp. 204–210). Ypsilanti, MI: High Scope Press.

Roberts, R., Wasik, B., Casto, G., & Ramey, C. (1991). Family support in the home: Programs, policy, and social change. *American Psychologist, 46*(2), 131–137.

Rutherford, B., & Billig, S. H. (1995). Eight lessons of parent, family, and community involvement in the middle grades. *Phi Delta Kappan, 77*(1), 64–68.

Sallinen-Kuparinen, A. (1992). Teacher communicator style. *Communication Education, 41*(2), 153–156.

Sarason, S. (1995). *Parental involvement and the political principle: Why the existing governance structure of schools should be abolished*. San Francisco: Jossey-Bass.

Stone, C. (1995). School/community collaboration: Comparing three initiatives. *Phi Delta Kappan, 76*(10), 794–800.

Stone, J. (1993). Caregiver and teacher language: Responsive or restrictive? *Young Children, 48*(4), 12–18.

Swick, K. (1991). *Teacher-parent partnerships to enhance school success in early childhood education*. Washington, DC: National Education Association.

Trawick-Smith, J., & Lambert, L. (1995). The unique challenges of the family child care provider: Implications for professional development. *Young Children, 50*(3), 25–32.

Weissbourd, R. (1996). *The vulnerable child: What really hurts America's children and what we can do about it*. Reading, MA: Addison-Wesley.

Williams, D. (1992). Parental involvement and teacher education preparation: Challenge to teacher education. In L. Kaplan (Ed.), *Education and the family* (pp. 243–254). Boston: Allyn and Bacon.

CURRICULAR TRENDS AND ISSUES
AFFECTING PRACTICE

A perpetually challenging question raised by early childhood educators throughout history is the one that we have used to frame Part II: *What are the best ways of optimizing every young child's growth, development, and learning?* We turn to the case of a particular child we know to illuminate this issue as well as to underscore the need to consider the interactions between development and learning.

Bonnie is a second grader who has a rare and poorly understood disease that afflicts approximately 250 children in the United States. Although an aggressive regimen of radiation and chemotherapy leaves Bonnie feeling ill, she expresses concern about missing school and wants desperately to keep up with her peers, who are "learning to do cursive writing." Her illness causes her to miss school frequently but is not so debilitating that she qualifies for a teacher who would visit her home and help her with her schoolwork. In this dramatic case, it would be inhumane for a teacher to ignore Bonnie's physical condition and pile on the homework in the interest of "covering" a set second-grade curriculum. The goal of pushing Bonnie to keep pace with her peers diminishes in importance in light of her situation. Yet in less dramatic cases, this emphasis on academic learning to the virtual disregard of growth and development is a frequent occurrence in classrooms.

There are many ways of conceptualizing curriculum. The word has its origins in the Latin *currere,* meaning a path or road. That pathway can go in many different directions. Most educators of the very young recognize that they are "learning how to learn" and focus on process as well as on content. Yet as children enter the primary grades, the more traditional emphasis on content frequently takes over and creates developmental discontinuity in programs for preschool and the primary grades. An even more important point about the curricular road early childhood educators select is that what a teacher believes he or she is teaching and what the children are learning is consistent. There is also a "hidden curriculum"—all of the things that children learn about by observing adults and peers in action rather than from the lesson plan. Discrepancies between and among what is actually learned, what is taught, and what is evaluated make the field of curriculum in general and curriculum in early childhood in particular a perpetually challenging one.

The four chapters in Part II confront curricular issues—the heart and soul of teachers' daily practice. Each of these chapters reflects current controversies inherent in curriculum reform in an era of educational change. The uncertainty and uneasiness within our profession have resulted in movements and countermovements to rectify past educational ills. Be it the new focus on standards, federal initiatives, or school innovations, the current educational reform aims to improve education for all children and has direct implications for the field of early childhood.

In Chapter 5, Shirley Raines confronts the issues emanating from developmentally appropriate practice. She identifies commonly encountered problems in attempting to use the terminology associated with developmental appropriateness and revisits its theoretical and philosophical influences. She then challenges those misconceptions, paying particular attention to the what, the how, and the why of curriculum design and implementation. She calls into question some long-held beliefs about time, depth, and process "that are part of the quest for definitive educational answers." The author concludes with numerous challenges for the field with regard to curriculum.

In Chapter 6, Daniel Shade and Bernadette Davis address some of the dilemmas relating to children and technology from three perspectives: where early childhood education has been, where it is now, and where it should be headed as we enter the third millennium. The authors conclude with key recommendations about the role of technology in young children's lives.

In Chapter 7, Sue Wortham reviews major trends and contemporary issues in alternative assessment. She argues that assessment is a thorny issue in early childhood education because the young child's active approach to learning is so inconsistent with formal, standardized testing methods. Wortham discusses recurring issues and concerns in reporting and evaluating children's progress. She also examines persistent issues such as time, teacher accountability, and the efficacy of performance assessment for young children to document what children think, know, feel, and can do.

The final chapter of Part II continues the examination of curricular issues and focuses on play. In Chapter 8, Pat Monighan-Nourot addresses the ever so controversial issues surrounding the learning potential of play and creative expression as foundational for a productive, long-term disposition toward learning. She looks at a new organizational framework for studying play "to express the depth and complexity of knowledge about play in educational settings that is available in the research literature." In the process, she distills a large body of literature to wrestle with the struggles in (1) defining play, (2) articulating the value of play to children's total development, (3) understanding the contextual and situational influences (e.g., time, gender, materials) on children's play and their development, and (4) using play as the unifying catalyst for learning.

Together, the four chapters of Part II analyze early childhood curriculum from the standpoint of what early childhood professionals know about educating young children, how they have arrived at these understandings, why they teach as they do, and how they go about documenting children's growth, development, and learning.

Chapter 5

Developmental Appropriateness: Curriculum Revisited and Challenged

SHIRLEY C. RAINES

Sage observers of educational change note that when a reform effort has a significant number of leaders and followers, it will be challenged mightily. "Developmentally appropriate practice" (DAP), widely and enthusiastically embraced by early childhood teachers, is now being challenged from within the field of early childhood education and from without by representatives of other fields (Johnson & Johnson, 1993; Kaminski & Carey, 1993; Kostelnik, 1992; Willis, 1993).

Another observation from the sage observers is that when a reform effort becomes so well known that it generates its own slogans, then it is no longer a reform but a mainstream idea. Nearly every booth at the National Association for the Education of Young Children (NAEYC) annual conference uses the developmental appropriateness phrase liberally. Whether describing a new book, instructional programs, or playground equipment, the phrase is invoked by an abundance of written advertisements, podium speakers, and workshop leaders. We now have disposable diaper companies calling their products "developmentally appropriate" and multimedia wizardry labeled "developmentally appropriate."

According to Bredekamp (1987), "the concept of developmental appropriateness has two dimensions: age appropriateness and individual appropriateness" (p. 2):

1. Age appropriateness. Human development research indicates that there are universal, predictable sequences of growth and change that occur in children during the first 9 years of life.
2. Individual appropriateness. Each child is a unique person with an individual pattern and timing of growth, as well as individual personality, learning style, and family background. (pp. 2–3)

Used, abused, and misunderstood, the "developmentally appropriate-ness" nomenclature has been elevated to the ranks of mainstream educational language. For the purposes of clarification, in this chapter, common misconceptions about DAP are explored, and theoretical influences from developmentalists/interactionists including Piaget, Vygotsky, and Dewey are reviewed. Additionally, overarching curriculum development issues are discussed, and, finally, inferences are drawn for some future challenges. Note that I have relied heavily on five sources: Bredekamp (1987); Bredekamp & Rosegrant (1992); Goffin (1994); Raines (1995); and Raines and Canady (1990).

COMMON MISCONCEPTIONS ABOUT DAP

While there are numerous misconceptions about developmentally appropriate practice, four common misconceptions surface regularly. These include the belief that the teacher is not in charge; that there is no structure; that few skills are taught; and that DAP is a set curriculum (Bredekamp & Rosegrant, 1992; Kostelnik, 1992; Willis, 1993).

Misconception About Who Is in Charge

The first misconception is that teachers are not in charge of the DAP classroom. In classrooms that reflect developmentally appropriate practices, teachers are in charge, but the environment is organized so that children have choices of numerous hands-on learning experiences. A balance is sought between child-choice and teacher-directed experiences.

The teacher's and children's interaction patterns in DAP classrooms versus traditional teacher-directed classrooms differ greatly. Classrooms are operated with a great deal of child autonomy during choice activities conducted during large blocks of time when youngsters choose from an array of centers and activities. When the children become accustomed to the class routines and expectations, there is even less need for the teacher as super manager of time, resources, and classroom rules.

Depending on the task, there are whole-class groups led by the teacher, small groups, partners, and individuals. Similarly, children are cooperatively organizing and disbanding these groups, with and without the direction of the teachers. Given a high-choice learning environment with many different activities, materials, resources, and size of groups, children develop more autonomy as learners and as socially responsible participants of the classroom. Cooperative learning and grouping for tasks support the sense of community that is developed.

Misconception About Structure

A second misconception is that there is no structure in the early child-hood DAP classroom. Every developmentally appropriate practice class-room is structured; however, this is not as readily apparent as the struc-ture of the teacher-directed classroom. Teachers orchestrate the classroom. The orchestration is organized around the elements of time, space, and the conceptual framework of the curriculum. Early childhood teachers organize the schedule, the space of the classroom, and the cur-riculum with the child's physical, social, emotional, and cognitive needs in mind, while seeking a balance of child-choice and teacher-led activi-ties. Individual appropriateness is considered as teachers assist children in the overall participation within the time, space, direction, and curricu-lum elements.

Misconception About the Role of Skills

Another misconception about DAP in early childhood classrooms is that few skills are taught. Teachers do teach for skill acquisition; however, the processes used and the application of the skills is in more authentic in-struction and assessment cycles than in drills and worksheets. In a DAP classroom, there is a meaning-making orientation, and skills are learned directly and indirectly in activities (Johnson & Johnson, 1993).

A teacher in a DAP classroom plans for children to construct knowl-edge based on what they already know and what they want to find out. The teacher's perspective is a developmental one, in which children are expected to develop over time and move from gross approximations toward refinement of skills and concepts. For example, in an early child-hood classroom, children would be encouraged to write using whatever letters they know. At first, the children may know only the letters of their names, but as they learn more about the sound/symbol relationships and learn letters, they will incorporate these symbols into their writing. In traditional classrooms, children are not encouraged to use the informa-tion they presently know, but are expected to wait until they know all the letters and all the sound/symbol relationships before they write.

The "individual appropriateness" section of the definition of develop-mentally appropriate is often omitted from discussion. Taken at its face value, individual appropriateness should encompass teaching young chil-dren with exceptionalities; however, early intervention methods have often been very directed with sequential skills, rather than the more broadly based goals sought by DAP teachers (Kaminski & Carey, 1993). Given the move away from behavioral and stimulus/response modifications to a variety of ecologically based strategies, such as child-initiated tasks and daily routine tasks, there may be more grounds for DAP teachers and special education teachers to work together (Wolery, Strain, & Bailey, 1992). However, the debate continues about instructional practices among many teachers of special needs children and early childhood educators.

Misconception About the Curriculum

A fourth misconception is that DAP is a set curriculum. Developmentally appropriate practices are not one curriculum; however, developmentally appropriate practice is reflected in the way the curriculum is organized and carried out.

> Curriculum is an organized framework that delineates the content that children are to learn, the processes through which children achieve the identified curricular goals, what teachers do to help children achieve these goals, and the context in which teaching and learning occur. The early childhood profession defines curriculum in its broadest sense, encompassing prevailing theories, approaches, and models. (Bredekamp & Rosegrant, 1992, p. 10)

An underlying question guides the teacher's design and implementation of the curriculum: What are the significant facts, concrete examples, and basic understandings we can examine in studying this topic? Obviously, what would interest and motivate 3–5 year olds is different from what would interest and motivate 8–10 year olds. Bredekamp and Rosegrant (1992) describe the transformational curriculum of the DAP classroom as one that uses conceptual organizers, such as themes, units, and projects, and is informed by child development knowledge, subject matter disciplines, and the individual children's needs and backgrounds.

If the "meaning-making" concept is taken as a driving force behind curriculum development, then the teacher considers how topics have been explored by the specialists in the field, how the stories and "truths" of the field are transmitted, and what is known about the students. Teachers are guided by children's answers to such questions as What do you *know* about the topic? What do you *want* to know about the topic? If we begin with what children already know, then we know what is missing. If we also consider what they want to know, we have a point of motivation (Ogle, 1986). Often young children learn a slice of interesting information selected by the teacher about a topic, and this beginning set of information prompts them to want to know more.

The significance of the teacher, of teacher-led activities, of teacher decision making about curriculum, and of teacher control should not be misinterpreted by the critics of developmentally appropriate practices. This does not negate the child. If we consider the age of the children we teach and understand them as individuals, we will make a few over-arching choices about the scope and potentials of the "what" of the curriculum. In addition, we will make decisions about the "how"—and the how includes a great deal of child-choice.

THEORETICAL INFLUENCES ON DAP

Developmentally appropriate practice views draw heavily on a family of theoretical perspectives that focus on the whole child (Goffin, 1994). Piaget's theory of the construction of knowledge is seen as the basis for the cognitive-developmental approach with an emphasis on cognition (DeVries, 1992; Kamii, 1992; Weikart & Schweinhart, 1987). The developmental perspective is derived from the psychodynamic theory, as described by Biber, and the Bank Street Developmental/Interaction Approach, with roots traced back to Dewey's educational philosophy (Goffin, 1994). Social development and emotional development are focal points. While the salient features of these theoretical perspectives are mentioned, the reader is encouraged to return to authorities in each of these theoretical perspectives for deeper understandings.

Constructivist Influence in DAP

The constructivist view is sometimes called the interactionist/constructivist view. Drawing on the philosophical underpinnings of cognitive theorists Piaget (1951) and Vygotsky (1978), the teacher organizes the classroom to take advantage of the children's stages of cognitive development. Piaget's emphasis on the physical manipulation of materials and his descriptions of children's abilities to conserve ideas are reflected in the early childhood classroom, with its varied physical activities and projects. The view also incorporates the Vygotskian belief that children learn from each other and function socially in a shared context.

According to Piaget, learning takes place through assimilation and accommodation. Learners make predictions by sampling information, then confirming or rejecting their predictions. If the learners' predictions are confirmed or verified, the information is assimilated, and they continue sampling. If their predictions are rejected, they must either abandon or adjust their predictions and sample for additional information.

New information may cause learners to organize their thinking into new constructs or schemata, indicating a process of accommodation. Depth of the learning will be determined by the quality of the predictions, the samples of information, and the prior knowledge of the learners (Raines & Canady, 1990).

Vygotsky (1962) emphasized that the child's concept development can be described in stages, but that children also operate in a "zone of proximal development." As the learner attempts to develop concepts, he or she is able to operate in the next level of development—the zone of proximal development—through the assistance and mediation of adults and other children.

Socially, developmentally appropriate practice classrooms are highly interactive. While the Piagetian focus is cognitive development, and the cognitive/interactionist approaches or constructivist theory of how knowledge is constructed, the developmental/interactionist theories are based on psychosocial theories of development. The whole-child emphasis of DAP classrooms is formulated from the tenets of the developmental psychologists. According to Goffin (1994), approaches to early childhood education such as those of Biber and the Bank Street Model are considered developmental/interactionist. The commonality of these developmental and cognitive interactionist approaches is that they embrace as best practice the child-centered, experience-centered, and process-oriented practices. They also share the commonality of views of learning occurring in developmental stages, with children able to understand, process, and construct knowledge at different levels and in different ways in successive stages.

Given the views of DAP teachers that children must be active learners and language producers, social-development and cognitive-development perspectives are congruent with the developmentally appropriate practices literature. Programs for young children have been influenced by social psychologists and by the derived approaches to early childhood education, as well as the Piagetian and Vygotskian views of how children construct knowledge.

Children learn to live together and to develop social competence. In DAP classrooms, the social and emotional development and the personal interactions of the children are valued. Yet, two curriculum questions continue: What is one to construct knowledge about and what is one to learn with one's peers in a socially interactive classroom? Whether the approach is constructivist, cognitive/interactionist or developmental/interactionist, a critical question remains: "What is the place and meaning of subject-matter and of organization within the experience?" (Goffin, 1994, p. 91). Child-centered, experience-centered, and process-oriented beliefs guide practices in DAP classrooms, but there are still subjects, top-ics, and units of study to be chosen for the curriculum.

Dewey's Influence on Early Childhood Curriculum Development

John Dewey's (1916) contributions to learning theory and curriculum de-velopment can also be seen in DAP classrooms. The early childhood cur-riculum remains child-centered and experience-centered. Perhaps be-cause the early childhood educator is dealing with the youngest groups of children, there is a recognition that the children are inexperienced; therefore, their experiences should be broadened. Harriet Cuffaro (1995) reminds us of the famous Dewey dictum: "Everything depends upon the quality of the experience which is had" (p. 7).

The explanation of the experience-centered curricula can trace its legacy in this century to John Dewey and the laboratory schools where progressive educators organized model schools and curricula to demon-strate kindergarten practices for teacher education programs. Dewey's experienced-based curriculum was founded on what he described as the human impulses: to socialize, to construct, to inquire, to question, to experiment, and to express or to create artistically (Smith, Stanley, & Shores, 1957, p. 265).

INTEGRATING THE CURRICULUM THROUGH THEMATIC UNITS AND PROJECTS

Early childhood teachers often design the curriculum around the con-ceptual framework of a unit of study, centered around a specific theme or project, usually from social studies or science. Jarolimek and Foster (1989) define the unit as a "coordinated series of learning activities planned around a broad topic that will involve the whole class in a com-prehensive study" (p. 54).

Thematic Units

According to the Association for Childhood Education International (ACEI), the thematic unit "embraces the teaching of all content areas, presented as integrated experiences that develop and extend concepts, strengthen skills, and provide a solid foundation for learning in language, literacy, math, science, health, art and music" (Moyer, Egertson, & Isen-berg, 1987, p. 239). Integrated curriculum units provide the topics and the mechanism for planning. Length of time for the unit may vary, taking

2 weeks or 2 months. The amount of time depends on the topic and the interests of the children.

Themes from social studies might include My Family, My Neighborhood, or Community Helpers. Science themes might include The Estuary, Recycling, Taking Care of Pets, or Our Vanishing Animal Friends. Literature units of study can focus on certain genres, such as poetry or fantasy literature. Literature themes might also encompass cultural studies, such as Folk Tales from Around the World, Native American Literature, Tales from the Caribbean, or Hispanic Family Stories.

Units of study are designed to increase the "meaning-making" probabilities. As children encounter the concepts and skills required to think about the topic and to interact with each other, as well as perform tasks, they have more opportunities to construct meaning. In choosing unit themes, teachers are ever cognizant of the developmental needs and the age and stage of learners, as well as who they are as individuals from specific families and cultures.

Projects

Lilian G. Katz and Sylvia C. Chard (1989) describe the project approach as similar to the thematic unit approach: "A project is an in-depth study of a particular topic that one or more children undertake" (p. 2). Some topics they list include "going to the hospital," "building a house," and "the bus that brings us to school." Described as a means of "cultivating the life of the young child's mind," the project approach is often associated with John Dewey (1916), among others.

The project approach, like the thematic unit, includes children's representations of what they are learning. Learning may be behavioral and can be observed by the teacher, but often also includes representations, such as drawings, three-dimensional constructions, and narratives chronicling the experience. For example, the project "building a house" may include a visit to a construction site, looking at blueprints, reading books about styles of houses, hammering, sawing, and nailing.

Katz and Chard (1989) also discuss the value of the project approach for knowledge and skill development, which are apparent in the activities mentioned above. Dispositions toward learning can also be enhanced when children learn to be experimenters, problem solvers, and competent social group members as they cooperate to achieve shared goals.

Carolyn Edwards, Lella Gandini, and George Forman (1993) have brought the Reggio Emilia approach to early childhood education to the attention of North American educators in their book, *The Hundred Lan-*

guages of Children. Located in Italy, the city of Reggio Emilia supports community preschools, which include extensive parent involvement. Like the integrated thematic unit topic, the project approach that characterizes the preschools of Reggio Emilia is a developmentally appropriate means of interacting with young children; however, the emphasis is on the symbolic representation of what is learned. About the Reggio Emilia approach, Howard Gardner (1993) says: "The principal educational vehicle involves youngsters in long-term engrossing projects, which are carried out in a beautiful, healthy, love-filled setting" (p. x).

The emphasis on symbolic representation is a cognitive emphasis, but because of the manner in which the program is delivered, it is considered holistic in using children's natural languages of expression, such as speaking, moving, drawing, painting, sculpting, making models, playing, and music-making. Thus, our limited view of symbolism as reading, writing, listening, and speaking is expanded to multitudes of means whereby children express what they are learning—hence the book's title, *The Hundred Languages of Children.*

In addition to the expanded view of ways of representing what is learned, the question of depth of exploration of the topic appears to be a major difference in many North American versions of the project approach and in the Reggio Emilia approach, in which the amount of time to be spent on a project is not determined ahead of time. "With a firm conviction in young children's abilities to concentrate on and remain involved with topics of interest for extended periods, there is no anticipated time of closure for a project once it has begun" (New, 1993, p. 220).

CURRICULAR TRENDS

Descriptions of the Reggio Emilia projects have called into question some long-held beliefs about early childhood curriculum in regard to time, depth, and process versus product. North American teachers tend to spend less time than Reggio teachers during the academic day on projects and less time in the school year. Whether less time is a function of perceived curriculum pressures to cover more different topics, or prevalent practice, or evidence of less faith in the young child's abilities to sustain interest, the results are the same. When less time is spent on a topic, there are fewer opportunities to explore a topic in depth.

The depth-versus-breadth issue is a long-debated one. However, given our more recent emphasis on meaning-making, it appears that the trend is toward longer units and studying in more depth. Professional organizations that develop policy and fund special projects for curriculum development have embraced integration, but they have not deviated from their call to explore their discipline subjects in more depth.

Leaders in art, social studies, mathematics, and science are calling for curricular reform. Curriculum organizations such as the Getty Center for Education in the Arts (1985) believe that arts education should be integrated across the curriculum and include experiences in four related aspects: art production, art history, art criticism, and aesthetics (Isenberg, 1995).

According to Seefeldt (1995), numerous councils and commissions have developed programs of study for the purpose of organizing and synthesizing social studies into a coherent body of knowledge. Organizing social studies in early childhood around the discipline of history allows children to gain an "understanding of their own history, appreciate political and cultural diversity, and understand the economic and sociological realities of a rapidly changing world" (National Council for the Social Studies [NCSS], 1989, p. xi).

According to Charlesworth and Lind (1995), the National Council of Teachers of Mathematics proposed standards that stress three language-related areas: communications, connections, and reasoning. Opportunities for communication can help children "realize that representing, discussing, reading, writing, and listening to mathematics are a vital part of learning and using mathematics" (p. 157).

Science educators also have standard-setting commissions to decide what should be studied and through what processes. Advocates of activity-based science require instruction that makes connections with other disciplines through real-world experiences (Charlesworth & Lind, 1995). Common to all the groups from the arts to the sciences are the principles of integration, application by solving real problems, and a focus on meaning-making.

The process-versus-product argument is alive and well in early childhood curriculum debates. What children learn is both process and product. How it is learned is both process and product, but the realization that young children's products are symbolic representations of what they know has caused the pendulum to swing toward examining the products of children's learning. From expository writing of invented spelling texts to refinements of drawings to show the growth processes of plants, children move from gross approximations to refined specifics. As they interpret and reinterpret, present and represent what they are learning, their products are central to teachers' understanding children's thinking and to children's staying involved in the process (Raines, 1990).

RECURRING ISSUES

The amount of time, the amount of coverage, and the related issue of depth versus breadth are unresolved in early childhood education. When commissions of large, disciplined-based organizations set out plans for early childhood teachers about what is to be taught and how it is to be taught, we applaud them when their recommendations are compatible with DAP. Yet, while process is touted in the DAP materials, process versus product is called into question when we consider the success of Reggio Emilio schools and examine the high-quality work that young children in these schools produce.

Recurring questions and issues are part of the quest for definitive educational answers. Only a few years ago, kindergarten teachers swore that they did not teach reading. Many did not even allow the alphabet in their classrooms. Then, as the emergent literacy studies became more widely known, kindergarten teachers learned they could hold on to their values of child-centered, experience-centered, and process approaches and still embrace young children's learning to read and write (Raines & Canady, 1990). What is considered definitive changes as we learn more about young children and the processes of learning and constructing knowledge.

Startled by the depth of knowledge, the motivation to learn, and the quality of the products produced by Reggio Emilia youngsters, North American educators are forced to examine their long-held belief that it is the process that counts and not the product. The product does count. The child who is drawing the directions for the long-jump competition knows that the instructions must be drawn correctly for the competition to proceed properly (Forman, 1993). She or he refines the drawing and explicates the nuances of meaning. Three to six-year-olds were not thought to be able to do such elaborate drawings, but they do them in the Reggio Emilia schools.

Is the Reggio Emilia approach so successful because the Italians have much brighter children, or is it that they have found ways to allow their children to learn about the world in more depth? What could we North Americans learn from other successful early childhood programs around the world?

Meanwhile, as the ebb and flow of educational change is taking place, teachers, administrators, and parents of many cultures are looking for ways to help their children develop as knowledgeable, skillful, and active problem solvers, not passive, inactive consumers. We want a challenging, motivating, interesting curriculum. Most of the curriculum decisions will come from the teacher about the overall framework of the curriculum, but many decisions will be made by the children—the teacher will help the children invest in what is learned, and how it is learned, and consequently they become "meaning-makers" (Wells, 1986).

CHALLENGES

Numerous challenges remain for early childhood educators. As DAP advocates, we must continue to address the common misconceptions—the beliefs that the teachers are not in charge, that there is little structure, that few skills are taught, and that DAP requires a set curriculum (Bredekamp & Rosegrant, 1992; Kostelnik, 1992; Willis, 1993).

Knowing the theoretical influences on our present practices should not preclude us from examining new interpretations of the theoretical bases and research that further explicate the cognitive and social interactions of learning.

A profound challenge for early childhood educators is to learn from the expertise of special educators and make better provisions for the needs of exceptional children. We must not limit our debate to direct instruction for skills but instead focus on what skills are learned as children construct knowledge and how can we help exceptional children function well in our classrooms. Similarly, as the fields of early childhood and special education attempt to work together, the dichotomy of appropriate interventions will need further discussion. As teachers work in inclusion classrooms, they will construct knowledge of more individually appropriate interactions with special-needs children.

We have worlds of challenges, both macro and micro. In the macro sense, we need to grow as a profession and learn from other cultures around the world, as well as those underrepresented in our own country. If the single classroom is seen as micro, we must include teachers of young children in the knowledge construction that informs our profession.

As professional organizations outline discipline-specific curriculum recommendations, we must become informed participants. The curriculum specialists also must learn about child development and how our interactionist classrooms have evolved.

With the infusion of technology into the classroom, we will be further challenged to hold on to our experience-driven curriculum. As the knowledge explosion continues and we have access to more information through technology, we will find ourselves revisiting the breadth-versus-depth debate.

Early childhood educators can teach the specialists in exceptional education, subject areas, and technology many lessons. Learning from each other is also predicated on the willingness of the specialists to examine the wholeness of the DAP teachers' approaches to the child and the curriculum. Yet, as recent challenges to our beliefs, such as whole language and the Reggio Emilia results, have rightly changed our practices, so we must remain open to the new knowledge the field will inevitably encounter.

Developmentally appropriate practice as a momentum for change has been successful, as indicated by the frequency of usage of the phrase and the sheer volume of books, journal articles, and products evoking it. Our continuing growth as a profession means we must be willing to be challenged and find ways to incorporate new ideas and interpretations into a growing body of literature and practices. Challenged, but undaunted, the early childhood education profession can continue to interpret what it means to operate classrooms that are developmentally appropriate.

REFERENCES

Bredekamp, S. (Ed.). (1987). *Developmentally appropriate practice in early childhood programs serving children from birth through age 8.* Washington, DC: NAEYC.

Bredekamp, S., & Rosegrant, T. (Eds.) (1992). *Reaching potentials: Appropriate curriculum and assessment for young children. Volume I.* Washington, DC: NAEYC.

Charlesworth, R., & Lind, K. K. (1995). Whole language and primary grades mathematics and science: Keeping in step with national standards. In S. C. Raines (Ed.), *Whole language across the curriculum: Grades 1, 2, 3* (pp. 156–178). New York: Teachers College Press.

Cuffaro, H. K. (1995). *Experimenting with the world: John Dewey and the early childhood classroom.* New York: Teachers College Press.

DeVries, R. (1992). Development as the aim of constructivist education: How can it be recognized in children's activity? In D. G. Murphy & S. G. Goffin (Eds.), *Project Construct: A curriculum guide. Understanding the possibilities* (pp. 15–34). Jefferson City, MO: Department of Elementary and Secondary Education.

Dewey, J. (1916). *Democracy and education.* New York: Macmillan.

Edwards, C., Gandini, L., & Forman, G. (Eds.). (1993). *The hundred languages of children: The Reggio Emilia approach to early childhood education.* Norwood, NJ: Ablex.

Forman, G. (1993). Multiple symbolization in the long jump project. In C. Edwards, L. Gandini, & G. Forman (Eds.), *The hundred languages of children:*

The Reggio Emilia approach to early childhood education. (pp. 171–188). Norwood, NJ: Ablex.

Gardner, H. (1993). Foreword: Complementary perspectives on Reggio Emilia. In C. Edwards, L. Gandini, & G. Forman (Eds.). *The hundred languages of children: The Reggio Emilia approach to early childhood education* (pp. ix–xii). Norwood, NJ: Ablex.

Getty Center for Education in the Arts. (1985). *Beyond creating: The place for art in America's schools*. Los Angeles: John Paul Getty Trust.

Goffin, S. G. (1994). *Curriculum models and early childhood education: Appraising the relationship*. New York: Merrill/Macmillan.

Isenberg, J. P. (1995). Whole language in play and the expressive arts. In S. C. Raines (Ed.), *Whole language across the curriculum: Grades 1, 2, 3*. (pp. 114–136). New York: Teachers College Press.

Jarolimek, J., & Foster, C. D. (1989). *Teaching and learning in the elementary school*. New York: Macmillan.

Johnson, J. E., & Johnson, K. M. (1993). Clarifying the developmental perspective in response to Carta, Schwartz, Atwater, and McConnell. *Effective School Practices, 12*(2), 75–80.

Kamii, C. (1992). Autonomy as the aim of constructivist education: How can it be fostered? In D. G. Murphy & S. G. Goffin (Eds.), *Project Construct: A curriculum guide. Understanding the possibilities* (pp. 9–14). Jefferson City, MO: Department of Elementary and Secondary Education.

Kaminski, R., & Carey, S. (1993). Developmentally appropriate practice and early childhood special education: Bridging the gap. *Effective School Practices, 12*(2), 81–86.

Katz, L. G., & Chard, S. (1989). *Engaging children's minds: The project approach*. Norwood, NJ: Ablex.

Kostelnik, M. J. (1992). Myths associated with developmentally appropriate programs. *Young Children, 47*(4), 17–23.

Moyer, J., Egertson, H., & Isenberg, J. (1987). The child- centered kindergarten. *Childhood Education, 63*(4), 235–242.

National Council for the Social Studies [NCSS]. (1989). *Social studies for early childhood and elementary school children: Preparing children for the 21st century*. Washington, DC: Author.

New, R. (1993). Challenges to theory and practice. In C. Edwards, L. Gandini, & G. Forman (Eds.), *The hundred languages of children: The Reggio Emilia approach to early childhood education* (pp. 215–231). Norwood, NJ: Ablex.

Ogle, D. (1986). The K-W-L: A teaching model that develops active reading of expository text. *The Reading Teacher, 39*(6), 564–570.

Piaget, J. (1951). *The child's conception of the world*. Savage, MD: Littlefield Adams.

Raines, S. C. (1990). Representational competence: (Re)presenting experience through words, action, and images. *Childhood Education, 62*(4), 260–264.

Raines, S. C. (Ed.) (1995). *Whole language across the curriculum: Grades 1, 2, 3*. New York: Teachers College Press.

Raines, S. C., & Canady, R. J. (1990). *The whole language kindergarten.* New York: Teachers College Press.

Seefeldt, C. (1995). A complete whole: Social studies and the language arts. In S. C. Raines (Ed.), *Whole language across the curriculum: Grades 1, 2, 3* (pp. 137–155). New York: Teachers College Press.

Smith, B. O., Stanley, W. O., & Shores, J. H. (1957). *Fundamentals of curriculum development.* New York: Harcourt Brace Jovanovich.

Vygotsky, L. S. (1962). *Thought and language.* Cambridge, MA: MIT Press.

Vygotsky, L. S. (1978). *Mind in society.* Cambridge, MA: Harvard University Press.

Weikart, D. P., & Schweinhart, L. (1987). The High/Scope Curriculum for early childhood care and education. In J. L. Roopnarine & J. E. Johnson (Eds.), *Approaches to early childhood education* (pp. 195–208). New York: Merrill/Macmillan.

Wells, G. (1986). *The meaning makers.* Portsmouth, NH: Heinemann.

Willis, S. (1993, November). Teaching young children: Educators seek "developmental appropriateness." *Curriculum Update.* Alexandria, VA: Association for Supervision and Curriculum Development.

Wolery, M., Strain, P. S., & Bailey, D. B. (1992). Applying the framework of developmentally appropriate practice to children with special needs. In S. Bredekamp & T. Rosegrant (Eds.), *Reaching potentials: Appropriate curriculum and assessment for 3–8 year olds* (pp. 92–111). Washington, DC: NAEYC.

Chapter 6

The Role of Computer Technology in Early Childhood Education

DANIEL D. SHADE
BERNADETTE C. DAVIS

I remember very clearly a day in the fall of 1986, the first day I entered an early childhood classroom as a professional. I immediately felt comfortable in the classroom because of the familiarity of the surroundings. From every corner of the room came some subtle reminder of my own days—long ago—in kindergarten: the unmistakable smell of fingerpaint; the smooth waxiness of crayons; the cool, pliable texture of playdough. Nothing the children were doing was foreign to me. I could easily join with the four children building a tower in the block area, or with the three children using the felt board to tell the story of Stone Soup. This classroom offered the children time-honored, traditional materials that support the exploration and natural curiosity of childhood, in the same way that such classrooms had been doing for years.

Recently, I had the opportunity to visit another early childhood classroom, and I was again able to enjoy that feeling of immediate familiarity. Children were moving about the room, all engaged in purposeful play. One group of children created paper reptiles with brushes and paint at the art table; another group worked determinedly to sort plastic turtles, snakes, and frogs on the carpet. Overall, this might have been the same classroom I had seen 10 years earlier, or even the kindergarten I attended myself decades before—except for the group of children excitedly exploring a computer in the corner of the room. As I watched, the two girls and one boy worked together to build a scene for the multimedia book they were writing on the Amazon rain forest. One child operated the mouse to select and position objects in a scene, as the other children made suggestions and gave advice. The young artists were able

to animate the snakes and frogs they had selected, and they recorded their narration of the scene for other children to hear as
the picture was viewed.

The microcomputer is the newest, and possibly the most powerful,
addition to the repertoire of learning materials in the early childhood
classroom. While many adults still struggle with the notion of replacing
their typewriters with word-processing software, children as young as 4
have already accepted the computer as simply another tool in their world,
and are using this technology to create pictures, stories, songs, plays, and
movies—whatever their imaginations can concoct. The computer has
taken a permanent place in education, as it has in society, but its arrival
in the classroom, especially the early childhood classroom, has not been
without struggle, and its future is not without challenges.

WHERE WE'VE BEEN

Hardware and Software

Ten years ago, as computers were making a tentative entry into secondary
and middle schools, most kindergarten teachers had never even considered the possibility of putting a computer in their classrooms. The few
early childhood classrooms that did feature computers at that time did
so out of personal interest on the part of a teacher or an administrator,
or as part of a research study. The technology found in these classrooms
was painfully slow by today's standards; the computers had no hard drive,
so all programs were accessed directly from the 5.25-inch floppy disks, or
even from cassette tapes that required several minutes to load information to the memory. The complicated loading procedures meant that an
adult had to be present if a child wanted to use the computer, or elaborate
rebus card directions had to be designed by the teacher to "walk" young
children through the complicated process of starting a piece of software
(Davidson, 1989)
Software designed for children in the 1980s is archaic compared with
today's programs. Monochrome monitors limited the graphics and detail
that could be shown, so many programs were completely textual. This
severely limited children's ability to use the computer independently, or
to use the technology as a tool for exploration. Drill-and-practice software
dominated the market, so, unless a teacher was willing to write original
programs, the children spent much of their computer time completing
the electronic equivalent of worksheets.

Educational Posture

No new educational material has ever been introduced without challenges, and the computer is certainly no exception (Morgan & Shade,
1994). If anything, the relatively high cost and complexity of computer
technology, when compared with less sophisticated materials such as
blackboards, tape recorders, and headphones, increased the initial resistance to bringing computers into early childhood classrooms.

The 1980s, and even the early 1990s, heard numerous critics rail
against the use of computers with young children. Many of their arguments involved theoretical misunderstandings and misconceptions of
computer use. Among other atrocities, computers were accused of hur-
rying children to maturity (Elkind, 1987), depriving children of valuable
social interactions (Barnes & Hill, 1983), forcing programmed learning
(Elkind, 1987), and displacing traditional activities such as painting,
reading, and large-motor movement (Cuffaro, 1984).

Perhaps the most potentially damaging argument against computer
use with young children came from a misinterpretation of Piaget's ideas.
Some early childhood educators (Barnes & Hill, 1983; Cuffaro, 1984; Elkind, 1987) interpreted Piaget's theory, including his descriptions of the
preoperational and concrete operational stages, as implying that all children younger than age 7 develop cognitively only by manipulating materials with their hands, and therefore should not use a tool employing
symbolic content, such as a computer, in an educational setting (Morgan
& Shade, 1994).

There were many theoretical and research-based responses to these
unfounded claims. Sheingold (1986) pointed out that many activities
young children participate in are symbolic: finger play, modeling figures
with playdough, even singing. Piestrup (1985) stated that criticism of the
computer's flat, two-dimensional screen as being too abstract was nonsen-
sical in that children use picture books, which are at least as abstract as
a computer screen and far more static (the pictures don't move). Shade
and Watson (1990) responded that such criticism ignored 20 years of research on television and children's ability, and lack thereof, to learn from
electronic media. Early studies (Shade, Nida, Lipinski, & Watson, 1986)
clearly showed that young children could, given what we look back on as
prehistoric hardware and software, select the software they wanted (a
5.25 floppy disk), insert it into the machine, turn on the machine, and
navigate through the software. Not only can children complete the functional tasks of using the computer, but they also can talk meaningfully
about their computer activity, work successfully in dyads, help one another, take turns, and share the computer, while enjoying enhanced

development in each curriculum area (math, science, and so forth) (Clements, 1987). Shade and Watson (1987) were also able to show that children as young as 36 months could use and learn from computers when sitting on mother's lap.

The best response to criticism of computer use by young children is found in Clements and Nastasi's (1993) statement that "what is 'concrete' to the child may have more to do with what is meaningful and manipulable than with its physical nature" (p. 259). To a child, the computer graphics that can be picked up with a mouse-driven cursor, moved, stretched, and dropped are as real as any physical object that can be touched with fingers.

As these arguments are finally put to rest, educators no longer need concern themselves with the question of appropriateness; that computers are appropriate for use with young children has been established (Shade & Watson, 1990). The question has become *how* computers can best enhance the learning experiences of young children.

WHERE WE ARE NOW

Hardware and Software

As computer technology has become more powerful and, at the same time, more affordable, computers have become standard equipment in elementary, middle, and secondary schools, as well as in many early childhood educational settings. Compared with the technology of the 1980s, computers found in schools today process staggeringly large amounts of information at blinding speed. A typical middle-of-the-road model of computer in the mid-1990s features a hard drive with the storage capacity of one or several gigabytes (1 gigabyte has 1.2 million times the storage capacity of an 800K floppy disk from the 1980s), quad-speed CD-ROM drives, internal sound sources for recording and playback, and monitors capable of depicting the thousands (or millions) of colors.

As computer hardware capability has increased, so too has the software that takes advantage of this power. Where educational programs once consisted almost entirely of text-driven worksheets, current software for children is graphic-intensive, featuring realistic, colorful animations and photo/video scenes, which are accompanied by verbal directions and feedback. These sophisticated graphics and sounds reduce software's reliance on text, making it possible for pre- and early-readers to operate the computer independently.

Several "child-proof" interface programs have been developed that act as a buffer between the child and the hard disk drive; when running, these management programs allow young children to explore the computer, while protecting important system files from inquiring young minds. Not only do these management programs make a child's time on the computer fun and easy, they also put the child completely in control of the computer interaction. Using one of the child-proof interfaces, children as young as 3 can load and operate a program that has been designated for their use, then exit and change to another program, and finally shut down the machine, all without the assistance of an adult.

Unfortunately, improvement in the technical features of software has not been accompanied by a comparable increase in educational quality. Educators must not assume that all programs that look good or come on a CD-ROM offer sound educational content. Many programs marketed as educational still use drill-and-practice as the primary method of presentation, which clearly violates the principles of developmentally appropriate practice (Bredekamp, 1987).

Educators should not give up hope of finding appropriate software, however. Haugland and Shade (1990) developed the Developmental Software Evaluation Scale (DSES), which is congruent with the guidelines for developmentally appropriate practice (Bredekamp, 1987). Judged according to DSES, many programs produced each year have the features of appropriate learning materials; that is, the programs allow the child to learn through exploration and experimentation. It has been estimated (Haugland, 1994) that between 25 and 30% of the software available to children is developmentally appropriate (not drill-and-practice). As small as that proportion may be, this translates into roughly 150–165 good software programs out of the thousands produced.

Computer Labs and Curriculum Integration

With enormous advances in hardware and software, computers have more potential in the mid-1990s than ever before to empower young children. Yet, even at this relatively advanced stage of technology, many children have not explored the full potential of technology because many schools continue to house their computers in a centralized lab, under the control of a special teacher, which the students visit as rarely as once or twice a month. In numerous multi-age schools, older students have priority in the computer lab, leaving young children insufficient time on the machines.

Many have speculated on the rationale and development of the computer lab. Some suspect that schools looked at the computer lab as a cheaper way to put computers in a school; 10 machines in one lab cost less than two or three computers in each classroom. Papert (1993) has called the development of the computer lab the school's immune response to the intrusion of a foreign material. In other words, instead of integrating computers across classroom curriculums, schools have made the computer a topic or part of the curriculum. So, children go to the lab to be taught "computer literacy" or "word processing." In addition, rather than forcing untrained classroom teachers to deal with technology, administrators gave the task to a single individual who had some interest, and possibly even training, in the area.

The fatal flaw in this approach to teaching is the fact that any information learned *about* the computers today will be obsolete tomorrow (Papert, 1993). What children need to learn is the habit of using the technology as a tool for accomplishing whatever task is at hand. Computer literacy is *not* knowing how to operate the machine, but how to approach a learning situation in a manner that results from fluency in using the computer as a tool (Papert, 1993). This type of fluency will not derive from the lab approach to computer education, but will come only when computers are made an integral part of classroom instruction, and when they are applied to learning situations for which they are appropriate (Clements & Nastasi, 1993; Davis & Shade, 1994; Shade, 1991).

One might be tempted to blame this propagation of technophobia on teachers who entered the profession before the latest wave of the technological revolution. Though it is true that many educators currently in the classroom were trained long before the accessibility of the personal computer, it is also true that new teachers recently emerged from their preservice programs are becoming part of the problem, rather than the solution (Novak, 1991). Less than one-third of education majors near graduation perceive themselves as prepared to teach with computers (Fulton, 1988). In this world, where technology has become indispensable and is advancing at an astonishing rate, teacher preparation institutions continue to educate their students to teach with chalk and slate as their primary tools of instruction—materials that are no different from the technology used by ancient peoples to scratch drawings onto the walls of caves.

WHERE WE ARE GOING

Teachers are by no means cave dwellers. Nor are they as incapable of using computers as the cave dweller of using a ball point pen. All that stands in the way of teachers' maximizing the potential benefits of computers in education is a lack of training. In this section we are going to discuss teacher education in detail. We maintain that professional development must top the list of "things to do" when any school thinks of using computers.

Preservice Education

Recognition of the need for improved teacher education in the area of technology is spreading rapidly. Recent calls for the inclusion of technology in teacher education from nationally recognized certification and accreditation agencies demand that graduating teachers not only know how to use technology personally but also be able to use technology appropriately in their classrooms (Wise, 1995). The International Society for Technology in Education (ISTE; 1992) defined its curriculum guidelines for teacher preparation programs. These 13 requirements reflect the fundamental concepts and skills necessary for applying technology in educational settings, and are recommended by ISTE as a component of every teacher education program, regardless of the specialization.

The National Council for Accreditation of Teacher Education (NCATE; 1994), which certifies teacher preparation institutions, incorporated the ISTE recommendations into their standards regarding technology in teacher education. Among other requirements, NCATE standards dictate that candidates complete a well-planned sequence of courses and/or experiences with educational technology, including the use of computers and other technologies in instruction, assessment, and professional productivity.

Functional Knowledge. Hardware training is initially the most intimidating hurdle to overcome (Fulton, 1988). Therefore, direct instruction in the basic use of computers, databases, electronic mail, and other technologies must be provided, either as part of early foundation courses, or in independent sessions. For teacher education students who will one day face a computer in their own classrooms, hardware training must progress to slightly more advanced topics, such as installing programs on the hard drive, troubleshooting on hardware and software, and maintaining the equipment (assembling machines, loading printers and changing ink cartridges, cleaning mice, and so forth). Mastering this functional knowledge tends to demystify the technology and reduces a future teacher's anxiety about using the machines.

In addition, education students must come to view technology as a productive tool in their own lives. As more preservice courses include technology-related elements, such as using word processors to produce papers, communicating with the instructor over electronic mail, or gathering data from the Internet or World Wide Web, students are being ushered into the use of technology on a personal level. Not only does such an approach provide certification candidates with a variety of technology experiences, but it also demonstrates the usefulness of technology in an educational context.

Theoretical Foundation. As discussed above, there should no longer be any question as to whether computers belong in the early childhood classroom; the appropriateness of this technology has been established. Preservice teacher education, then, must be conducted under this paradigm, and should endorse a theoretical basis for the appropriate use of technology with children. Just as the works of Bruner, Piaget, and Vygotsky are studied for their contributions to educational theory, teacher education students must also examine how these theories relate to the use of technology as a tool for learning.

Software Evaluation. The appropriateness of computer technology as a learning tool has been convincingly argued, yet the appropriateness rests not in the hardware itself, but in how this technology is utilized. In terms of computers, the pivotal factor of appropriateness is the software that is used. Propelled by expensive marketing campaigns, tens of hundreds of educational software titles become available each year, and teachers can easily find themselves lost in a sea of colorful packages that disguise low quality. For teachers to make informed decisions regarding software, preservice programs must include training in evaluating software for its educational content, quality, and appropriateness. Teachers who become familiar with the characteristics of developmentally appropriate software (such as open-endedness, child-control, and equitable gender and multicultural representation) and who receive training in using evaluation instruments, such as the DSES (Haugland & Shade, 1990), or subscribe to Warren Buckleitner's *Children's Software Revue* are more likely to take an active role in selecting software for use in their own classrooms, and tend to make better software choices (Clements & Nastasi, 1993).

Implementation and Integration. Improving teacher education to include technology is not a goal to be satisfied by merely tacking a few courses onto the certification requirements. Teaching technology in an isolated context is analogous to requiring a separate course that teaches the operation and potential uses of chalk; such a class would thoroughly describe how to use chalk, but in no other class would these future teachers be expected to use chalk, nor would their instructors incorporate the use of chalk in their courses. Educators prepared with such limited opportunity would be highly unlikely to ever integrate this instructional tool into their curriculum, despite its potential benefits for teaching and learning.

Of course, this example is absurd, but the analogy is not unfounded. As long as technology is treated as an add-on in the preservice programs, it will continue to be considered an add-on in public education (Niess, 1991). Instead of adding courses that treat technology as a separate topic, existing foundations and methods courses must use the technologies that fit the course material. Because a large percentage of the technology being used today will be obsolete tomorrow, as was pointed out earlier regarding children, the only truly valuable technology skill to be instilled in teacher education students is the habit of using technology as a tool to accomplish whatever task is currently being addressed (Papert, 1993).

In-service Education

The computer-related industry is the fastest developing—and the fastest changing—industry in the history of the world (Dyrli & Kinnaman, 1995). So it is unreasonable to assume that effective teacher education in the area of technology can end with the completion of a certification program. Instead, technology education must continue throughout a professional career, and teachers need support from administrators and districts that promotes ongoing technology education to accomplish this goal.

Many teachers who are considered leaders in the use of technology in the classrooms recommend guided instruction and time to practice as two of the most important factors in staying proficient with technology (Ferris & Roberts, 1994). But the time needed for this instruction and practice simply does not exist in a teacher's day. Teachers will need more than just information about workshops or courses they can attend; this learning requires a commitment to bring qualified instructors to the schools and to support release time—and provision of substitute teachers—so that classroom teachers can participate in training sessions. Teachers should also be encouraged to explore the technology on their own turf, even taking computer equipment home over summer break, to gain comfort with the technology in a low-pressure setting. It is reasonable to assume that, due to the blinding rate of advance in the field of technology, the need for ongoing education will continue, and even increase.

TWO MAJOR ISSUES THAT REQUIRE IMMEDIATE ATTENTION

There are numerous issues that surround the use of technology by young children, but we want to focus on the two receiving the most attention and having the most impact on early childhood education. Developmental appropriateness has the potential to change how software is developed, how computers are used in the classroom, and how teachers are educated. Equity issues touch all children in many ways: gender, ethnic group, and the allocation of educational funds.

Developmental Appropriateness

Developmentally appropriate practice (Bredekamp, 1987) is an underlying premise for all educational experiences designed for young children. Although the theories of DAP have become pervasive in many aspects of the early childhood curriculum, developmental appropriateness is still largely absent from the methods in which the computer is used with young children. To ensure that computer technology enhances the learning experiences of young children, standards of DAP must be applied to this material, as they are to other materials and methods in the classroom. The National Association for the Education of Young Children recently undertook to write, establish, and publish guidelines for the DAP use of computers in all early childhood settings ("NAEYC Position Statement," 1996).

When thinking of computer integration across the classroom curriculum, it is helpful to think of software as a manipulative. And why not? That is how most children perceive the machine, as something to manipulate, something to control. Any teacher who has spent a few moments with quality early childhood software can see that the computer is not unlike other early childhood materials such as books, playdough, and blocks. With the right kind of software, computers are open-ended and discovery-oriented, with 3-dimensional screen manipulatives that are controlled with various input devices. One simply points the mouse, clicks, and drags the objects on the screen to the desired location. Sometimes the graphics are static, as in a picture book, and sometimes they are animated (birds fly, people walk). Therefore, computer graphics constitute manipulatives, as do blocks and puzzles.

Like other manipulatives, computers can be used in many ways. They can be used wisely in a way that enhances development or in less appropriate ways. No one would argue against crayons as a necessary staple in the early childhood program. Yet this does not mean we support having 2-year-olds use crayons to color shapes on a ditto page or trace

letters of the alphabet on a workbook page. Similarly, computers are advocated as an appropriate tool for use with young children, but only if they
are employed in a manner that encourages their use for supporting curiosity and exploration, not as an expensive worksheet.

Equity

Money seems to be an important variable when we look at most kinds of
computer inequities. Minority children, from low-income homes, are less
likely to have access to personal computers than are middle-income children. They are less likely to have a computer in their home, less likely to
live in a neighborhood with access through the public library, and less
likely to attend schools that have computers (Clements & Nastasi, 1993).

Currently, about 25–30% of American homes have personal computers (Edwards, 1993), and it is projected that by 1998, this figure will rise
to 50%. Buckleitner (1994) has shown that a machine adequate for the
quality of children's software today costs about $2,000. In other words, a
5-year-old computer might still function well as a word processor, but it
would be incapable of running much of today's early childhood software.
The "have-versus-have-not" issue is directly related to the cost of computers. Therefore, pressure should be applied to hardware companies to
develop a reliable educational machine for under $1,000. It is a matter of
economics: Is it better to sell 5 computers at $2,000 ($10,000) or 500
computers at $1,000 ($500,000)?

Gender equity reaches both schools and homes, but the cause does
not appear to be dollars. In preschool and kindergarten girls show little
difference from boys in their interest in computers (Lipinski, Nida,
Shade, & Watson, 1986). Some evidence suggests girls spend even more
time on the computer than boys at the kindergarten level (Adams, 1993).
There may be some gender differences in terms of software preferences,
but research is not clear in this area (Shade, 1994). Nevertheless, some-
where by the third grade, girls begin to receive a message that computers
are math, and math is for boys, and therefore computers are not for girls.
From that time on fewer females are found using the computer in class or
labs and in computer clubs (Hess & Miura, 1985; Loyd, Loyd, & Gressard, 1987).

This negative message may first reach girls at home. A study by Fillinger (1991) found that mothers and daughters receive very little computer time at home because the computer(s) is somehow "roped off" as
belonging to the men (fathers and sons) in the family. If this continues to
be the case, schools must redouble their efforts to bring computers and
young children—girls and boys—together in appropriate ways to ensure

that all children have an equal chance to become successful users of technology. Allowing minority or female children to take school computers home for the summer might be another solution.

FUTURE DIRECTIONS AND CONCLUSIONS

What will the next improvement in computer power be? We can be very confident that computers will continue to become smaller and more powerful, and to drop in price. Low-cost color printing is nearly here already. The perfection of reliable voice activation that could recognize each child's voice and respond to verbal commands is almost certainly imminent; imagine a 5-year-old saying, "Computer, print my picture," and having a color printout in her hands within a matter of seconds.

Also on the horizon is virtual reality software in which a young child is not just exploring a simulation of the Amazon jungle, but, by wearing special glasses and gloves, is, as far as their perceptions are concerned, *actually in the Amazon.*

Just as computing power will not remain quiescent, neither will the hurdles associated with the use of computer technology in education. Some of the past barriers to young children's computing are already falling ("K–12 Technologies," 1994), including funding, teacher resistance, and platform incompatibilities. There are still other barriers to overcome (Morgan & Shade, 1994), but the journey appears bright with potential. The time and effort required to overcome the obstacles will be a valuable investment in the future, for the children who use the technology of today will invent the technology of tomorrow.

References

Adams, J. H. (1993). *Free to choose: Learning area use and social relationships among kindergarten children.* Unpublished undergraduate senior thesis, University of Delaware, Newark.

Barnes, B. J., & Hill, S. (1983). Should young children work with microcomputers—Logo before Lego? *The Computing Teacher, 10*(9), 11–14.

Bredekamp, S. (Ed.). (1987). *Developmentally appropriate practice in early childhood programs serving children from birth through age 8.* Washington, DC: National Association for the Education of Young Children Press.

Buckleitner, W. (1994). Tips for buying a children's computer. *Children's Software Revue, 2,* 4.

Clements, D. H. (1987). Computers and young children: A review of research. *Young Children, 43*(1), 34–44.

Clements, D. H., & Nastasi, B. K. (1985). Effects of computer environments on social-emotional development: Logo and computer-assisted instruction. *Computers in the Schools, 2*(2/3), 11–31.

Clements, D. H., & Nastasi, B. K. (1993). Electronic media and early childhood education. In B. Spodek (Ed.), *Handbook of research on the education of young children,* (pp. 251–275). New York: Macmillan.

Cuffaro, H. K. (1984). Microcomputers in education: Why is earlier better? *Teachers College Record, 85,* 559–568.

Davidson, J. I. (1989). *Children & computers: Together in the early childhood classroom.* Albany, NY: Delmar.

Davis, B. C., & Shade, D. D. (1994, December). *Integrate, don't isolate! Computers in the early childhood curriculum.* (ERIC Document Reproduction Service No. EDO-PS-94-17)

Dyrli, O. E., & Kinnaman, D. E. (1995). Technology in education: Getting the upper hand. *Technology & Learning, 15*(13), 37–43.

Edwards, C. (1993). Life-long learning. *Communications of the ACM, 36*(5), 76–78.

Elkind, D. (1987). *Miseducation: Preschoolers at risk.* New York: Knopf.

Ferris, A., & Roberts, N. (1994). Teachers as leaders: Five case studies. *Educational Technology Review, 15*(7), 11–18.

Fillinger, B. A. (1991). *Computing at home: Gender-related issues.* Unpublished master's thesis, University of Delaware, Newark.

Fulton, K. (1988). Preservice and inservice: What must be done in both. *Electronic Learning, 8,* 32–36.

Haugland, S. W. (1994, November). *1994 developmentally appropriate software awards.* Paper presented at the National Association for the Education of Young Children, Washington, DC.

Haugland, S. W., & Shade, D. D. (1990). *Developmental evaluations of software for young children.* Albany, NY: Delmar.

Hess, R. D., & Miura, I. T. (1985). Gender differences in enrollment in computer camps and classes. *Sex Roles, 13,* 193–203.

International Society for Technology in Education. (1992). *Curriculum guidelines for accreditation of educational computing and technology programs.* Eugene, OR: International Society for Technology in Education Press.

K-12 technologies worth $1.02 billion in 1993. (1994, August). *Electronic Education Report, 1,* 4.

Lipinski, J. M., Nida, R. E., Shade, D. D., & Watson, J. A. (1986). The effect of microcomputers on young children: An examination of free play choices, sex differences, and social interactions. *Journal of Computing Research, 2,* 147–168.

Loyd, B. H., Loyd, D. E., & Gressard, C. P. (1987). Gender and computer experiences as factors in the computer attitudes of middle school students. *Journal of Early Adolescence, 7*(1), 13–19.

Morgan, G. G., & Shade, D. D. (1994). Moving early childhood education into the 21st century. In J. L. Wright & D. D. Shade (Eds.), *Young children: Active learners in a technological age* (pp. 135–149). Washington, DC: National Association for the Education of Young Children.

NAEYC position statement: Technology and young children—ages three through eight. (1996). *Young Children, 51*(6), 11–16.

National Council for the Accreditation of Teachers. (1994). *NCATE Standards* Washington, DC: National Council for the Accreditation of Teachers Press.

Niess, M. (1991). *Preparing teachers of the 1990s.* Greenville, NC: East Carolina University.

Novak, D. (Ed.). (1991). *An exploration of computer use by beginning elementary teachers.* Greenville, NC: East Carolina University.

Papert, S. (1993). *The children's machine: Rethinking school in the age of the computer.* New York: Basic Books.

Piestrup, A. M. (1985). Silicon chips and playdough. In A. M. Gordon & K. W. Browne (Eds.), *Beginnings and beyond: Foundations in early childhood education* (pp. 399–402). Albany, NY: Delmar.

Shade, D. D. (1991). Integrating computers into the curriculum. *Day Care and Early Education, 19*(1), 45–46.

Shade, D. D. (1994). Computers and young children: Software types, social contexts, age, and emotional responses. *Journal of Computing in Childhood Education, 5*(2), 177–209.

Shade, D. D., Nida, R. E., Lipinski, J. M., & Watson, J. A. (1986). Microcomputers and preschoolers: Working together in a classroom setting. *Computers in the Schools, 3*(2), 53–61.

Shade, D. D., & Watson, J. A. (1987). Microworlds, mother teaching behavior, and concept formation in the very young child. *Early Child Development and Care, 28,* 97–114.

Shade, D. D., & Watson, J. A. (1990). Computers in early education: Issues put to rest, theoretical links to sound practice, and the potential contribution of microworlds. *Journal of Educational Computing Research, 6*(4), 375–392.

Sheingold, K. (1986). The microcomputer as a symbolic medium. In P. F. Campbell and G. G. Fein (Eds.), *Young children and microcomputers,* Englewood Cliffs, NJ: Prentice-Hall.

Wise, A. E. (1995, Fall). Raising expectations for technology in teacher education. *NCATE Quality Teaching, 5,* 1–2.

Chapter 7

Assessing and Reporting Young Children's Progress: A Review of the Issues

SUE C. WORTHAM

Denzel is sitting in the hallway of Silver Lake Elementary School. He is 4 years old and has been brought to the school by his mother for screening tests for the prekindergarten class. Earlier Denzel worked with a teacher who asked him questions about pictures and gave him tasks to do with blocks and shapes of several sizes and colors. He was asked to cut with scissors and copy designs on a piece of paper with a large pencil. Now Denzel is waiting with his mother for a vision and hearing examination by the school nurse. Denzel is uneasy because the school looks very big and the halls are very long. His mother reassures him, but she, too, is anxious about the meaning of the tasks Denzel was asked to do and whether he did well. While they wait for the nurse to call Denzel's name, they look at a book together.

The construct of assessing young children's progress can have multiple characteristics. The initial assessment of a child's physical status and subsequent developmental progress begins before birth and continues through frequent examinations during the first days, weeks, and months of the infant's first year. As the young child enters the preschool years, more purposes for developmental assessment are added, and when the child enters kindergarten and the primary grades, assessment broadens to include progress in learning and achievement.

In this chapter we will examine the purposes for and methods of assessing young children's progress. Definitions of assessment will be accompanied by discussion of the purposes for assessment. Because there is dissonance between ideals of how young children should be assessed and actual practices currently used in assessing young children, issues in assessment will also be discussed. The issues are significant and give rise to questions about assessment of young children. When is assessment appropriate, and when is it inappropriate? What strategies should be used when appropriate assessment of young children is indicated? How can assessment results be used appropriately or inappropriately? Finally, perspectives and approaches for addressing appropriate assessment of the young child's progress and implications for future teaching and learning will be proposed.

UNDERSTANDING ASSESSMENT

To establish the characteristics of the construct of assessment of young children, the following questions will be addressed. What is meant by assessment of progress in young children? Who are the young children addressed in assessment? Why are young children assessed? Why is the assessment of young children an issue?

What is Meant by Assessment of Young Children's Progress?

The position statement developed by the National Association for the Education of Young Children (NAEYC) and the National Association of Early Childhood Specialists in State Departments of Education, "Guidelines for Appropriate Curriculum Content and Assessment in Programs Serving Children Ages 3 Through 8" (1992), proposes the following definition of assessment:

> Assessment is the process of observing, recording, and otherwise documenting the work children do and how they do it, as a basis for a variety of educational decisions that affect the child, including planning for groups and individual children and communicating with parents. Assessment encompasses the many forms of evaluation available to educational decision-making. (p. 10)

This position statement definition describes assessment in terms of educational programs and goals. From this perspective, assessment is conducted for the purposes of reporting to parents and for planning for instruction.

Assessment of young children's progress cannot be separated from the terms *measurement* and *evaluation.* Goodwin and Goodwin (1993) discuss the measurement of young children in broader terms:

> Measurement is defined here as the process of determining through observation, testing, or other means, an individual's traits or behaviors, a program's

characteristics, or the properties of some other entity, and then assigning a number rating, score, or label to that determination. It usually involves numbers, scales, constructs, reliability, and validity. This definition includes many measuring devices other than paper-and-pencil tests such as observation systems and nonreactive measures. (p. 441)

This description of measurement includes standardized tests as part of the assessment process of the young child, a source of the issues or concerns about assessment that will be discussed later.

Shepard (1994) separates the definition of measurement of young children into two categories, testing and assessment. Although she acknowledges that both terms mean the same thing, Shepard prefers to define *tests* as the traditional, standardized measures and *assessment* as developmentally appropriate procedures that are used for observing and evaluating young children.

It seems clear, then, that even the terms used in regard to the assessment of young children are ambiguous, difficult to differentiate, and subject to individual interpretation. For the purposes of this chapter, the term *assessment* will be defined broadly enough to encompass all of its purposes. If we are to discuss why and how we assess young children, we must go beyond programmatic purposes. In this context, assessment includes all the strategies used to measure development and learning that affect decisions that are made and planning that is conducted on behalf of young children.

Who Are the Young Children Addressed in Assessment?

All young children are addressed in the "who" of assessment. When we describe the importance of understanding how best to assess young children, we must be inclusive in describing the population. The types of assessments used and the purposes for which assessments are conducted depend on children's individual characteristics and backgrounds. Young children are diverse in development, culture, language, abilities, and life experiences. All of these factors affect the nature and course of development and learning that influence the child's status and needs at a particular time. Our interest in and concerns for assessment must include the possibilities for diversity that inform how and why assessments are conducted. The population of young children addressed in assessment in this chapter ranges from birth through age 8, the years of early childhood.

Why Are Young Children Assessed?

Jacob is 2 years old. Although he seems very bright, and is curious about everything in his environment, he speaks very little. His parents are anxious about his delay in language development. They asked the pediatrician about Jacob at his 2-year checkup. After the doctor asked questions about Jacob's speech, he agreed with the parents that Jacob needed to be further evaluated. Because Jacob has had many respiratory infections, the pediatrician referred him for a hearing assessment. The results showed that Jacob had some hearing loss that was affecting his language development. Jacob was put under the care of the hearing specialist for further diagnosis and treatment.

Depending on individual characteristics and diversities, young children are assessed for many purposes. Taking the broader perspective of development and learning described earlier, it is proposed here that assessment serves the following purposes, especially for infants and toddlers:

- To monitor the course of physical, language, cognitive, and socio-emotional development
- To identify and serve infants and young children who are at risk for development and successful later learning
- To identify and serve infants and young children who have a disabling condition that would respond to early intervention (Wortham, 1996)

Assessment in the early weeks, months, and years of life is conducted to evaluate or measure the course of the young child's development. Early indicators that a child's development is not progressing normally provide the opportunity to use intervention services and programs to address the child's needs. Thus children who are born prematurely, suffer trauma during the birth process, present a disability such as mental retardation, or encounter an experience that results in injury are assessed to determine if they are at-risk for development and later learning. Young children in the preschool years might also be assessed for other risk factors such as language differences, family instability resulting in poor social skills, or a lack of experiences needed for cognitive development.

Hills (1992) suggests additional purposes for assessment of young children when they are enrolled in early childhood programs. She proposes that assessment should help determine if a child needs to be placed in a particular program, can benefit from a particular program, or a specialized or individualized program is indicated. The child's progress in a program should be assessed as well as the appropriateness of programs and strategies.

There are a variety of preschool and early elementary programs available to serve young children. The uses for assessment cited above

facilitate the identification, program planning, and program evaluation
for all types of young children in all types of early childhood programs.
Although assessment has a necessary role in these programs, there are
also concerns about that role. We will identify these concerns by discussing why assessment is an issue.

Why Is the Assessment of Young Children an Issue?

> Anabella entered kindergarten after Christmas. Her parents moved
> into the community when her father was able to obtain work in a
> local restaurant. In April the kindergarten children were adminis-
> tered a readiness test to determine if they were to be placed in kin-
> dergarten again or promoted to first grade. Although Anabella's
> score on the test was just below the mean, her teacher has recom-
> mended that Anabella repeat kindergarten. Anabella's parents are
> very concerned. They feel that Anabella should go to first grade
> with her peers. The school believes that Anabella is not ready for
> first grade based on test results and will benefit from the additional
> time in kindergarten.

Some of the purposes for early childhood assessment have been subject
to debate and controversy during the last 10 years. The conflict revolves
around not only why young children are assessed, but also how young
children are assessed and how test results are used. More specifically,
there are appropriate and inappropriate uses for assessment of young
children.

The appropriate uses of assessment are to serve teachers and children. Assessment methods should help the teacher understand the child's
development and how to design developmentally appropriate curriculum
and instruction to meet the child's needs and maximize his or her potential. The assessments used should be convenient and useful to the
teacher. Barnes (1991) suggests the following criteria for assessment instruments. They should provide the following:

- Guidelines and levels that are appropriate and helpful for the appraisal of
  child development, in a range that covers all the children in the classroom
- A measure that corresponds with the curriculum of the classroom and assesses progress towards the goals of that curriculum
- Information on the development of each child in many areas, including
  academic skills, social competence, problem solving, and physical development, as well as such personal attributes as persistence, responsibility,
  and initiative.

- Information on each child on a continuing basis during the year, documenting the child's progress in many developmental areas
- Information on the learning needs of each child to assist the teacher in planning classroom materials and activities that meet children's needs
- A process that does not demand time taken away from teaching but can be integrated with the teaching process
- Information that can be shared with parents and administrators to document children's progress during the year. (p. 22)

Assessment should also serve the needs of the child by being nonintrusive, nonstressful, and available to the child and family. Ideally, young children should play an important role in the assessment process.

Unfortunately, other applications are made for assessments used with young children. Inappropriate uses include the use of standardized test scores to compare teachers, schools, and school districts; and the use of screening, readiness, or other test instruments to place children in programs, to retain children, or to deny them access to prekindergarten, kindergarten, or first grade. In this "high stakes testing" (Meisels, 1987, 1989), the central issues are whether standardized tests should be used with young children and the misuse of standardized test results for the placement of young children in early childhood classrooms (Shepard, 1989, 1994; Shepard & Graue, 1993; Shepard & Smith, 1988). These concerns will be discussed in more detail in the next section.

HOW AND WHY YOUNG CHILDREN SHOULD BE ASSESSED

Homero Ruiz is a first-grade teacher in an inner-city school whose population is 98% Hispanic children. Each year many of Homero's students are retained in first grade because of poor classroom performance and low performance on a standardized achievement test. This year Homero is very encouraged because his school is piloting a project in multi-age education. Retention has been eliminated for the time being as children are grouped into classrooms that span two grade levels. Homero will have some of his children for 2 years, which will permit him to work intensively with his students who are at-risk for failure. He and his fellow teachers in multi-age settings will not be administering standardized tests. Instead they will be using performance assessments based on a continuum of learning objectives to help their students learn more effectively.

Early childhood educators discourage the use of standardized tests because of the limitations and difficulties when they are administered to young children (Bredekamp, 1987; NAEYC, 1988). Additionally, how test results are used to make decisions about young children is the subject of debate and controversy (Meisels, Steele, & Quinn-Leering, 1993; Perrone, 1990, 1991; Shepard & Graue, 1993).

The Increased Use of Standardized Tests

Educational reform and concerns about accountability for learning have resulted in the increased use of standardized testing in the public schools. State-level achievement tests are mandated in many states in secondary and elementary schools. Criticism of standardized tests has focused on the limited usefulness of such tests (Perrone, 1981) and the impact that testing has imposed on instruction (Durkin, 1987). Although such testing is advocated as a method to improve the quality of education (Popham, 1987), those who oppose the practice (Calfee, 1987) propose that mandated tests now dictate the curriculum that has been labeled *measurement-driven*.

The increased use of tests is also prevalent in preschool and early elementary classrooms. Measurement-driven curriculum has forced changes in instruction in early childhood grade levels, including a more academic approach and more difficult content. As will be discussed later, curriculum changes and increased expectations for achievement in young children have been accompanied by concerns about poor performance by many children in the primary grades.

Inappropriateness of Standardized Tests for Young Children

Of major concern in using standardized tests is the difficulty of designing valid and reliable instruments for assessment. One source of difficulty in obtaining validity and reliability is the rapidity of developmental change in young children. Because children change rapidly, results of single administration of an instrument can be inaccurate (NAEYC, 1988). Another criticism is the limitations of the content of standardized tests developed for young children. Katz (1985) noted that achievement tests for young children measure only cognitive objectives, thus neglecting other areas such as social competence, self-esteem, and creativity.

There are difficulties in administering standardized tests to young children. Reliability is affected when tests are administered to young children in groups. On the other hand, when tests are administered individually or to small groups, the time required is a problem. The time factor is also a problem when instruments are lengthy and require young children to attend for long periods of time that are beyond their developmental capacities.

Also at issue is who administers tests to young children. Although it is important that young children be tested by individuals who are qualified to administer the test and knowledgeable about the developmental needs of young children (NAEYC, 1988), this is not always the case. Frequently children are given tests used to make important decisions in an unfamiliar environment by an examiner who is a stranger. Cryan (1986) described the issues and difficulties in using standardized tests with young children as a potential plague. He proposed that the problems in testing can mislabel children and that test results are subject to error.

The issue when using standardized tests with children with cultural, language, and socioeconomic differences is whether they are fair (Goodwin & Goodwin, 1993). Efforts have been made to design tests that are free of bias; nevertheless, there are still concerns about test context and language, culture, ethnic, and gender bias (Duran, 1989; Hilliard, 1990).

A related issue is the fairness of standardized tests when used with children from school-disadvantaged backgrounds. The socioeconomic background of a child may influence the opportunity to acquire the skills and knowledge measured in a standardized test, leading to lower performance. When combined with language and cultural differences, the child's low socioeconomic status increases the chances for error or unreliable results (Harman, 1990; Oakland, 1977; Taub, Love, Wilkerson, Washington, & Wolf, 1980).

Inappropriate Use of Standardized Tests for Denial of School Entry, Placement, and Retention

The most controversial issue is the use of standardized tests to deny children entry to early childhood classrooms, to place children in special education programs, to place children in transitional classrooms, or to retain them. The misuse or misapplication of test results for these purposes is questioned strongly by early childhood specialists as well as experts in measurement (Goodwin & Goodwin, 1993; Perrone, 1990, 1991; Shepard, 1994; Shepard & Graue, 1993).

As noted earlier, the school reform movement that put pressure on school districts to increase achievement scores impacted instructional practices used with young children and resulted in inappropriate uses of standardized tests. The pressure to raise children's achievement and provide accountability for that achievement resulted in the increased use of achievement tests. Another effect was the "trickle-down" curriculum (Meisels et al., 1993) whereby the content and difficulty of curriculum formerly covered at one grade level was pushed down to a lower grade level in an effort to accelerate learning. This practice in turn resulted in the academization of kindergarten and the phenomenon of young children not performing well in the primary grades, particularly in first grade.

In the effort to address rising rates of failure in first grade and concerns about achievement scores in the primary grades, practices were initiated to maximize the potential of children to perform well and test well. The solutions to the dilemma were to keep some children in kindergarten an extra year, place them in a prekindergarten or pre-first grade classroom, or deny them entry to a preschool program. The use of standardized tests to make these decisions led to concerns about the misuse of tests and test results with young children.

School Readiness Screening. Screening to determine where children should be placed in the early childhood grades or if they should delay a year in entering school has become the norm in addressing the issues related to improving learning and raising achievement scores (Gnezda & Bolig, 1988). Developmental screening instruments and readiness tests used for screening and placement have become the target for concern. It has become common practice to use developmental screening instruments such as the *Brigance Screen K and 1* (Brigance, 1982) and readiness tests such as the *Gesell School Readiness Screening Test* (Ilg, Ames, & Gillespie, 1978) and the *Metropolitan Readiness Test* (Nurss & McGauvran, 1976) to evaluate children's readiness for school entry or promotion (Meisels, 1987; Shepard, 1991; Shepard & Smith, 1986).

Meisels and colleagues (1993) categorized both developmental screening tests and readiness tests as inappropriate for those purposes because they are criterion-referenced readiness tests that measure only the child's current performance on individual test objectives. They further propose that the purpose of readiness tests is "to evaluate a child's relative preparedness to profit from a particular curriculum" (p. 283). In addition, they submit that criterion-referenced measures can be used to assess current achievement, but not to predict what young children can achieve in the future. Shepard and Graue (1993) support this position on the use of readiness tests. They further agree that developmental screening tests should not be used for special education or placement decisions. Rather, the purpose for their use is to ascertain the child's current developmental status and whether additional assessment measures should be conducted to collect additional data.

Retention and Placement in Transitional Classrooms. A parallel issue is the use of standardized tests for retention of a child or placement in a transitional classroom. The criticisms noted above pertain to the validity of using screening instruments or readiness measures to determine if a child should be promoted or remain at a grade level.

In addition, there is concern about the efficacy of the practice of retention. Decisions to retain a child in kindergarten or place him or her in a transitional classroom were originally made with the thought that this would enhance the child's potential for later success. The belief was that children would benefit from such placements because they would have time to mature. Although many educators and parents believe that retention benefits the child, research does not support the practice. A review of the research on retention (Holmes & Matthews, 1984) determined that children make progress when a grade is repeated, but not as much progress as children who are promoted. Gredler (1984) found similar results for children placed in transitional classrooms—they benefited no more than children who were retained. Teachers' perception that children benefit from retention or placement in a transitional classroom is apparently based on their observation that the children make progress; nevertheless, the same or more progress might have been made if the child had been promoted (Foster, 1993; Pierson & Connell, 1992; Tanner & Combs, 1993). Allington and McGill-Franzen (1995) studied retention practices in school districts where administrators and teachers believed their retention programs were effective. After following the longitudinal progress of cohorts of children who entered kindergarten together in these schools, they concluded that the retention practices were not effective in the long run. Students who were retained experienced a slight gain during the year of retention, but gradually slid downward in the following years. Allington and McGill-Franzen (1995) concluded that retention and transitional classrooms do not benefit children.

HOW SHOULD YOUNG CHILDREN'S PROGRESS BE ASSESSED AND REPORTED?

Denzel has spent the past 9 months in the prekindergarten program at Silver Lake Elementary School. The initial assessment prior to the beginning of school and his fear about the school are long forgotten. He has had a happy year with many friends at school and has enjoyed having his mother as a helper in his room often during the year. Denzel and his mother are proud of what he has learned. Denzel has a portfolio of materials that document what he has learned. In addition, Denzel's teacher has records of other assessments she has conducted with Denzel and the other students during the year. She has compared Denzel's progress with the assessment results at the beginning of the year. This information will be forwarded to Denzel's kindergarten teacher next year. During the last week of school Denzel and his mother visit the kindergarten classroom during an open house held in the evening. They get acquainted with the kindergarten teacher and study displays of work and projects completed by the kindergarten students this year. Both Denzel and his mother feel comfortable that kindergarten will be another good year, and they look forward to the beginning of school in the fall.

We now return to the central question of this chapter. Considering all of the concerns about standardized testing as an inappropriate method of assessment, how can early educators assess children in the most appropriate manner?

Appropriate Uses of Standardized Testing

Despite the controversies over the inappropriate uses of standardized testing with young children, there are beneficial uses for standardized tests. Screening instruments are used for periodic screening of development as well as health and learning problems. Children who have disabilities at birth or are at risk for developing a disability are evaluated frequently using developmental measures and other standardized instruments to diagnose the extent of the disabling condition. Standardized instruments contribute to the assessment of these infants and young children who are later identified as exhibiting developmental delay. Identification and diagnosis of delays and/or disabilities lead to essential intervention services for infants and young children. Although there are also concerns about the use of tests for this purpose (Lehr, Ysseldyke, & Thurlow, 1987), standardized tests, when used in combination with other assessment strategies, can make an appropriate contribution to the assessment of young children (Wortham, 1996).

Standardized tests are also used to identify children for preschool intervention programs such as bilingual programs and classes for children at risk for success in school. In combination with interviews and background information about the child and family, standardized tests are one part of the screening and assessment process to select children who will benefit from preschool programs prior to kindergarten.

Authentic and Performance Assessment of Young Children

There are numerous strategies for assessment that are considered appropriate for young children. For many decades early childhood educators have used observation, checklists and rating scales, work samples, and teacher-designed assessments for assessment purposes (Goodwin & Goodwin, 1993; Wortham, 1995). These strategies are still part of the repertoire available to teachers; moreover, they contribute to the current emphasis on assessments that are contextual to the child's learning experiences. Two terms that are used to describe this type of assessment are *authentic assessment* and *performance assessment*.

While standardized tests and other more traditional forms of assessment have as their purpose to assess what the child knows or has learned, authentic assessment includes an assessment of what the child can do or apply. Moreover, authentic assessment is conducted within a meaningful context for the child. Performance assessment, or performance-based assessment, refers to authentic assessment whereby the child demonstrates learning or understanding through performing an activity. The assessment activity is meaningful in that it is connected to the real world (Bergan & Feld, 1993). Performance-based assessments are particularly useful with young children because developmental progress can be measured as well as learning. In addition, performance assessments permit the teacher to observe the processes the child uses to learn (Meisels et al., 1993).

There are three central purposes for performance-based assessments. As mentioned above, performance assessments are used to evaluate the child's progress in development. A second purpose is to make the connection between curriculum and assessment. Because the performance activity is closely related to instruction and desired outcomes of the curriculum, performance assessment enables the teacher to understand the child's progress and how to plan for further instruction. Both curriculum and instruction and the child's progress are assessed. Third, performance-based assessment can be used to evaluate the preschool program—evidence of the child's progress also reflects success in program goals (Hills, 1992; Schweinhart, 1993).

There are many strategies that can be used to facilitate the child's demonstration of progress and learning, among them:

• *Work Samples.* Work samples are the types of assessment data most commonly thought of in terms of portfolio collections. Teachers are familiar with collecting samples of children's work. In the context of performance-based assessment, there is a specific purpose for the samples selected (Grace & Shores, 1992).

• *Interviews.* Seefeldt (1993) suggests that interviews can be used to assess what children understand about concepts. A teacher can conduct an informal interview that takes place while children are working in centers and is initiated when the teacher notices that relevant behaviors are occurring. In contrast, a structured interview involves prior planning on the teacher's part with specific questioning to elicit the child's thought (Engel, 1990). A third type of interview, the diagnostic interview, is conducted to determine why a child is experiencing difficulty in learning a concept.

• *Games.* Teachers can design games for specific learning objectives so that children demonstrate their thought processes in showing what they have learned. Teachers observe the children as they are engaged in the game and study how the children employ game strategies (Kamii & Rosenblum, 1990).

• *Portfolios.* Portfolios facilitate authentic assessment by providing a method of organizing various types of materials into a collection that can be used to evaluate the progress of the child. Portfolios can be organized in many ways and can be collections of the child's work selected by the teacher, the child, or the teacher and child together. Depending on the type of curriculum and instruction that is conducted in the classroom, the portfolio can be organized by developmental domain, by content area, or by integrated curriculum units or projects. The goals and objectives for the curriculum serve as the foundation for assessment as a framework for the portfolio contents (Glazer, 1993; Grace & Shores, 1992; Wortham, 1995).

REPORTING YOUNG CHILDREN'S PROGRESS

How should we report young children's progress? Given that teachers use authentic assessments that are performance-based, how are these assessments interpreted and reported appropriately? Strategies to report children's progress complement the assessment process that is performance-based. Likewise, the reporting process should reflect curriculum and instruction that are appropriate for the development of young children. In sum,

> alternative systems of reporting that use authentic or performance assessments provide more than letter grades. They can include (1) a continuum of development and learning, (2) information about the whole child, (3) diagnostic information that allows the teacher to adjust instruction and activities, and most importantly, (4) examples of what the child has done to demonstrate understanding. (Wortham, 1995, p. 200)

The major function of reporting the child's progress is to communicate information about the child to the parents. To develop a quality approach to report progress, the system that is designed should include documentation of the results of authentic assessments, a vehicle for interpreting the collected data, and an effective method for communicating with parents. It is suggested that portfolios and narrative reports are effective strategies to use for reporting children's progress to parents.

As described in the previous section, portfolios facilitate the collection of information and materials relative to the child's assessment. The content of a teacher-and-child portfolio can include a section for work selected by the child, a section for work selected by the teacher, and a section for teacher assessment records such as observation reports, checklists and rating scales, and other documentation of the child's progress.

Before the child's progress can be reported to parents, an evaluation or interpretation must be made of the material and data that have been collected. The evaluation of assessment data should be connected to specific criteria established for assessment of learning goals, and performance should be compared to this standard. The standards that are developed must be both appropriate for the child's level of development and consistent with the teacher's curriculum.

The combined assessments are used to develop a profile of the child. The profile includes conclusions about the child's progress and reports information about the child's strengths and weaknesses, achievements, and instructional needs. Evaluation can include process and product assessments. The teacher conducts frequent process assessments with the child, discussing portfolio materials and progress that has been made. Product evaluation includes review of portfolio materials to sum up a student's progress prior to sharing the evaluation with parents in a conference (Farr, 1993). The portfolio materials serve as the resource for the teacher, child, and parents to discuss the child's evaluation through a review of portfolio contents.

A written report of the child's evaluation can be used with the portfolio as a reporting tool or as a separate alternative to report progress. Including all assessment materials and record-keeping forms, the teacher's written report constructs a profile or picture of the child in terminology that is meaningful and understandable for the parents (Horm-Wingerd, 1992; Krechevsky, 1991).

Current practices in how we should assess and report young children's progress favor the use of performance-based assessments. Authentic assessment methods combined with portfolios and written summary reports are proposed as models for assessment and reporting. Project Spectrum (Krechevsky, 1991), the Work Sample System (Meisels et al., 1993), and the Child Observation Record (Schweinhart, 1993) all use a combination of authentic, performance-based assessment strategies, a record-keeping system, portfolio materials, and a written summary report.

All three models have been carefully researched to ensure a quality assessment and reporting process that can be disseminated to early childhood educators.

PERSISTENT ISSUES IN THE ASSESSMENT AND REPORTING OF YOUNG CHILDREN'S PROGRESS

In spite of the positive steps being taken in developing appropriate assessment and reporting procedures, there are concerns associated with their use. The time needed to initiate and maintain portfolios and compose written reports on children's progress is an issue for many teachers. Other issues focus on teacher accountability for portfolio assessment. Teachers are insecure about the validity and reliability of the assessment and reporting method. They are uncertain whether they are grading the child's work appropriately. In some schools teachers are encouraged to use portfolios for assessment, but are required to give letter grades. They find this a source of conflict and confusion (Goodwin & Goodwin, 1993; Guskey, 1994; Shepard, 1995).

Performance assessments and reporting are still in early stages of implementation. While performance assessments and portfolios are being accepted and used throughout the United States, there is uncertainty about how well they are understood and implemented. Grant Wiggins expressed concern about the future of this assessment innovation (in Brandt, 1992):

> I think some assessment boats are already sinking—or at any rate, they're taking on water. I see parallels here between kids and adults: if students need models, criteria, and feedback, so do adults. Teachers now face the same situation as students who are asked to do a nonroutine task: how do they design new forms of assessment, the likes of which they've never seen? They know what they don't like about conventional testing—and they are absolutely right—but they don't know what this new vision looks like. When you consider that performance assessment is complicated logistically and technically, you've got a serious problem, particularly if it's a high-stakes situation. (p. 35)

There is currently little research available on the efficacy of using performance assessment to report children's progress. Herman and Winters (1994) reported that of 89 articles on portfolio assessment published in the last 10 years, only 7 reported technical data or used accepted research methods. Early childhood educators need to be aware that the performance-assessment boat could sink. While many materials are available on the advantages of performance assessment and strategies for developing portfolios, more information on how to ensure that performance assessments are reliable and valid is needed. Also needed are more models on how the teacher makes the connections between assessment and instructional planning. Teachers of young children need to be comfortable and confident that performance assessments are suitable for evaluating, reporting, and planning instruction. Shepard (1995) suggests that teachers who are changing to performance assessment need sustained support for an extended period of time as they try out new practices in assessment. Extensive staff development is recommended with time to reflect and develop new instructional and assessment approaches.

In these closing years of the 20th century, teachers have an accumulation of instruments and strategies at hand. Some measures are required by policy; others are within the choices that teachers may make for assessment. This chapter has explored both appropriate and inappropriate measures. Many issues about appropriate assessment are unresolved at this time. While performance assessments do not yet have longitudinal evidence of their effectiveness, they are a promising approach that serves the needs of teachers and children, as well as documentation of learning and achievement. It is important that educators of young children be able to use assessment measures that are effective and beneficial for children. Teachers now need the time to address the use of appropriate approaches such as performance assessment to better serve their students. If inappropriate uses of assessment continue, negative consequences for young children will also continue. It is in the best interests of educators, children, and families to eliminate inappropriate strategies and to continue to develop improved methods of assessment. The effective education of young children will be influenced by the quality of assessment practices used in the coming years and into the new century.

REFERENCES

Allington, R. L., & McGill-Franzen, A. (1995). Flunking: Throwing good money after bad. In R. L. Allington & S. A. Walmsley (Eds.), *No quick fix* (pp. 45–60). New York: Teachers College Press.

Barnes, H. V. (1991, Winter). Assessment: Current problems, promising practices. *High/Scope Resource*, pp. 22–23.

Bergan, J. R., & Feld, J. K. (1993). Developmental assessment: New directions. *Young Children, 48*, 41–47.

Brandt, R. (1992). On performance assessment: A conversation with Grant Wiggins. *Educational Leadership, 49*, 35–37.

Bredekamp, S. (Ed.). (1987). *Developmentally appropriate practice in early childhood programs serving children from birth through age 8.* Washington, DC: National Association for the Education of Young Children.

Brigance, A. H. (1982). *Brigance K & 1 Screen for Kindergarten and First Grade.* North Billerica, MA: Curriculum Associates.

Calfee, R. C. (1987). The school as a context for assessment of literacy. *The Reading Teacher, 40,* 738–743.

Cryan, J. R. (1986). Evaluation: Plague or promise? *Childhood Education, 62,* 344–350.

Duran, R. P. (1989). Testing of linguistic minorities. In R. L. Linn (Ed.), *Educational measurement* (3rd ed.; pp. 573–587). New York: Macmillan.

Durkin, D. (1987). Testing in the kindergarten. *The Reading Teacher, 40,* 766–770.

Engel, B. (1990). An approach to assessment in early literacy. In C. Kamii (Ed.), *Achievement testing in the early grades: The games grown-ups play* (pp. 119–134). Washington, DC: National Association for the Education of Young Children.

Farr, R. C. (1993). *Portfolio assessment teacher's guide grades k–8.* Orlando, FL: Harcourt Brace Jovanovich.

Foster, J. E. (1993). Retaining children in grade. *Childhood Education, 63,* 38–42.

Glazer, S. M. (1993, January). Assessment in the classroom: Where we are, where we're going. *Teaching k–8 ,* pp. 68–71.

Gnezda, M. T., & Bolig, R. (1988). *A national survey of public school testing of prekindergarten and kindergarten.* Washington, DC: National Academy of Sciences.

Goodwin, W. L., & Goodwin, L. D. (1993). Young children and measurement: Standardized and nonstandardized instruments in early childhood education. In B. Spodek (Ed.), *Handbook of research on the education of young children* (pp. 441–465). New York: Macmillan.

Grace, C., & Shores, E. F. (1992). *The portfolio and its use: Developmentally appropriate assessment of young children.* Little Rock: Southern Early Childhood Association.

Gredler, G. R. (1984). Transition classes: A viable alternative for the at-risk child? *Psychology in the Schools, 21,* 463–470.

Guskey, T. R. (1994). What you assess may not be what you get. *Educational Leadership, 51,* 51–54.

Harman, S. (1990). Negative effects of achievement testing in literacy development. In C. Kamii (Ed.), *Achievement testing in the early grades: The games grown-ups play* (pp. 111–118). Washington, DC: National Association for the Education of Young Children.

Herman, J. L., & Winters, L. (1994). Portfolio research: A slim collection. *Educational Leadership, 52,* 48–55.

Hilliard, A. G., III. (1990). Discussion on "What is test misuse?" In *The uses of standardized tests in American education: Proceedings of the 1989 Fiftieth ETS Invitational Conference* (pp. 27–35). Princeton, NJ: Educational Testing Service.

Hills, T. W. (1992). Reaching potentials through appropriate assessment. In S. Bredekamp & T. Rosegrant (Eds.), *Reaching potentials: Appropriate curriculum and assessment for young children* (pp. 43–65). Washington, DC: National Association for the Education of Young Children.

Holmes, C. T., & Matthews, K. M. (1984). The effects of nonpromotion on elementary and junior high school pupils: A meta-analysis. *Review of Educational Research, 54,* 225–236.

Horm-Wingerd, D. M. (1992). Reporting children's development: The narrative report. *Dimensions of Early Childhood, 21,* 11–15.

Ilg, F. L., Ames, L. B., & Gillespie, C. (1978). *Gesell school readiness test kit.* Rosemont, NJ: Programs for Education Publishers.

Kamii, C., & Rosenblum, V. (1990). An approach to assessment in mathematics. In C. Kamii (Ed.), *Achievement testing in the early grades: The games grown-ups play* (pp. 146–162). Washington, DC: National Association for the Education of Young Children.

Katz, L. (1985). Dispositions in early childhood education. *ERIC/EECE Bulletin, 18,* 1, 3.

Krechevsky, M. (1991). Project Spectrum: An innovative assessment alternative. *Educational Leadership, 48,* 43–48.

Lehr, C. A., Ysseldyke, J. E., & Thurlow, M. L. (1987). Assessment practices in model early childhood special education programs. *Psychology in the Schools, 24,* 390–399.

Meisels, S. J. (1987). Uses and abuses of developmental screening and school readiness testing. *Young Children, 42,* 4–6, 68–73.

Meisels, S. J. (1989). High stakes testing in kindergarten. *Educational Leadership, 46,* 16–22.

Meisels, S. J., Steele, M., & Quinn-Leering, K. (1993). Testing, tracking, and retaining young children: An analysis of research and social policy. In B. Spodek (Ed.), *Handbook of research on the education of young children* (pp. 279–292). New York: Macmillan.

National Association for the Education of Young Children. (1988). Position statement on standardized testing of young children 3 through 8 years of age. *Young Children, 43,* 42–47.

National Association for the Education of Young Children and National Association of Early Childhood Specialists in State Departments of Education. (1992). Guidelines for appropriate curriculum content and assessment in programs serving children ages 3 through 8. In S. Bredekamp & T. Rosegrant (Eds.), *Reaching potentials: Appropriate curriculum and assessment for young children* (pp. 9–27). Washington, DC: National Association for the Education of Young Children.

Nurss, J. R., & McGauvran, M. E. (1976). *Metropolitan readiness tests.* Orlando, FL: Harcourt Brace Jovanovich.

Oakland, T. (Ed.). (1977). *Psychological and educational assessment of minority children.* New York: Brunner/Mazel.

Perrone, V. (1981). Testing, testing and more testing. *Childhood Education, 58,* 76–80.

Perrone, V. (1990). How did we get here? In C. Kamii (Ed.), *Achievement testing in the early grades: The games grown-ups play* (pp. 1–13). Washintgon, DC: National Association for the Education of Young Children.

Perrone, V. (1991). On standardized testing. *Childhood Education, 68,* 132–142.

Pierson, L. H., & Connell, J. P. (1992). Effect of grade retention on self-system processes, school engagement, and academic performance. *Journal of Educational Psychology, 84,* 300–307.

Popham, W. J. (1987). The merits of measurement-driven instruction. *Phi Delta Kappan, 68,* 679–682.

Schweinhart, L. J. (1993). Observing young children in action: The key to early childhood assessment. *Young Children, 48,* 29–33.

Seefeldt, C. (1993). *Social studies for the preschool-primary child* (4th ed.). New York: Merrill/Macmillan.

Shepard, L. A. (1989). Why we need better assessments. *Educational Leadership, 46,* 35–40.

Shepard, L. A. (1991). The influence of standardized tests on early childhood curriculum, teachers, and children. In B. Spodek & O. N. Saracho (Eds.), *Yearbook in early childhood education* (pp. 166–189). New York: Teachers College Press.

Shepard, L. A. (1994). The challenges of assessing young children appropriately. *Phi Delta Kappan, 76,* 206–213.

Shepard, L. A. (1995). Using assessment to improve learning. *Educational Leadership, 52,* 38–45.

Shepard, L. A., & Graue, M. E. (1993). The morass of school readiness screening: Research on test use and validity. In B. Spodek (Ed.), *Handbook of research on the education of young children* (pp. 293–305). New York: Macmillan.

Shepard, L. A., & Smith, M. L. (1986). Synthesis of research on school readiness and kindergarten retention. *Educational Leadership, 44,* 78–86.

Shepard, L. A., & Smith, M. L. (1988). Escalating academic demand in kindergarten: Counterproductive policies. *Elementary School Journal, 69,* 135–145.

Tanner, C. K., & Combs, F. E. (1993). Student retention policy: The gap between research and practice. *Journal of Research in Childhood Education, 8,* 69–76.

Taub, H. P., Love, J., Wilkerson, D. A., Washington, E. D., & Wolf, J. M. (1980). *Accept my profile: Perspectives for Head Start profiles of program effects on children.* Black Rock, CT: Mediax Interactive Technologies.

Wortham, S. C. (1995). *Measurement and evaluation in early childhood education* (2nd ed.). Englewood Cliffs, NJ: Merrill (an imprint of Prentice-Hall).

Wortham, S. C. (1996). *The integrated classroom: The assessment-curriculum link in early childhood education.* Englewood Cliffs, NJ: Merrill (an imprint of Prentice-Hall).

Chapter 8

Playing with Play in Four Dimensions

Patricia Monighan-Nourot

As a teacher with many years of experience in the early childhood class-room, and more recently as a teacher researcher and teacher educator, I have let questions about the value of play in classrooms for young children guide my career for over a decade. Why is play an issue for educators of young children? Is it really as valuable to future learning and development as many of us claim, or does our romantic attachment to images of ideal childhood cloud our views (Almy, 1984; Isenberg & Quisenberry, 1988)? We might consider the following scenarios:

The High Chair

Amy, Bettina, and Kimi are playing in the housekeeping area. Amy sits in the high chair and announces, "I'm the baby now."

Kimi puts the food tray on the high chair, and Amy pounds on the tray with her fists, "Ga-Ga Ga-ga Ga-ga. I want something to eat!"

Kimi says, "Pretend I'm the auntie."

"And I'm the visitor," adds Bettina.

Bettina says to Kimi, "What do you want her to eat?" She gives Amy a small plastic dish. Amy throws the dish to the floor, laughing "No! No! No! No!" Kimi gives her a plastic pineapple, a cooking pot, a plastic cauliflower, and two more dishes in succession. Amy throws each to the floor chanting "Na-na-na-na!"

Mitch comes into the play area and tries to put a plastic banana in Amy's mouth. "Eat it, baby."

Amy throws the banana on the floor. Bettina offers her the plastic cauliflower. "Amy, eat this!"

Amy says "Cauliflower" in a high-pitched voice, and laughs and throws it from the high chair to the floor.

Bettina offers her the plastic banana. "Want this?"

Amy agrees "OK" in a high-pitched voice and makes smacking sounds as she holds the banana near her mouth.

Bettina, Mitch, and Kimi then take turns "feeding" her all the toy food, and pots and pans previously thrown on the floor. Amy smacks her lips and pretends to eat. Bettina brings a dress. Amy pretends to eat the dress, smacking her lips, then throws it on the cupboard. Mitch gives her a baby bottle. She pretends to suck on it and throws it on the cupboard. Kimi brings a long, stuffed toy snake and offers it.

"No, no I don't like snakes," Amy says shaking her head emphatically and laughing.

Mitch brings her a suitcase, and she pretends to eat it. They all fall down, laughing hysterically.

The Three Pigs

Nathan sits at the playdough table playing alone. He builds a three-tiered structure, and then pokes holes in it with a toothpick. He rolls several small pieces of playdough and places them adjacent to one another around the structure, like stepping stones. Using a stick, he presses ridges into the small pieces of dough and hums a melody softly to himself. "There! A tower," he says sotto voce.

He picks up a cookie cutter shaped like a human figure, and "walks" it along the playdough stones. In a high-pitched voice he sings, "I'm walkin' on the sidewalk! I'm walkin' on the sidewalk! I'm walkin' on the sidewalk!" He tips the cookie cutter over. "Ahhhh!" Picking up the cookie cutter, he hops it up and down in front of the playdough "tower." "Little pig, little pig, let me come in! I'll huff and I'll puff and come in!" he chants in a low, gruff voice.

He switches to a high-pitched voice. "Not by the hair on my chinny-chin-chin!"

"Whoa! Br-rkk. Boom!" he exclaims, as he pushes the cookie cutter into the playdough tower and it crumbles.

Here are two examples of play occuring in classrooms for young children. The episodes have elements of the real, the fantastic, and the humorous. They involve problem solving and intense feelings. One is social, and one, very private. Each reflects the development of individual children and the influence of the peer culture and the culture at large. Each is embedded in the life of the classroom, and each contributes rich information about children and classroom learning to the teacher who understands and respects children's play. So why does play in some early childhood programs remain controversial?

First of all, play is an issue for many teachers and administrators because its definition is elusive and it defies "packaging" into neat curriculum activities. Its emphasis on process over product sometimes makes teachers uncomfortable, and they ask, How can I show that children are learning when they play?

What children are learning as they play is the next frequently asked question. The relationship of play to a variety of domains of development and to academic achievement in schools is not always easy to discern. Play is deeply embedded in children's capacity to make meaning of their experiences in the world and their emerging symbolic and cognitive capacities. It is frequently idiosyncratic, always culture bound, and requires the teacher to view it through a complex set of lenses in order to fully understand its role in the classroom culture and in curriculum.

While play is the source of creativity and innovation, it is also the source of rebellion and parody in our classrooms, and demands flexibility, a sense of humor, and playfulness that busy teachers may not always command at a moment's notice. A complex dance of intuition and intellect is called for on the part of the teacher to skillfully use play to assess and orchestrate the learning and development of young children. What is the role of the sensitive teacher with regard to play in educational settings? How is play viewed in the age-appropriate development of children? Who defines "good" play and "poor" play, developmentally advanced play and delayed play, and how are these values reflected in teacher's decisions about curriculum and interactions with children (Jones & Reynolds, 1992; King, 1992; Van Hoorn, Nourot, Scales, & Alward, 1993)?

Three issues frame this chapter's review of research and theory regarding the place of play in the early childhood curriculum:

1 How is play defined?
2. What is the role of play in learning and development?
3. What is the teacher's role in interpreting and orchestrating play?

Embedded in these issues are questions regarding the values and goals of early education in American culture, and the ways in which teachers and researchers have conceptualized the study of play, development, and learning.

FRAMING THE ISSUES

Metaphors for the roles of educators have changed from purveyors of information to investigators, architects, gardeners, and scaffolders of children's learning. With this shift in the conception of teachers' roles, it becomes increasingly desirable and important for teachers to develop the ability to apprehend the qualities of human intelligence, creativity, and the capacity for integration as a whole person in each child who comes to school (Isenberg & Jalongo, 1997; Wassermann, 1990).

Constructivist ideas that lead the way in contemporary educational dialogues, drawing on theories of Piaget (1962), Vygotsky (1978), Mead (1934), and Dewey (1916), find in play the source of abstract thought, self-regulation, experimental inquiry, and creative imagination. What, then, do theory and research offer on the value of play in the educational life of young children and their teachers, and how can we learn to understand its complexity and value?

From a paucity of research in the 1960s and 1970s, the literature on play that attempts to define it, explain it, and value its place in our lives has expanded exponentially. In revisiting these questions I looked for new patterns of organization to express the depth and complexity of knowledge about play in educational settings that is available in the research literature.

One new pattern of organization is based on Einstein's work in the early part of this century, and on the work of others who elaborated and refined his models. They challenged the either-or way of viewing the universe within the field of physics, and emphasized the paradoxical relationships of observer and observed (Kaku, 1994; Weber, 1985a; Zukav, 1979). Researchers in social science have begun to experiment with this paradigm in relation to disciplinary models (Diesing, 1971; Fein, 1984; Weaver, 1994), and it seems to hold promise for play. Multiple dimensions of play continue to exist holistically, but what we choose to foreground as players, teachers, or researchers shapes our interpretations and actions. Play expresses an implicit holographic order in which discrete factors are enfolded into the whole of the play experience. These factors become explicated as play unfolds and players negotiate its features. They also become explicated when teachers and researchers choose a particlar aspect of play as more important or more relevant than others (Pribram, 1985; Weber, 1985b). The ability to select among a set of lenses that illuminate particular qualities of play at the expense of leaving others in the shadows is one that serves both teachers and researchers, but remains dependent on the underlying awareness that play, as we perceive it, is constantly defined, redefined, and shaped by transactions between observer and observed (Van Hoorn et al., 1993).

As a teacher of young children, I frequently responded to research I read in my efforts to understand play in a "Yes, but . . . " manner. Each day in my classroom I found individuals and situations that verified the conclusions I read; just as often I found examples that did not support research conclusions. It seemed that I would have to selectively attend to some features of play, while negating others in order to understand it, and it always felt like a song half-finished. Like a character in a lower dimension trying to apprehend a reality I could sense but not see, I struggled to wrap my mind around the multiple layers and perspectives that characterized the play life of early childhood classrooms. I began to conceptualize play in spatial metaphors, first as a one-dimensional line, then as a two-dimensional surface, and then as a cube or sphere. Finally I conceptualized play as it might be grasped from a metaphoric dimension beyond our physical world of space and time. I turned first to the issue of identifying play as play in early childhood classrooms, conceptualizing it as a linear continuum marked by play and not-play.

PLAY IN THE FIRST DIMENSION: WHAT IS PLAY?

As we contemplate play in its first dimension, teachers and researchers alike struggle with defining play. Perhaps as Fromberg (1992) points out, part of the difficulty arises in conceptualizing play as both a noun and a verb. Play *is* and we *do* play so that play is not simply a clearly delineated package of activities but also a process or a "frame" that transcends physical and social contexts, materials, and time (Bateson, 1972). For example, what are the common qualities that emerge in analyzing the high-chair play and the three pigs enactment? In each episode behavior is taken out of its usual context and enacted in an imaginary one, with symbolic representation as the tool of thought and communication, and with intellect and feelings closely interwoven. But which of these qualities actually defines play?

Early philosophers such as Comenius (1953), Pestalozzi (Anderson, 1931), and Rousseau (1762/1964) defined play most simply by its qualities and by its intrinsic relationships to childhood, finding its origin in sensory experience and remarking on its fundamental qualities of free expression (Isenberg & Jalongo, 1997; Nourot, Henry, & Scales, 1990). Froebel (1896) saw play as basic to children's unfolding understanding of the unity and interconnected nature of the universe. Huizinga(1950) constructed complicated definitions of play, viewing play from nearly every aspect of civilization and in numerous languages, and contrasted it to work, earnestness, and seriousness:

> The significance of play, on the other hand, is by no means defined or exhausted by calling it "not earnest," or "not serious." Play is a thing by itself.

The play concept itself is of a higher order than is seriousness. For seriousness seeks to exclude play, whereas play can very well include seriousness. (p 45)

Huizinga concludes that play is the primary evidence for the existence and power of mind in relation to the apparent order of the universe, an attribute of play elaborated by Vygotsky (1976) when he speaks of the development of will power within a play frame.

Ignoring Huizinga's cautionary remarks, some theorists have defined play by what it is not (not work, not serious, not coerced) or play in opposition to work. For example, Klinger (1971) describes play as behavior that is displaced from the "normal" motivational context that constitutes "work," a position that fuels our Protestant work ethic, placing work at the center of awareness and everything else on the margins, and thus implicitly not valuable.

More open is the continuum described by Dewey (1916) in which foolery appears at one end, drudgery at the other, and play and work in the middle, with playful seriousness or serious playfulness as the "ideal" mental condition (Fromberg, 1992). Bergen (1988) characterizes play and work along a similar continuum, ranging from free play to guided play, directed play, "work disguised as play," and work.

Play as Viewed by Children, Teachers, and Theorists

Views about the definition of play are by necessity shaped by our places vis-à-vis play frames: children, teachers, and developmental theorists may describe play in differing terms.

In interviews with schoolchildren, King (1987) reports that children see play as self-selected, desirable, and pleasurable, a view that seems to be contextualized by the implicit and explicit values assigned by teachers to play (King, 1992; Polito, 1994).

Wing (1995) proposes a play-work classification based on children's perceptions of school experiences. She includes voluntary versus obligatory activity, the need to finish a product, adult judgment or evaluation, teacher direction, and fun. Fein's (1985) interviews with children regarding play indicate locus of control as the most central feature of play.

Teachers' views of play are shaped by their knowledge, beliefs, and experiences. Cuffaro (1995) captures the range of these curricular contexts well:

In early childhood play is used by teachers as a label in a variety of ways, reflecting different perspectives and understanding of the activity. The word may be used to distinguish between teacher-directed and child-initiated activities (the former being work, the latter play); refer to the activities of an area (house play, outdoor play, water play); describe activity that by the adult's standards does not seem goal directed or purposeful ("they're just playing with those shapes"); describe a child's or children's activity that seems to have some element of narrative within it that has been initiated by the participant(s) (commonly referred to as dramatic play); refer to the social make-up of the activity or to a developmental stage (solitary, parallel, cooperative, group play). (p. 79)

Some theorists who have studied the role of play in development and learning ascribe to play "assimilation of reality to the ego" (Piaget, 1962, p. 149). From the Piagetian perspective, as the reciprocal processes of assimilation and accommodation fluctuate in early childhood, children progress toward a more stable equilibrium between internal cognitive structures and the demands to accommodate imposed by the external world. This constant fluctuation and contradiction that marks the development from unreliable and idiosyncratic concepts about the way the world works to the more stable concepts of middle childhood is directed by play. Because of the emerging and changing nature of early logical concepts reflected and generated in play, behavior is always characterized by the child's own immediate viewpoint and his or her active engagement of current cognitive structures for making sense of the world. For example, in the high-chair episode, the shared humor comes from the implicitly negotiated agreement among players that suitcases and dresses and snakes (even pretend ones) are not in the category of things to eat. This inversion of what children know to be sensible in the real world to its opposite in play is the source of humor in communication (McGhee, 1984; Van Hoorn et al., 1993).

The view of play as the source of abstract thought, imagination, and practical intelligence is echoed in Vygotsky's theory in which play is seen as the "leading" activity of early childhood. This designation as "lead" activity means that play has the most significant impact during the early years of development. Leading activities such as play give rise to new competencies, form the foundation for future development, and facilitate the construction and restructuring of cognitive structures already in place (Bodrova & Leong, 1996; Moll, 1990; Vygotsky, 1978). The representational play of children reveals new skills, concepts, and competencies as they are emerging in the intuitive repertoire of the child. Play stretches children beyond the limits of what has already been achieved and provides the impetus for expanded mental possibilities.

"Play is the source of development and creates the zone of proximal development" (ZPD), according to Vygotsky (1976, p. 552). This view of the ZPD differs from that usually studied by educational researchers. Play as the ZPD is not dependent on expert-novice apprenticeship in problem solving solutions; the source of development is the collaborative construction of an imaginary playing field that is invented by, and subject to implicit rules negotiated by, players (Nicolopoulou, 1994; Nourot, Henry, & Scales, 1990). Because of the child's desire to participate in this imaginary world, symbolic meanings are invented and accepted, self-regulation of impulses triumphs, and the collaborative construction of pretend pulls all the players into their "zone" of higher psychological functioning.

Play Unifies Paradox

The very elusiveness of the definition of play points to its function in human development as central to the ability to apprehend the aesthetic, the ambiguous, and the paradoxical in human experience, and thus suggests play as the essence or "implicate order" of both intuitive and logical processes in the making of meaning (Egan, 1988; Huizinga, 1950; Nachmanovitch, 1990; Weber, 1985a, 1985b).

Those who study play and cognition focus on the mental structures generated in play, naming such constructs of play as means over ends, symbolic activity, representational competence, freedom from external rules, and self-referenced behavior (Rubin, Fein, & Vandenberg, 1983).

Those who study play from the psychodynamic perspective highlight affective qualities of play such as masterful, voluntary, pleasurable, relaxing, exciting, joyous, wish-fulfilling, and compensating for reality (Erikson, 1963; Fraiberg, 1959; Gould, 1972; Griffin, 1982; Hartley, Frank, & Goldenson, 1957; Issacs, 1933; Winnicott, 1971).

This apparent dichotomy between the cognitive and the affective in play gives rise to one of the most compelling attributes of play, and one that makes it so difficult to define. Play is essentially integrative and unifies apparently paradoxical qualities (Nachmanovitch, 1990; Van Hoorn et al., 1993). This unifying property of play seems to capture the essence of its definition. For example, while play is frequently described as pleasurable, it may just as easily be frustrating or difficult. Vygotsky (1976) elucidated this view when he described play as entry into an imaginary world in which implicit or explicit rules govern actions and children's desires to inhabit this play world give rise to willpower and self-control. As such, the cognitive ability to transform the world of the "here and now" to that of the "there and then" frees children from the constraints of the real world and invites them to voluntarily abide by the constraints of an invented world.

Bateson (1972) elaborates this transformative aspect of play into the analogy of "frames," which define play as it is played in a particular context of time and space negotiated by the players. These frames serve as doorways into the "play-sphere" of children (Huizinga, 1950) as they signal to one another (and to themselves) that "the meaning (of objects, words, gestures, actions) in this situation is something other than it appears to be" (p. 56).

Expanding on Bateson's (1972) "framing" of play, Reifel and Yeatman (1993) describe play as a "family of simulations, including pretense, dramatic play (including storytelling), games, arts and crafts, rough and tumble, joking, and word play, and motor exploration, any of which can be done as an end in itself" (p. 353).

Focusing on play within the single dimension of what qualities define it clarifies play for me as an educator. I think about play and work along a linear continuum and identify the properties that help me discern whether an activity is play:

- Does it integrate experience?
- Is it paradoxical?
- Does it involve symbolic meanings?

Once I believe I can identify play in children's behavior with some appreciation for its variety, I turn to the second issue: How can teachers understand the role of play in development and learning? This brings me to the metaphor of a two-dimensional perspective on play.

PLAY IN THE SECOND DIMENSION: DEVELOPMENT AND LEARNING

When one moves from a one-dimensional view of what play is (and isn't), the constructs of relationships and change over time enter the picture. In addition to describing play by its qualities or by analogy to other aspects of experience, a two-dimensional view addresses the question of what play is good for. With play on one axis and selected aspects of behavior, learning, or development on another, researchers are able to map play in two conceptual dimensions, and the dimension of time becomes important.

Time and Development

Perhaps it is because play moved from the domain of the philosopher to that of the developmental psychologist that concepts of time have become so prevalent in research and theory in play. Stages of play-as-play based on Piaget's work form the foundation for one branch of studies, tracking in great detail the cognitive developmental life of play in childhood (Dansky, 1980; Eifermann, 1971; Feitelson & Ross, 1973; Smilansky, 1968, 1990). Other studies (King, 1987; Nourot, Henry, & Scales, 1990) look at play in relation to other aspects of development: language, narrative competence, problem solving, metacognition, socialization, moral development, and creativity. In these studies rest the arguments for the "instrumental" value of play as a component of planned curriculum for young children that contributes to the developmental aims of education.

Time is most familiar to educators and psychologists in the linear form that theories about the development of play usually take: Play leads to competence or complexity in another domain of development. An exception to this linear view is the reconstructive view of Corsaro regarding the role of play in the continual creation and recreation of peer cultures in which play development is recursive (Gaskins, Miller, & Corsaro, 1992). Another "wrinkle" in the time sequence is the dilemma presented by Csikszentmihalyi (1979) in discussing the evolution of flow and its relationship to play; he raises interesting questions about the links between productive work and play in childhood and adulthood.

As we see in the multidimensional views of play that come later in this chapter, constructs of "developmental time" are relative to many contextual factors, including situation, culture, language, and social relationships, and allow us to view play as development from more multifaceted perspectives.

Time as a Variable in Play

While one focus of playing with time rests with the theorist, another is situated in the playing out of play itself. Children manipulate and negotiate the variable of time within play frames characterized by "shared predictability and collaborative novelty" (Fromberg, 1992, p. 49). They also use spatial reasoning and representation to mark the passage, both backward and forward, through time in their play enactments. For example, in order to mark events in sequence within a storyline, or to achieve a "meanwhile back at the ranch" effect, players mark areas of the stage on which they enact their stories as "the house they used to live in" or "the forest they will get lost in" as well as designating backstage areas where players wait until their part comes into the story (Nourot et al., 1990). The planning of play, in terms of both events and roles, marks entries and exits to and from the play frame, and language frequently marks the passage of "pretend" time for players:

> "Pretend it was too hot and so we had to go swimming," says Kevin to Georgann.

"And then we put on our bathing suits and got splashed," Georgann adds.

"Then, pretend the rain came and we had to run real fast to the
car. It's cold! Brr-rr!" as Kevin and Georgann shiver and clutch
imaginary towels to their chests.

In playing with time young children experiment with their emerging
notions of cause and effect—"vertical" patterning of space–time—such
as the sequence of events pretended by Kevin and Georgann. Children
also experiment with synchronicity, or events connected by meaning in
their play, such as the implicit shared meaning of what is edible and not
edible in the high-chair episode. These meaning-connected events form
a "horizontal" pattern of space-time that intersects with the sequence
of events expressed in a play episode, and the connections may only be
apprehended by the players themselves. Interactions within the "playing
field" created by children are analogous to the quantum fields of physics
in which time may move both "forward" and "backward" from the events
marked by observers (or players) in their joint negotiation of pretend (Zukav, 1979).

What Does Play Lead To?

In placing play at the center of developmentally sensitive curriculum for
young children, the views that emphasize play as the construction of
meaning dominate (DeVries & Kohlberg, 1987; Diaute, 1989; Van Hoorn
et al., 1993). In play children employ their imagination and problem-
solving skills to make connections among experiences and to link past
experiences and characteristic ways of approaching the world to future
possibilities (Cuffaro, 1995).

According to constructivist and social constructivist theories, child-
initiated action fuels cognitive development, mediated by the cultural
symbols and signs represented in play. Although children also learn
through the imitation characterized by memorization and practice, imitated skills and concepts serve development more fully when children
appropriate them for play, leading to the construction of mental models
characteristic of abstract thought.

The interaction between spontaneous and culturally transmitted
ideas is seen clearly in Vygotsky's (1978) discussion of spontaneous and
scientific concepts. Children's informal intuitive concepts develop out of
their daily experience and provide the structure to make sense of future
experience. Scientific concepts are part of the "cultural tool kit" (Bruner,
1976) imparted by experts or elders in a society or within a discipline
and are formally taught. These scientific concepts give form to the sponta-

neous concepts that make them more readily accessible to interpretation by others from the culture, and provide an organizing framework for future cognitive development (Moll, 1990; Vygotsky, 1978).

Dewey (1916) describes similar reciprocity between intuitive and cognitive modes in the process of experimental inquiry. Reflective thought is provoked by the "indeterminacy" of situations that challenge children's existing structures of meaning, giving rise to feelings of confusion, uncertainty, or ambiguity. This "felt" quality of the disequilibration posited by Piaget (1962, 1969) is frequently expressed in play; children intuitively express elements of an experience or situation that do not fit neatly into already developed structures for interpreting and expressing meaning. In reflecting on their play, be the play dramatic, constructive, artistic, or physical, children formulate their inquiry. Like the "beginner's mind" called for in both artistic and scientific trailblazing, in successful experimental inquiry children approach their problems with both logical hypothesis formation and the affective dispositions of open-mindedness, wholeheartedness, and intellectual responsibility, in which they consider the consequences of their actions explored in play (Cuffaro, 1995; Zukav, 1979).

Given these theoretical models for the development of thinking and problem solving, the importance of self-initiated spontaneous play and representation, coupled with images and behaviors derived from the culture, is apparent. Researchers have studied these relationships in play and to play for several decades (Rubin et al., 1983).

As play in childhood grows in complexity, it encompasses the use of increasingly abstract symbols to represent feelings, ideas, objects, and situations that are removed from their immediate space–time context. Early on, the sensorimotor play of infancy gives rise to the construction of pretense, in which the meaning is created in the mind and expressed in gesture and/or language (Copple, Cocking, & Matthews, 1984; Fein, 1981; Fenson & Ramsay, 1980; McCune, 1985).

A related area of research that draws on children's ability to make symbolic transformations and to reflect on those transformations is the research on the development of "theory of mind" (Astington, 1993; Leslie, 1988). Children's ability to enter "as if" frames and to negotiate with others within those frames marks the human capacity to enter wholly mental realms of experience, and to reflect on those experiences as distinct from experience in the real world. Researchers studying these processes in young children do not agree on the nature of "meta-representational" thought in play, but do agree that pretense contributes in a significant way to children's understanding of their own psychological worlds and those of others.

In both cognitive and social domains, play provides the context for the resolution of problems (Connolly & Doyle, 1984; Howes, Unger, & Matheson, 1992; Pepler, 1986; Trawick-Smith, 1992, 1994). A key feature of the ability to solve problems is flexibility in thinking, the open-mindedness described by Dewey that frees one to entertain multiple possibilities and suspend current strategies and judgments while doing so (Adams, 1976; Christie, 1985; Isenberg & Jalongo, 1997; Pellegrini, 1984; Pepler & Ross, 1981). In the same way that adults "talk through" processes and possible outcomes to problems they face, children "play through" alternatives (Hutt, 1971).

In the social realm, flexibility in thinking and the ability to entertain multiple perspectives on a situation relate to peer popularity and to the qualities observed in "master players" (Farver, 1992; Fein, 1985; Garvey, 1977/1990; Hazen & Black, 1984; Jones & Reynolds, 1992; Reynolds & Jones, 1996; Trawick-Smith, 1988, 1992), who by compromising and suggesting alternatives in roles and scripts keep play going, and invite imaginative elaboration of themes and characters (Doyle & Connolly, 1989; Kamii & DeVries, 1980; Reifel & Yeatman, 1991). Creative thinking is closely linked to the flexibility of thought required for effective problem solving and seems such an integral part of children's play that teachers may take it for granted (Isenberg & Jalongo, 1997; Van Hoorn et al., 1993).

Play as the source of novelty and adaptive flexibility is a position taken by Ellis (1988) when he writes about the contribution of play to evolution, an idea also elucidated by Bruner (1976) and Csikszentmihalyi (1979, 1993). Csikszentmihalyi relates playfulness in childhood and adulthood to clear goals and immediate feedback, opportunities for mastery and control, concentrated attention, intrinsic motivation, loss of self-consciousness, altered sense of time, and autotelic nature of experience (worth doing for its own sake), all of which characterize the psychological states described by those who engage in productive, fulfilling work as adults.

Noddings and Shore (1984), on the other hand, write about the intuitive modes that underlie play processes as these modes involve immediate apprehension of objects of knowledge or feeling without the mediation of conceptual schemes. Both objects and ideas when considered outside the dimension of logical operations may become the focus of intuition, the necessary partner to the cognitive qualities described by others who study creativity. Mozart, for example, described "hearing" melodies in his head when his attention was concentrated in this intuitive mode. Tom Robbins (1995), a contemporary novelist, describes his process in writing a novel; he thinks of a title and then "holds auditions" for the characters in his mind. This internalized integration of the mental processes of both the conscious and intuitive mind drives the forces of artistic creativity, and has its roots in the primal life function of fantasy and play (Egan, 1988). Cuffaro (1995), in describing Dewey's (1916) notion of "aesthetic experiencing," also likens the creative process to flow that is holistic and complete in its immediacy:

> There are moments, sometimes fleeting, when a young child moves a block along the floor, lifts it abruptly, whirs with swaying, lilting motions of the body across the room. Immediate time and space are transcended. The child and the block become one, a unity expressing the essence of *helicopterness*. It is an instance of wholeness. (p. 81)

It is the flowing, integrated, and more "textured" view of play that I turn to next.

PLAYING IN THE THIRD DIMENSION: PLAY IN CONTEXT

Like the character in *Flatland* (Abbot, 1884/1952) who is suddenly lifted from his two-dimensional universe, entry into a three dimensional view of play opens new horizons. The two-dimensional surface on which I characterize play in relation to a series of developmental variables expands in this view to a cube metaphor, much like a three-dimensional chessboard, or a cube of jello. This dimensional view focuses attention on the patterns, contexts, and interrelationships that qualify, modify, and clarify relationships between play and other aspects of human development and learning.

King (1992) provides a useful framework for entry into a three dimensional model by reminding us that all play is contextualized; it is the very essence of play to transform and control contextual and situational frames. Play derives its meaning from these frames. King describes in detail contextual variables that influence play in school settings. Physical contexts consist of amounts and arrangements of space and materials for play. For example, researchers have studied physical environments in preschool settings, noting that enough space for children to move around and make choices, plus clear boundaries and pathways, helps children focus attention and protect their interactive space (Corsaro, 1985; Jones, 1973; Phyfe-Perkins, 1980).

Arranging furniture in ways that connect to children's lives outside of school is vividly illustrated by Curry's story (1971) of the Navajo children who "discovered" the housekeeping area only after the furniture had been left against the wall, an arrangement more familiar to those who lived in round hogans. Preferences of outdoor to indoor play space may also influence the degree and kind of play children engage in (Sutton-Smith & Heath, 1981).

Materials influence play from both cultural and developmental stances. Having both replicas and unstructured objects such as blocks available serves children's need to make choices based on symbolic distancing skills or previous experience (McLloyd, 1983, 1986; Pulaski, 1970). Including items familiar to children in their homes and cultural contexts is thought to facilitate play in schools (Derman-Sparks & A.B.C. Taskforce, 1989).

Time is another physical variable that influences both the duration and complexity of play (Christie & Wardel, 1992; Smilansky, 1968). Christie and his colleagues found that a minimum of 30 minutes was required to become fully engaged in play in the sample of children they studied. Researchers who have used Parten's (1932) categories of social play (unoccupied, onlooker, solitary, parallel associative, group) frequently cite time as a major factor in the social organization of play (Monighan-Nourot, Scales, Van Hoorn, & Almy, 1987; Rubin et al., 1983; Takhvar & Smith, 1990). For example, an onlooker may observe play long enough to find an appropriate entry point and strategy into the flow of play (Campbell, 1995; Monighan-Nourot et al., 1987); a parallel player may be invited to join the group, or a group player may become a solitary one as his or her focus shifts. Too little time allocated for play may destroy its essence, at least from the child's point of view (Polito, 1994).

From the researcher's stance, adequate time to apprehend the nature of play as expressed in its flow is a significant methodological issue (Reifel & Yeatman, 1993; Takhvar & Smith, 1990). Reifel and Yeatman describe how the contextual variables of materials, social relationships, real-world experience, play decisions, and the transformations within a timed play frame influence interpretations of play, and that the fluctuating elements cannot be easily labeled as a single kind of play. This is a particuarly important issue in light of the large number of studies that draw conclusions about "good play" and "poor play," developmentally advanced and delayed play, from very brief observations and inferences made by observers of the play. The transactions of the observer and the observed within a time period as well as consideration of a variety of contextual factors is essential for apprehending the complex nature of play. In addition, developmental stages of play that come out of decontextualized studies associate a particular set of behaviors unfolding in a particular order with developmental norms. This knowledge may bias teachers' interpretations of children's behavior and limit views of the possible.

Personal characteristics, what Dewey (1916) called "habits" or characteristic styles and sequences of approaching experience, influence play as well (Cuffaro, 1995; King, 1992; Van Hoorn et al., 1993), as do temperamental characteristics and configurations of intelligence (Gardner, 1983; Thomas & Chess, 1977). For example, Nathan was frequently a solitary player in the kindergarten classroom, and his three pigs enactment was typical play for him, while Amy, who played the baby role in the highchair episode, was more frequently engaged in social play with others. Children's primary language and the status and availability of peers who speak their home language also affect their interest in play materials and themes and their intentional styles within play (Meyer, Klein & Genishi, 1994; Orellana, 1994).

Children's histories within their families, cultural groups, and socioeconomic classes provide interesting food for thought for teachers (Griffin, 1982; Jones & Reynolds, 1992; Van Hoorn et al., 1993), and can guide the interventions of teachers and the interpretations of researchers (D'Amato, 1989; Meyer et al., 1994; Orellana, 1994; Tizard & Hughes, 1984).

Gender and the interactive construction of gender identity within play contexts has proven to be a topic for lively discussion among teacher researchers, since boys and girls have very distinctive play styles (Halliday & McNaughton, 1982; Liss, 1986). Boys are thought to be more likely to engage in rough-and-tumble play (Pellegrini, 1989; Pellegrini & Perlmutter, 1988) and weapon and war play (Carlsson-Paige & Levin, 1990), and to construct narratives that are more disorderly and with more exciting and incongruous elements than do girls (Nicopoulou, Scales, & Weintraub, 1994; Scales & Cook-Gumperz, 1993). Girls are more likely to use a pretend frame to persuade others to their play agenda, a strategy Sheldon (1992) calls "double voiced discourse."

The interaction of the development of gender identity and genderstyled play presents provocative dilemmas for classroom teachers as well, with children frequently resisting well-intentioned attempts to "unisex" their play (Barrs & Pidgeon, 1993; Paley, 1984).

Closely related to personal and family characteristics are children's relationships with others in school. Research on peer cultures in classrooms (Corsaro, 1985; Elgas, Klein, Kantor, & Fernie, 1988; Kantor, Elgas, & Fernie, 1993) highlights the importance of social status for the possession of territories in the classroom (e.g., blocks, climbing structure), materials (e.g., sticks, capes), and roles ("bosses" and followers) as well as the out-of-frame negotiations that create patterns of alliance, control, and exploitation (Trawick-Smith, 1988, 1992, 1994; Paley, 1990, 1992; Van Hoorn et al., 1993).

Children's relationships with teachers and other adults are critical for both individual and peer group development. Corsaro (1985) introduces the term *secondary adjustments* to describe how the mischievous, sometimes destructive elements of play may characterize the efforts of children to outwit the system and collectively oppose adult boundaries. Everyday classroom experience reveals incidents of "group glee" in which children's silliness overwhelms them, such as the hysterical laughter in the high-chair episode, and "procedural display" ("it's not really a rifle, it's just a horse") as challenges to social conventions and rules. Corsaro (1985) claims that the social cohesion among peers that is constructed in these "boundary contacts" with adult/school culture is essential to children's identity formation, first as part of the "we" in a group of children, and later as part of individual identity.

Related to this mischievous play is Schwartzmann's (1978) observation that we as adults may flatter ourselves when we interpret children's play as imitated adult behavior in an emulative way. The truth is they may be making fun of us. In a recent study of play in her third-grade classroom, Campbell (1995, p. 77) describes how a group of girls plan their play to parody their experiences of parents' adult friends who give children unwanted physical attention:

Caia: I already have an idea.
Emily: Tell me the idea.
Caia: The idea is there is a parent, she's gonna have a party 'cause she just made a lot of money on her jewelry—lots of people—invited to the party—Ladies who pull your cheeks! And we can put fake cheeks on, and then a kid spikes the punch and its all over.
Emily: Yeah, let's do it.
Caia: (Using the voice of a pirate) OK, we got to go find some more people to get their cheeks pulled.
Emily: No, to be the ladies, we're the kids.
Caia: OK, we go to find the "cheek pullers."

Factors outside the classroom in the "macrosystem" (Bronfenbrenner, 1979) have less apparent but no less powerful influences on children's play. These include historical views of children, childhood, education, and play (King, 1992; Nourot et al., 1990; Sutton-Smith, 1986); war and oppression, such as Eisen's (1988) study of play and the Holocaust and a study of play during the Gulf War (Klugman & Smilansky, 1996); and natural disasters, such as earthquakes, floods, and fires. Social phenomena such as HIV/AIDS, violence, and homelessness documented by the anecdotal reports of teacher researchers also have a significant impact on the context of play (Silin, 1995; Van Hoorn et al., 1993). This context for play brings home the value and power of play as a therapeutic tool, as the affective foundation for play reveals children's innate capacity to cope, make meaning, assimilate, and survive (Kohlberg & Fein, 1987).

I turn now to the metaphor of the fourth dimension to encompass the patterns of human experience found in play but not readily expressible in logical terms or spatial models, instead relying on the intuitive and even the spiritual for their grounding.

PLAY IN THE FOURTH DIMENSION:
PLAY, CREATIVITY, AND CONSCIOUSNESS

When Charles Dodgson, an Oxford mathematician writing as Lewis Carroll, took his readers "through the looking glass" (1865/1946), he incorporated the fourth spatial dimension and the concept of "wormholes" or tunnels between parallel universes into Alice's adventures in wonderland. Although the concept of pathways between our universe and higher dimensions has long been the raw material of science fiction and mystical writing, as well as inspiring the work of such artists as Picasso, Duchamps, and Dali, recent work in theoretical physics revisits these concepts in newly powerful ways (Kaku, 1994).

The concept of dimensions beyond three-dimensional space, in which space–time and matter–energy are unified constructs, is analogous to the way that imaginative play manipulates and unifies these constructs to suit the needs of the play-world created by the players. The relationships between play and other dimensions of development and learning, interacting with physical contextual variables and time and influenced by cognitive, affective, physical, social–moral, and historical forces, are necessary components to adequately apprehending the complexity of play in childhood. But there is something beyond these components of rational analysis: Play can be apprehended as a unifying force for all dimensions of experience, including those that elude the intellect. Quantum physicists look for language like the language of "mythos" used in both story and play that expresses experience with a more permissive set of rules than those of classical logic. The immediate apprehension of memory and feeling characteristic of myth and fantasy give life and spirit to the rational (Egan, 1988; Gleick, 1987; Zukav, 1979). The concept of "playing fields" then is similar to that of quantum fields in freeing participants and observers from the boundaries of classical logical thought. If such modes of expression are on the frontiers of science, perhaps the innate human ability to use symbolic tools to explain, distort, and recreate the known universe in new ways is but a shadow of the higher dimensional understanding that awaits the evolution of playful consciousness in the future.

We do have access to these higher dimensions of experience, or parallel universes, in our daily lives. For children the doorways are opened in play. For adults, the aesthetic experiences of our culture invite access, as do a variety of human activities that fall into the realm of the sacred.

The Fool, the Coyote, the Trickster, the Koshari, "Beginner's Mind," the Child, are images of the spirit of play that seems to filter through from other dimensions and appears in the sacred myths and symbols of many cultures. The "wisdom of the fool" is found in stories from the Native American Coyote to the "Emperor's New Clothes" to Zen koans to Shakespeare. This spirit represents the "galumphing" child, the risk-taker, the experimenter, whose energy is spontaneous and unfettered by fear.

The combination of the spirit of the Fool, the Child, the Coyote, with the disciplined skill that comes from practice leads humans to the source of expression in the arts, the sciences, and most important, the self, in transaction with others. Both are necessary; neither is sufficient on its own to release the creative power of the Muse. In play we find it all.

SUMMARY

I have reviewed three issues related to play in early childhood educational settings: How is play defined? How is play understood as contributing to learning and development? and What considerations guide teachers of young children in interpreting and orchestrating play? In doing so I framed research on play within spatial models. In a one-dimensional view I saw play qualities ranged along a continuum that helps teachers to define play as it is observed and experienced. Moving to two dimensions, I saw play in relation to other aspects of learning and development and the changes in each over time. As I expanded my mental graphs of play to cubic models, I found multiple contexts that influence play's development and its relationship to other aspects of experience. Finally like the multiple profiles represented in Picasso's painting "Portrait of Dora Maar," I pointed to other dimensions of consciousness and experience that we can apprehend but not readily represent in our study of play.

Drawing on concepts from physicists, I explored paradoxes such as observer and observed, space and time moving in multiple directions, and the creative and dissipative forces that fluctuate in patterns of play consciousness, linking the world of perceived reality to the possibilities of the imagined.

REFERENCES

Abbott, E. (1952). *Flatland: A romance of many dimensions* (6th ed.). New York: Dover Publications (Original work published 1884)

Adams, J. (1976). *Conceptual blockbusting: A pleasurable guide to better problem solving.* New York: Norton.

Almy, M. (1984). Reaffirmations: Speaking out for children: A child's right to play. *Young Children, 39*(4), 80.

Anderson, L. F. (1931). *Pestalozzi.* New York: AMS Press.

Astington, J. (1993). *The child's discovery of the mind.* Cambridge, MA: Harvard University Press.

Barrs, M., & Pidgeon, S. (Eds.). (1993). *Reading the difference: Gender and reading in elementary classrooms.* York, ME: Stenhouse.

Bateson, G. A. (1972). *Steps to an ecology of mind.* New York: Ballantine Books.

Bergen, D. (Ed.) (1988). *Play as a medium for learning and devlopment: A handbook of theory and practice.* Portsmouth, NH: Heinemann.

Bodrova, E., & Leong, D. (1996). *Tools of the mind: The Vygotskian approach to early chilhood education.* Columbus, OH: Merrill/Prentice Hall.

Bronfenbrenner, U. (1979). *The ecology of human development: Experiments by nature and design.* Cambridge, MA: Harvard University Press.

Bruner, J. (1976). The nature and uses of immaturity. In J. S. Bruner, A. Jolly, & K. Sylva (Eds.), *Play: Its role in development and evolution* (pp. 1–64). New York: Basic Books.

Campbell, G. (1995). *Can we play? Play in a third grade classroom.* Unpublished Master of Arts thesis, School of Education, Sonoma State University, Rohnert Park, CA.

Carlsson-Paige, N., & Levin, D. (1990). *Who's calling the shots?* Santa Cruz, CA: New Society Publishers.

Carroll, L. (1946). *Alice in wonderland.* New York: Random House. (Original work published 1865)

Christie, J. (1985). Training of symbolic play. *Early Childhood Development and Care, 19,* 42–46.

Christie, J., & Wardel, F. (1992). How much time is needed for play? *Young Children, 47*(3), 28–31.

Comenius, J. A. (1953). *The analytical didactic of Comenius* (V. Jelinek, Trans.). Chicago: University of Chicago Press.

Connolly, J. A., & Doyle, A. (1984). Relation of social fantasy play to social competence in preschoolers. *Developmental Psychology, 20,* 797–806.

Copple, C. E., Cocking, R. R., & Matthews, W. S. (1984). Objects, symbols, and substitutes: The nature of the cognitive activity during symbolic play. In T. D. Yawkey & A. D. Pellegrini (Eds.), *Child's play: Developmental and applied* (pp. 105–123). Hillsdale, NJ: Lawrence Erlbaum.

Corsaro, W. (1985). *Friendship and the peer culture in the early years.* Norwood, NJ: Ablex.

Csikszentmihalyi, M. (1979). The concept of flow. In B. Sutton-Smith (Ed.), *Play and Learning* (pp. 257–274). New York: Gardner.

Csikszentmihalyi, M. (1993). *The evolving self: A psychology for the third millenium.* New York: Harper Collins.

Cuffaro, H. (1995). *Experimenting with the world: John Dewey and the early childhood classroom.* New York: Teachers College Press.

Curry, N. E. (1971). Consideration of current basic issues on play. In N. Curry and S. Arnuad (eds.), *Play: The child strives toward self-realization* (pp. 51–62). Washington, DC: National Association for the Education of Young children.

Daiute, C. (1989). Play as thought: Thinking strategies of young writers. *Harvard Educational Review, 59,* 1–23.

D'Amato, J. J. (1989). Rivalry as a game of relationships: The social structure created by the boys of a Hawaiian primary school class. In M. N. Bloch & A. D. Pellegrini (Eds.), *The ecological context of children's play* (pp. 254–281). Norwood, NJ: Ablex.

Dansky, J. L. (1980). Make-believe: A mediator of the relationship betweeen play and associative fluency. *Child development, 51,* 576–579.

Derman-Sparks, L., & the A.B.C. Taskforce. (1989). *The anti-bias curriculum: Tools for empowering young children.* Washington DC: National Association for the Education of Young Children.

DeVries, R., & Kohlberg, L. (1987). *Constructivist early education: Overview and comparison with other programs.* Washington, DC: National Association for the Education of Young Children.

Dewey, J. (1916). *Democracy and education.* New York: Macmillan.

Diesing, P. (1971). *Patterns of discovery in the social sciences.* Chicago: Aldine-Atherton.

Doyle, A. B., & Connolly, J. (1989). Negotiation and enactment in social pretend play: Relations to social acceptance and social cognition. *Early Childhood Research Quarterly, 4,* 289–302.

Egan, K. (1988). *Primary understanding: Education in early childhood.* New York: Routledge.

Eifermann, R. (1971). Social play in childhood. In R. E. Herron & B. Sutton-Smith (Eds.), *Child's play* (pp. 270–297). New York: Wiley.

Eisen, G. (1988). *Chldren and play in the Holocaust: Games among the shadows.* Amherst: University of Massachussetts Press.

Elgas, P., Klein, E., Kantor, R., & Fernie, D. (1988). Play and the peer culture: Play styles and object use. *Journal of Research in Childhood Education, 3*(2), 142–153.

Ellis, M. (1988). Play and the origin of species. In D. Bergen (Ed.), *Play as a medium for learning and development: A handbook of theory and practice* (pp. 23–25). Portsmouth, NH: Heinemann.

Erikson, E. (1963). *Childhood and society* (2nd ed.). New York: Norton.

Farver, J. (1992). Communicating shared meaning in social pretend play. *Early Childhood Research Quarterly, 7*(40), 501–516.

Fein, G. (1981). Pretend play in childhood: An integrative review. *Child Development, 52,* 1095–1118.

Fein, G. (1984) New wine in old bottles. In F. Kessel & A. Goncu, (Eds.), *Analyzing children's play dialogues* (pp. 71–85). San Francisco: Jossey-Bass.

Fein, G. G. (1985). Learning in play: Surfaces of thinking and feeling. In J. Frost & S. Sunderlin (Eds.), *When children play: Proceedings of the international confernce on play and play environments* (pp. 45–51). Wheaton, MD: Association for Childhood Education International.

Feitelson, D., & Ross, G. S. (1973). The neglected factor—play. *Human development, 16,* 202–223.

Fenson, L., & Ramsay, D. S. (1980). Decentration and integration of the child's play in the second year. *Child Development, 47,* 232–235.

Fraiberg, S. (1959). *The magic years: Understanding and handling the problems of early childhood.* New York: Scribners.

Froebel, F. (1896). *Pedagogics of the kindergarten* (J. Jarvis, Trans.). New York: Appleton.

Fromberg, D. (1992). A review of research on play. In C. Seefeldt (Ed.), *The early childhood curriculum: A review of current research* (2nd ed.; pp. 42–840). New York: Teachers College Press.

Gardner, H. (1983). *Frames of mind: The theory of multiple intelligences.* New York: Basic Books.

Garvey, C. (1990). *Play.* Cambridge, MA: Harvard University Press. (Original work published 1977)

Gaskins, S., Miller, P., & Corsaro, W. (1992). Theroetical and methodological perspectives in the interpretive study of children. *New directions in child development, 58,* 5–23.

Gleick, J. (1987). *Chaos: Making a new science.* New York: Viking Penguin.

Gould, R. (1972). *Child studies through fantasy.* New York: Quadrangle Books.

Griffin E. (1982). *Island of childhood: Education in the special world of the nursery school.* New York: Teachers College Press.

Halliday, J., & McNaughton, S. (1982). Sex differences in play at kindergarten. *New Zealand Journal of Educational Studies, 17,* 161–170.

Hartley, R. E., Frank, L., & Goldenson, R. M. (1957). *The complete book of children's play.* New York: Crowell.

Hazen, N., & Black, B. (1984). Social acceptance: Strategies children use and how teachers can help children learn them. *Young Children, 39*(6), 26–60.

Howes, C., with Unger, O., & Matheson, C. (1992). *The collaborative construction of pretend: Social pretend play functions.* Albany: State University of New York Press.

Huizinga, J. (1950). *Homo ludens: A study of the play element in culture.* London: Routledge & Kegan Paul.

Hutt, C. (1971). Exploration and play in children. In R. E. Herron & B. Sutton-Smith (Eds.), *Child's play* (pp. 231–251). New York: Wiley.

Isenberg, J., & Jalongo, M. (1997). *Creative expression and play in early childhood* (2nd. ed.). Upper Saddle River, NJ: Merrill Prentice-Hall.

Isenberg, J., & Quisenberry, N. L. (1988). Play: A necessity for all children. *Childhood Education, 64*(3), 138–145.

Issacs, S. (1933). *Social development in young children.* London: Routledge & Kegan Paul.

Jones, E. (1973). *Dimensions of teaching-learning environments: Handbook for teachers.* Pasadena, CA: Pacific Oaks College.

Jones, E., & Reynolds, G. (1992). *The play's the thing: Teachers roles in children's play.* New York: Teachers College Press.

Kaku, M. (1994). *Hyperspace: A scientific odyssey through parallel universes, time warps, and the 10th dimension.* New York: Doubleday.

Kamii, C., & DeVries, R. (1980). *Group games in early education*. Washington, DC: National Association for the Education of Young Children.

Kantor, R., Elgas, P., & Fernie, D. (1993). Cultural knowledge and social competence within a preschool peer culture group. *Early Childhood Research Quarterly, 8*(20), 125–148.

King, N. (1987). Elementary school play: Theory and research. In J. Block and N. King (Eds.), *School play: A source book* (pp. 143–166). New York: Garland.

King, N. (1992). The impact of context on the play of young children. In S. Kessler & B. Swadner (Eds.), *Reconceptualizing the early childhood curriculum* (pp. 43–61). New York: Teachers College Press.

Klinger, E. (1971). *Structure and functions of fantasy*. New York: John Wiley.

Klugman, E., & Smilansky, S. (1996). (Eds.). *Play, policy, and practice*. St. Paul, MN: Red Leaf Press.

Kohlberg, L., & Fein, G. (1987). Play and constructive work as contributors to development. In L. Kohlberg et al. (Eds.), *Child psychology and childhood education* (pp. 392–449). New York: Longman.

Leslie, A. M. (1988). Some implications of pretense for mechanisms underlying the child's theory of mind. In J. Astington, P. Harris, & D. Olson (Eds.), *Developing theories of mind* (pp. 19–46). New York: Cambridge University Press.

Liss, M. B. (1986). Play of boys and girls. In G. Fein & M. Rivkin (Eds.), *The young child at play: Reviews of research, Vol. 4.* (pp. 127–140). Washington, DC: National Association for the Education of Young Children.

McCune, L. (1985). Play-language relationships and symbolic development. In C. C. Brown & A. W. Gottfried (Eds.), *Play Interactions* (pp. 38–45). Skillman, NY: Johnson & Johnson.

McGhee, P. (1984). Play, incongruity, and humor. In T. D. Yawkey & A. D. Pellegrini (Eds.), *Child's play: Developmental and applied* (pp. 219–236). Hillsdale, NJ: Lawrence Erlbaum.

McLloyd, V. (1983). The effects of the structure of play objects on the pretend play of low-income preschool children. *Child Development, 54,* 626–35.

McLloyd, V. (1986). Scaffolds or shackles? The role of tags in preschool children's pretend play. In G. Fein & M. Rivkin (Eds.), *The young child at play: Review of the research Vol. 4.* (pp. 63–67). Washington, DC: National Association for the Education of Young Children.

Mead, M. (1934). *Mind, self, and society*. Chicago: University of Chicago Press.

Meyer, C., Klein, E., & Genishi, C. (1994). Peer relationships among 4 preschool second language learners in "small group time." *Early Childhood Research Quarterly, 9,* 61–85.

Moll, L. (1990). Introduction. In L. Moll (Ed.), *Vygotsky and education: Instructional implications and applications of sociohistorical psychology* (pp. 1–30). Cambridge: Cambridge University Press.

Monighan-Nourot, P., Scales, B., Van Hoorn, J., with Almy, M. (1987). *Looking at children's play: The bridge between theory and practice*. New York: Teachers College Press.

Nachmanovitch, S. (1990). *Free play: The power of improvisation in life and the arts.* New York: Putnam.

Nicolopoulou, A. (1994). Narrative devlopment in social context. In D. Slobin, J. Gerhardt, A Kyratzis, & G. Jiansheng (Eds.), *Social interaction, social context, and language.* Hillsdale, NJ: Lawrence Erlbaum.

Nicolopoulou, A., Scales, B., & Weintraub, J. (1994). Gender differences and symbolic imagination in the stories of four-year-olds. In A. H. Dyson & C. Genishi (Eds.), *The need for story: Cultural diversity in classroom and community* (pp. 102–123). Urbana IL: National Coucil for the Teachers of English.

Noddings, N., & Shore, P. J. (1984). *Awakening the inner eye: Intuition in education.* New York: Teachers College Press.

Nourot, P. M., Henry, J., & Scales, B. (1990, April). *A naturalistic study of story play in preschool and kindergarten.* Paper presented at the annual meeting of the American Educational Research Association, Boston.

Orellana, M. (1994). Appropriating the voice of the superheroes: Three preschoolers bilingual language uses in play. *Early Childhood Research Quarterly, 9*(2), 171–193.

Paley, V. (1984). *Boys and girls: Superheroes in the doll corner.* Chicago: University of Chicago Press.

Paley, V. (1990). *The boy who would be a helicopter.* Cambridge, MA: Harvard University Press.

Paley, V. G. (1992). *You can't say you can't play.* Cambridge, MA: Harvard University Press.

Parton, M. B. (1932). Social participation among preschool children. *Journal of Abnormal Psychology, 27,* 243–269.

Pellegrini, A. D. (1984). The effects of exploration and play on young children's associative fluency: A review and extension of training studies. In T. D. Yawkey & A. D. Pellegrini (Eds.), *Child's play: Developmental and applied* (pp. 237–253). Hillsdale, NJ: Lawrence Erlbaum.

Pellegrini, A. D. (1989). Elementary school children's rough and tumble play. *Early Childhood Research Quarterly, 4*(2), 245–260.

Pellegrini, A., & Perlmutter, J. (1988). Rough and tumble play in the elementary school playground. *Young Children, 43*(2), 14–17.

Pepler, D. (1986). Play and creativity. In G. Fein and M. Rivkin (Eds.), *The young child at play: Reviews of Research* (Vol. 4, pp. 143–154). Washington, DC: NAEYC.

Pepler, D., & Ross, H. S. (1981). The effects of play on convergent and divergent problem-solving. *Child Development, 52,* 1202–1210.

Phyfe-Perkins, E. (1980). Children's behavior in preschool settings—A review of research concerning the influence of the physical environment. In L. G. Katz (Ed.), *Current topics in early childhood education* (Vol. 3, pp. 91–125). Norwood, NJ: Ablex.

Piaget, J. (1962). *Plays, dreams and imitation in childhood.* New York: Norton.

Piaget, J. (1969). *The language and thought of the child.* New York: World Publishing.

Polito, T. (1994). How play and work are organized in a kindergarten classroom. *Journal of Research in Childhood Education, 9*(1), 47–56.

Pribram, K. H. (1985). What the fuss is all about. In K. Wilber (Ed.), The holographic paradigm and other paradoxes: Exploring the leading edge of science (pp. 27–34). Boston: Shambala.

Pulaski, M. (1970). Play as a function of toy structure and fantasy predisposition. *Child Development, 41*, 531–537.

Reifel, S., & Yeatman, J. (1991). Action, talk and thought in block play. In B. Scales, M. Almy, A. Nicolopoulou, & S. Ervin-Tripp (Eds.), *Play and the social context of development in early care and education* (pp. 156–172). New York: Teachers College Press.

Reifel, S., & Yeatman, J. (1993). From category to context: Reconsidering classroom play. *Early Childhood Research Quarterly, 8*(1), 347–367.

Reynolds, G., & Jones, E. (1996). *Master Players.* New York: Teachers College Press.

Robbins, T. (Speaker). (1995). *City arts of San Francisco* (videotape). Petaluma, CA: City Arts and Lectures, Pacific Vista Productions.

Rousseau, J. J. (1964). *Emile.* In S. E. Frost, Jr. (Ed.), R. L. Archer (Trans.), *Emile, Julie and other writings.* New York: Barron's Educational Series. (Original work published in 1762)

Rubin, K., Fein, G., & Vandenberg, B. (1983). Play. In E. M. Hetherington (Ed.), *Handbook of child psychology: Volume 4. Socialization, personality, and social development* (pp. 698–774). New York: Wiley.

Scales, B., & Cook-Gumperz, J. (1993). Gender in narrative and play: A view from the frontier. *Advances in Early Education and Day Care, 5*, 167–195.

Schwartzman, H. B. (1978). *Transformations: the anthology of children's play.* New York: Plenum.

Sheldon, A. (1992). Conflict talk: Sociolinguisttic challenges to self-assertion and how young girls meet them. *Merrill-Palmer Quarterly, 38*(1), 95–117.

Silin, J. (1995). *Sex, death, and the education of children: Our passion for ignorance in the age of AIDS.* New York: Teachers College Press.

Smilansky, S. (1968). *The effects of sociodramatic play on disadvantaged preschool children.* New York: Wiley.

Smilansky, S. (1990). Sociodramatic play: Its relevance to behavior and achievement in school. In E. Klugman & S. Smilansky (Eds.), *Children's play and learning: Perspectives and policy implications* (pp. 18–42). New York: Teachers College Press.

Sutton-Smith, B. (1986). The spirit of play. In G. Fein & M. Rivkin (Eds.), *The young child at play: Reviews of research,* (Vol. 4, pp. 3–16). Washington, DC: National Association for the Education of Young Children.

Sutton-Smith, B., & Heath, S. B. (1981). Paradigms of pretense. *The Quarterly Newsletter of the Laboratory of Comparative Human Cognition.* San Diego: University of California.

Takhvar, M., & Smith, P. K. (1990). A review and critique of Smilansky's classification scheme and the "nested hierarchy" of play categories. *Journal of Research in Childhood Education, 4*, 112–122.

Thomas, A., & Chess, S. (1977). *Temperament and development.* New York: Brunner Mazel.

Tizard, B., & Hughes, M. (1984). *Young children learning.* Cambridge, MA: Harvard University Press.

Trawick-Smith, J. (1988). "Let's say you're the baby, OK?" Play, leadership and following behavior of young children. *Young Children, 43*(5), 51–59.

Trawick-Smith, J. (1992). A descriptive study of persuasive preschool children: How they get others to do what they want. *Early Childhood Research Quarterly, 7*(1), 95–114.

Trawick-Smith, J. (1994). *Interactions in the classroom: Facilitating play in the early years.* Columbus, OH: Merrill.

Van Hoorn, J., Nourot, P. M., Scales, B., & Alward, K. (1993). *Play at the center of the curriculum.* Columbus, OH: Merrill.

Vygotsky, L. S. (1976). Play and its role in the mental development of the child. In J. S. Bruner, A. Jolly, & K. Sylva (Eds.), *Play: Its role in development and evolution* (pp. 537–554). New York: Basic Books.

Vygotsky, L. S. (1978). *Mind in society: Development of higher psychological processes.* Cambridge, MA: Harvard University Press.

Wassermann, S. (1990). *Serious players in the primary classroom: Empowering children through active learning experiences.* New York: Teachers College Press.

Weaver, C. (1994). Parallels between new paradigms in science and in reading and literacy theories: An essay review. In R. Ruddell, M. Ruddell, & H. Singer (Eds.), *Theoretical models and processes of reading* (4th ed.; pp. 1185–1202). Newark, DE: International Reading Association.

Weber, R. (1985a). Field consciousness and field ethics. In *The holographic paradigm and other paradoxes: Exploring the leading edge of science* (pp. 35–43). Boston: Shambala.

Weber, R. (1985b). The enfolding-unfolding universe: A conversation with David Bohm. In *The holographic paradigm and other paradoxes: Exploring the leading edge of science.* (pp. 44–104). Boston: Shambala.

Wing, L. (1995). Play is not the work of the child: Young children's perceptions of work and play. *Early Childhood Research Quarterly, 10*(2), 223–248.

Winnicott, D. W. (1971). *Playing and reality.* New York: Basic Books.

Zukav, G. (1979). *The dancing Wu Li masters: An overview of the new physics.* New York: Macmillan.

TRENDS AND ISSUES AFFECTING TEACHER PREPARATION AND PROFESSIONAL DEVELOPMENT

The three chapters in Part III focus on effective ways to prepare newcomers to the field of early childhood education as well as strategies for supporting the professional development of experienced educators of young children. When we asked a group of early childhood majors to select a metaphor, a symbol to characterize their professional role, these were some of their responses:

- A student teacher said: *"I picture myself as a bird in a cage. I can't escape, yet everyone else can casually walk by and see what I do and how I am struggling."*
- A rather traditional kindergarten teacher remarked: *"It's like building with blocks—first you make the base, then you stack them, one at a time, on top of one another."*
- An experienced Montessori teacher said: *"I chose the metaphor of a swimmer. You can dive in or wade in. You might find yourself in deep water or in freezing cold water or even turning to the lifeguard (support services) for help. When you swim, you can rely on a flotation device for a while but eventually, you select and develop your own style. Above all, if you are a swimmer, you swim."*
- An early childhood major with a background in special education said: *"I see myself as a tightrope walker, balancing many jobs on each side of my pole. When tightrope walkers hear a gasp or a burst of applause, they know how to respond. As a teacher, I have to stop, look, and listen to the responses of the children and let them be my guide."*

As this sampling of metaphors suggests, teachers view their professional role very differently. Issues surrounding teacher preparation and the professionalization of teaching continue to attract the attention of the media and the general public. Thus, it is not surprising that the authors in the three chapters of Part III are dealing with the controversy about inclusion of young children with disabilities in the "regular" classroom, international trends concerning the care and education of young children, and the issue of the low social and professional status of early childhood education and early childhood educators.

149

In Chapter 9, Doris Bergen addresses the issues surrounding the current emphasis on inclusion of children with disabilities in mainstream early childhood classrooms and presents differing viewpoints concerning the challenges and opportunities of inclusion. Bergen delineates problems related to professional preparation, system structures, and personnel resources and offers suggestions for what will make inclusion work well in the future.

In Chapter 10, Jim Hoot and Mary Jalongo, with Jyotsna Pattnaik, Weiwei Cai, and Sunhee Park, examine early childhood education from an international perspective. They begin with the assertion that cross-cultural comparisons of programs for young children would suggest that the United States is not a leader in early childhood care and education. These authors call for an international dialogue and global perspective on policies, programs, and practices affecting the young child. They formulate a series of questions that can be used as a reflective tool to gain a more profound understanding of what early childhood educators around the globe can learn from one another and then apply this reflective tool to brief profiles of three countries' struggles to provide for their youngest citizens—China, India, and Korea. Chapter 10 concludes with strategies for broadening our perspectives on the field to encompass a world view, a perspective that holds the greatest promise for enabling early childhood educators to expand their vision as child advocates and act on our commonly held commitment to nurture and educate every child.

In the final chapter, Doris Fromberg takes a fresh look at the social, political, and educational factors that have contributed to the low status of the early childhood profession. She presents a working definition of professionalism followed by a perspective on historical and philosophical traditions of the field, an interpretation of its knowledge base, and other pertinent trends. She continues with implications for the field, contending that there is a difference between a professional and a technician and that "early childhood education needs to be a distinctly ethical profession because the clientele are vulnerable and relatively powerless." The chapter concludes with issues and future trends such as the underrepresentation of minority group teachers, the problems inherent in career-ladder initiatives, the need to improve staff-development services to all early childhood personnel, and the redistribution of staff-development funds. Fromberg is clear in her call for a self-standing early childhood certificate but acknowledges that in reality we will have to engage in considerable advocacy initiatives in order to achieve this ideal.

Together, these three chapters address teacher professional development issues and raise the question that provides a framework for Part III: *How can practitioners in the field be best prepared to meet challenges now and in the future?*

Chapter 9

Perspectives on Inclusion in Early Childhood Education

Doris Bergen

In the second-grade classroom that was Dee's first teaching assignment, there were four children with special needs, only one of whom was "identified." This child had a physical handicap resulting from an infectious disease, which required her to wear braces. The three children that Dee identified as having special needs were a child with a learning disability that affected his symbolic memory and reading skill, a child who was intellectually gifted but a social isolate, and a child whose disruptive behavior required constant monitoring. Unfortunately, Dee's early childhood education program had not included any preparation in working with special education children. It had, however, prepared her very well for providing a developmentally appropriate classroom, and she used that skill to try adaptations to accommodate the needs of these children. Dee's second teaching assignment was in a preschool, and, at various times during the years when she worked in that setting, she had children with mental retardation, hearing impairment, juvenile diabetes, celiac disease, Legg-Perthes disease, seizures, attention deficit/hyperactivity, and language delays. Her role included initially identifying some of the children's problems, gaining information about the children from their parents, and helping her volunteer staff of parents learn to work with these children. When she later served as director of a number of preschool programs, she had to assist her staff in adapting their teaching for children with Down syndrome, visual impairment, autism, disfigurement from facial burns, language delays, neurological impairments, and a variety of problems resulting from abuse and neglect. Her work also included conferring with related service personnel, such as speech therapists and pediatricians, as well as with the parents of these children. She presently supervises

151

a collaborative toddler program of "reverse inclusion," in which a number of typically developing children are enrolled with children who have been identified as having disabilities or who are at risk for developmental delay. This program is a collaborative one with a human services agency and uses an interdisciplinary-team approach that includes professionals from a wide range of disciplines, as well as students in training for these disciplines.

Is this a vision of an early childhood educator of the future? It certainly could be, given the emphasis of recent years on including all children in the early childhood classroom. In actual fact, however, this scenario is part of this author's biography. A similar teaching history could probably be obtained from many people who have been early childhood educators in the past 20–30 years. This example should serve as a reminder that the idea of including children with disabilities in their classrooms is not a new concept for early childhood educators, many of whom have always taught children with a wide range of special needs within their regular program. Indeed, most early childhood classrooms, with their emphases on individualized and developmentally appropriate learning, child choice and control, and facilitated peer interaction, can be an ideal setting for inclusion, and early childhood educators have usually been very successful in managing such classrooms even though the label "inclusion" was not applied to them until recently.

Why is the issue of inclusion of such great concern now to early childhood educators and early childhood special educators? What has changed in the present environment that makes inclusion both a positive opportunity and a subject of concern for teachers and parents? This chapter will address the issues surrounding the current emphasis on inclusion of children with disabilities in regular early childhood classrooms at preschool, kindergarten, and primary levels. Differing viewpoints concerning the challenges and opportunities of inclusion will be outlined, and the historical/theoretical/social context of this movement will be reviewed. A discussion of some of the problems in implementing inclusion that have been identified and suggestions for removing some of the barriers to effective inclusion, especially in programs for children in the early childhood age range, will conclude the chapter.

DIVERSE VIEWPOINTS ABOUT THE MEANING OF INCLUSION

It is a rare early childhood educator or special educator who would not agree that all children can learn and that they should have the opportunity to learn in environments that encourage them to reach their highest potential. The proponents of full inclusion and those who oppose it are both committed to the idea that all children should be in environments that give them maximum learning opportunities. Their difference in viewpoint revolves around the question of what that environment should be like and how it can be achieved. What is really best for children with special needs and for their typical peers? The debate is not as vociferous in early childhood as it is among those who teach older children, but the basic differences in viewpoint are expressed by teachers and parents at all levels. These conflicting views of inclusion-related education reform provide the context for examining inclusion in early childhood education.

As is the case with many newly advocated practices, the meaning of the term *inclusion* is often ambiguous and varied. There are also contrasting opinions as to when, how, and even *if* it should be the preferred practice for meeting the needs of children previously served in special education classrooms. The most far-reaching model, in terms of effects on both children and teachers, is that of "full inclusion." Full inclusion has all children, no matter what their disability, present in the regular education classroom, with both special and regular educators sharing joint responsibility in a team teaching or teaching/consulting model that adapts the curriculum to meet the needs of all learners.

At the opposite end of the continuum from full inclusion is the completely self-contained special education classroom, which has been the model commonly used to serve the needs of children identified as having disabilities. On the continuum between full inclusion and no inclusion are models that incorporate special education children in regular education for various time periods less than the full day, involve the regular and special educator in varied balanced or unbalanced role responsibilities, and include or exclude children with severe or multiple disabilities. For the purposes of outlining the prevailing viewpoints, this discussion will center on the debate between the advocates for "full" inclusion and those who favor "partial/optional" inclusion because this is the area where the debate is presently focused. Few educators are presently advocating the old model of completely separate education for children with disabilities.

The Full Inclusion Argument

Those who want full inclusion believe that a "separate but equal opportunity" approach does not give children with disabilities the best forum for reaching their potential achievement levels (Shapiro, Loeb, & Bowermaster, 1993; Van Dyke, Stallings, & Colley, 1995). They are particularly concerned that children with severe disabilities need to be in integrated settings in order to give them "normalized" experiences so that they can learn the social interaction skills that will make it possible for them to be included in the broader society (Gartner & Lipsky, 1987). They also believe that these children will have an improved self-concept and gain in cognitive skills by being surrounded by peer models of achievement. They cite research evidence that special "pull-out" programs have had little effect on improving performance of children with disabilities (e.g., Deno, Maruyama, Espin, & Cohen, 1990). Further, they believe that by being in the regular classroom, even those children with severe disabilities will have the opportunity to interact with peers and to get to know them well enough that friendships can be formed (Hamre-Nietupski, Hendrickson, Nietupski, & Sasso, 1993). The importance of opportunities for developing friendships has been stressed in a number of inclusion models (Bergen, 1993; Perske, 1988).

The advocates see full inclusion as also benefitting typical children. By having children with disabilities as classroom peers, these children will lose their fears and stereotypic thinking about persons with disabilities, which will have long-term benefits for society as a whole (Covert, 1995). They believe that the increasing diversity of the social world makes it imperative that all children learn the attitudes and behaviors that make them good citizens of such a society and that experiences with people of diverse cultural, socioeconomic, and disability conditions will provide such learning opportunities.

Proponents do not believe that having special-needs children in the regular class will prevent typical children from continuing to learn at their highest potential and that an added benefit of the inclusion philosophy of individualization of instruction will be that many children who are at risk for school failure but who don't presently "qualify" for special education services will have their learning needs met more effectively. These children often have difficulty with the "standard curriculum applied to all" approach but their needs for individualization have usually been ignored (Stainback & Stainback, 1991).

In order for the full inclusion model to work in schools, however, proponents do indicate that some rethinking of present regular education methods of instruction and staffing patterns is needed. They believe there must be curricular reforms and team teaching approaches, with regular and special educators working together in the classroom, although the regular education teacher should take ultimate responsibility for all children in the class (Jenkins, Pious, & Jewell, 1990). They do not suggest a reduction in special education personnel, however, because having a sufficient number of special education consultants who have skills in helping other teachers adapt their methods to meet individualized needs is essential for the model to be effective. They believe that, with these changes in regular classroom structure, all children can benefit. For children with severe disabilities, the addition of individual child aides may be necessary so that these children can function well in the inclusion classroom but these individual child aides must also work as part of the integrated team.

The Partial/Optional Inclusion Argument

Although some voices have been raised in opposition to any type of inclusion (e.g., Shanker, 1994), most opposition to a full inclusion approach comes from people who want to maintain the present continuum of options that range from special education self-contained classrooms, resource rooms that provide assistance on an as-needed basis, and other "mainstream" options, as well as the full inclusion option. Their argument is drawn from two types of concern, one of which is related to the social skill/self-concept dimension and one to academic achievement goals. The proponents of this view are concerned about children with severe and with mild/moderate disabilities, but they are more likely to focus on the problems that children with moderate special needs, such as learning disabilities or mild developmental delays, might have with full inclusion. They are not sanguine that the ideal classroom envisioned by full inclusion proponents will be available for most children (Mather & Roberts, 1994). Rather, they are fearful that there will be a return to conditions of the past in which many children who needed learning assistance were overlooked in the "standard curriculum for all" classroom.

The academic achievement argument—that children with mild or moderate disabilities are often overlooked in a classroom in which teachers gear the curriculum to the typical children—is of great concern to many special educators and parents. They believe that, without the options of special classrooms and teachers, these children may not be able to achieve at the level that they could achieve if they had a one-to-one or small-group environment with a teacher who focused on their particular learning modalities, and they also cite research that shows support for this view (e.g., Mather & Roberts, 1994). Joining this argument are those concerned about gifted children, whose needs have also been often overlooked in the regular classroom (Zigmond et al., 1995).

In regard to the social and self-concept dimension, the "range of option" advocates assert that while labeling and segregating children may not have been conducive to social skill or self-concept improvement, there is little indication that having all children in the regular classroom will be likely to solve this problem. The research they cite shows mixed effects or even negative effects of the inclusion classroom because when children lack social skills they may be rejected by peers rather than having the peers assist them in gaining those skills (Roberts, Pratt, & Leach, 1991; Sabornie, Marshall, & Ellis, 1990). There is also evidence that certain conditions are needed to promote peer friendship development because this acceptance will not happen automatically. Friendship development must be a structured goal and plans for adult facilitation of peer interactions must be implemented if friendships are to occur (Bergen, 1993).

Further, proponents of partial/optional inclusion assert that if children with disabilities have repeated failure in doing classroom academic tasks, they will not develop a positive self-concept (Dickman, 1994). Thus, they also agree that teachers in inclusion settings must be prepared to adapt the curriculum and instructional methods to enable these children to feel success in their academic work. Because effective full inclusion models require more adults (and more highly skilled adults) in the educational environment, they would also be expensive to implement. The partial/optional inclusion advocates believe they are more realistic about what models can be embraced given teacher skill levels and personnel resources of most schools.

Many of the objections to full inclusion that have been expressed arise from such practical concerns rather than from value issues. That is, although both teachers and parents have a generally positive view of the need for inclusion and support its goals, they also identify problems in implementing these models (Peck, Carlson, & Helmstetter, 1992; Semmel, Abernathy, Butera, & Lesar, 1991). Thus, while most would agree that the goals of inclusion are ones they support, they may disagree on what environment might be best for which children with what types of disabilities, how and by whom placement decisions should be made, and how the costs of providing such environments can be borne by schools.

Inclusion Arguments and Early Childhood Practices

The arguments opposing full inclusion make presumptions about regular classroom environments and teaching styles that may not be accurate for most early childhood and early childhood special education settings. For example, while many early childhood regular education classrooms at the primary level still use a whole-group instruction, individual workbook-oriented approach that does not differentiate among children on the basis of their needs (Baker & Zigmond, 1990), the early childhood classrooms at preschool and kindergarten levels are more likely to provide opportunities for meeting individual children's needs. Choices of activities are available, peer interaction is encouraged, and teacher goals and plans often include methods to meet the varying learning needs of children. This is even more the case in early childhood special education classrooms, which usually combine developmentally appropriate curriculum approaches with attention to individual needs of children with disabilities or delay. Thus, when proponents of full inclusion suggest what the classroom environment should be like to make inclusion work, they describe a classroom that is quite similar to many of those in early childhood, at least at the kindergarten and preschool level.

Moreover, the educational goals and recommended practices of early childhood educators and early childhood special educators are very similar, making it much more possible for them to work together in team approaches (Bergen, 1994a). For example, both early childhood and early childhood special education models use a team of staff members, individualize children's learning experiences, stress social skill development, and include curriculum opportunities for children to use a range of learning modalities. The majority of preschool educators do support the value of inclusion and are willing to make the transition to inclusion as long as support services are available.

Because early childhood teachers have typically had other staff members in the classroom, when they do have inclusive classrooms, they are usually more accepting of having special educators and other resource personnel, such as physical therapists, observing and working with the children, and of incorporating teacher aides who are specified to assist children who have severe impairments or behavioral problems. Regular preschool programs rarely have an early childhood special educator available to act as a team member or consultant on a regular basis, however (Wolery et al., 1994). Some teachers have had preparation to teach in both early childhood and special education so they have skills to use in meeting the educational needs of both typical children and those with disabilities. Until recently, publicly funded programs have served only children with disabilities, although some of them include children who are at risk for developmental delay. The majority of early childhood special education programs are now moving to "reverse inclusion" models that incorporate some typical children in their classrooms. The Head Start program has long had a mandate to include a portion of children with special needs in their classrooms, and many private preschool programs also have accepted such children, but usually without the support of special educators or related personnel services.

Implementing inclusion is often a different matter for teachers in early childhood classrooms at the kindergarten and primary grade levels, because the teachers' structural constraints, personnel resources, and instructional methods differ. For example, teachers rarely have even one other adult in the classroom even though there may be 25–30 children in the class. Moreover, there has been increasing pressure on these teachers to focus on getting every child in the class to meet a certain level of performance, regardless of their special needs, learning modalities, or developmental status. Thus, although individual teachers may wholeheartedly embrace a developmentally appropriate philosophy, they may still be subjected to external pressures from state-mandated proficiency tests beginning at primary level and the subsequent directives from administrators to meet standard test score criteria. The problems they face in implementing an effective inclusive classroom are therefore more similar to those of teachers of older children. Although primary teachers may see the same potential benefits from inclusion that parents and teachers of preschool children have noted, they must resolve their concerns in regard to academic achievement and social/behavioral issues and gain the support of the educational system to make the changes that are needed for effective inclusion classrooms.

CONTEXTS OF THE INCLUSION DEBATE

If many of these arguments seem familiar, it may be because the controversy over inclusion, by whatever name it is called, is not a new one. These viewpoints are rooted in historical and political grounds. They are also strongly influenced by the social value structure of American society, which sends conflicting messages to parents, teachers, and children. These contexts must be considered if the inclusion debate is to be understood.

Historical/Political Context

Before the 1960s, there was little focus on special education except for children with severe sensory, motor, or cognitive problems. Educational service, if these children received any at all, was given within the confines of an institutional setting or in a privately funded special day facility. When the Education of All Handicapped Act was passed in 1975 (P.L. 94–142), it signaled a major paradigm shift in thinking about education for these children. Not only were all children with disabilities to be identified and educated, but the law stated that "to the maximum extent appropriate, handicapped children are . . . [to be] . . . educated with children who are not handicapped" (89 Stat 781). If this was not possible, special education children were to be educated in whatever environment was most similar to a regular classroom that also met their special needs. Supplementary services were also required to meet the goals of the individual educational plan. Although the original bill and its subsequent revisions included preschool age children (from age 3) in the mandate, states were exempt if this mandate was "inconsistent with State law or practice" (89 Stat. 780). Thus, states could choose to start services at age 3, but because they were mandated only to provide education for children at age levels where the schools already had services, preschool services were initiated in only a few states that chose to do so (e.g., Michigan).

As identification and placement decisions began to be made by schools, and in response to the way restricted funding sources were accessed, there was often a limited set of options available for child placement. Options may or may not have included receiving service within the regular classroom, but usually placement was in a separate classroom within existing school buildings. Even this "inclusion" in the same building was initially considered a potentially traumatic change because, before that time, children with disabilities were rarely even seen by typical children. For approximately the last 20 years, special education placements have been primarily in these self-contained settings staffed with teachers trained to work specifically with children who had been identified as having a particular type of disability (e.g., learning disabled, multi-handicapped). Although some of these children were "mainstreamed" into regular art, music, and other classes for part of the day, their basic instruction took place in a separate or segregated setting. States and local districts varied greatly in the ways they implemented the law, but, by the 1980s, the model of "range of options" was becoming more popular.

In 1986, the effectiveness of these separate special education classrooms or "resource" rooms began to be questioned. The catalyst for change was a report by the Assistant Secretary of the Office of Special Education and Rehabilitative Services, Madeleine Will (1986), in which she proposed the Regular Education Initiative (REI), which would return many of the children to regular classrooms and remove categorical labels. She stated:

> Although for some students the "pullout approach" may be appropriate, it is driven by a conceptual fallacy: that poor performance in learning can be understood solely in terms of deficiencies in the student rather than deficiencies in the learning environment. . . . The major flaw in this argument is the premise that to improve student performance we always have to create a new educational environment. Recent experience has shown there is an alternative. This is to adapt the regular classroom to make it possible for the student to learn in that environment. (pp. 10–11)

This movement became a part of regular education reform and was advocated by number of theorists and researchers (e.g., Gartner & Lipsky,

1987; Reynolds, Wang, & Walberg, 1987). Parents, especially those who had children needing intensive services, also began to advocate for having more integrated approaches, as did teachers of children with severe disabilities (e.g., The Association for Persons with Severe Handicaps—TASH). As identification and service mandates were extended to preschool age children in 1986 (P.L. 99–457) and its subsequent revision (Individuals with Disabilities Education Act of 1990, 101.476), the least-restrictive-environment requirement was maintained. The 1986 amendments (P.L. 99–457) required schools to be responsible for the education of children age 3 to 5 who had been identified as having disabilities or who were at-risk for developmental delay. Each state, however, had to determine the extent and types of "at-risk" that would be included in the services provided. The vast majority of programs at the preschool level were segregated, due to the fact that funding was provided only for those children with identified disabilities. If typical children were included, their parents usually had to pay for the preschool program.

The term *inclusion* arose from a group of the proponents of the Regular Education Initiative who noted that there were really two systems of education—regular and special—and suggested that the two systems should merge. According to Fuch & Fuch (1994), "increasingly, special education reform is symbolized by the term inclusive schools" (p. 299). They assert that the movement to full inclusion is a "radicalization" of the reform movement and is based on the view that the separateness of special education has made regular educators unused to adapting the curriculum, thus jeopardizing the education of all children. Stainback & Stainback (1992) further assert that regular education no longer concerns itself with children with learning problems because special education has taken on that task. According to proponents, full inclusion would force regular educators to address the needs of all children and thus needed educational reform would occur across the entire system. The ultimate goal of this movement is to "radicalize" the entire system of education. As noted earlier, this radical approach includes ideas such as team teaching, cooperative learning with peers, planning individualized instruction, and adapting curriculum materials and methods to meet learner needs, all of which are ideas that have been long espoused in the developmentally appropriate practice of early childhood.

Social/Value Context

The concept of "development as achievement," which assumes that children's attainment of higher developmental stages and their learning of increasingly complex skills are measures of their achievement, is a strong

value of American culture (Feinman, 1991). The role of the early childhood educator has long been to facilitate that achievement in the domains
considered important for educational success (e.g., social, emotional, language, cognitive, physical). In some eras one or another of these domains
has been stressed; in particular, emphasis on achieving competence in
social/emotional or in cognitive/language domains has alternately waxed
and waned (Raver & Zigler, 1991).

Feinman (1991) argues that viewing development as progress rather
than as merely change may be problematic, quoting Bruner's (1983) com-
ment that "human beings, whatever their age, are completed forms of
what they are" (p. 138). Nevertheless, the "development as achievement"
viewpoint is pervasive in American society and is reflected in terms such
as "developmental milestones," "developmental delay," "readiness," and
all other concepts that imply that children must strive to achieve developmental and learning goals and be "prepared" for the next level of challenge (Bergen, 1994b). It is also the rationale on which both recommendations to include *and not to include* children with disabilities or
developmental delays are often based. Those who advocate full inclusion
say that this environment is the best one for children with disabilities to
meet developmental goals, while those opposing such inclusion assert
that other, more specialized, environments may be most conducive to
developmental achievement for some children.

Concomitant with the social goal of development as achievement
is another value of American society: fair competition. While this has not
been a concern of many preschool teachers, it does affect the thinking of
kindergarten and primary teachers because curriculum adaptations for
children with disabilities are difficult to reconcile with the requirement
to rate children's performance on comparative standards. Although not
discussing inclusion per se, Bricker (1989) provides some insight into
this dilemma. He describes the balancing of excellence and equity as a
dilemma all teachers face because American social goals include both
equality and excellence and these are often in conflict when teachers
must make decisions. For example, teacher concern about "fairness" is
often difficult to reconcile with decisions required in an inclusion classroom to give some children special assistance, additional time, or adaptations of the curriculum that may result in the "lowering of standards."
Bricker quotes one teacher as saying that teachers might wish to "reward
that low-ability student" but if they do so they worry that the high-ability
student will say, "I worked too hard ... I may as well back off on the
effort" (p. 107). The inclusion debate has not really resolved the issue of
teachers' (and parents') concerns about fairness. In the early childhood
classroom, of course, the emphasis on fairness usually is not equated with

doing equal types or quantities of academic work, but rather takes the form of permitting every child some individualization and encouraging all to achieve in developmentally appropriate ways. One of the advantages of multiage grouping in the kindergarten-primary grades is that teachers become freed of the "everyone must be the same" perspective and individualization for all children is more likely to occur.

Another social/value issue that affects effective inclusion practice is that of diversity. The fact that the population of the United States now comprises a wide range of cultural and ethnic groups has made the valuing of diversity a major goal of many people. However, there are others who see embracing diversity and having tolerance for individuals with nondominant values as harmful to the fabric of this society. The ambivalence of many people toward valuing diversity has affected children with disabilities in two ways. First, acceptance of children who are "different" may vary among child peers (and among educators!) because of their family, cultural, or religious values. Second, the identification of children as having a disability or being at-risk for developmental delay has long been suspect when children are from nondominant cultural or ethnic groups, and much has been written about misidentification due to cultural/ethnic or socioeconomic factors (Bergen & Mosley-Howard, 1994). A result of either the full or partial inclusion approach could be to increase the valuing of diversity, as its advocates predict. On the other hand, careful planning is needed to ensure that the experience does not result in a reinforcement of stereotypes and a reaction against inclusion as a viable educational model.

Given these contextual factors within which the inclusion experiment is taking place, what are the implications for practice in early childhood and early childhood special education? In addition to the commitment to following an inclusion model of education, there are a number of systemic, resource, and practice issues that must be addressed if the promise of the model is to be realized.

IMPLICATIONS FOR PRACTICE

Teachers and administrators who are trying to implement either full or partial inclusion models have identified a number of practical problems and barriers that have prevented these models from being effectively implemented. While these concerns are especially salient for early childhood classrooms at kindergarten and primary levels, and for upper-grade levels as well, many also apply to preschool inclusion settings. The problems and some suggestions to consider in removing barriers to effective inclusion are discussed in this section. If early childhood educators are to make inclusion goals a reality, they will have to join with other teachers, administrators, and parents to address these issues.

Problems and Suggestions Related to Professional Preparation

Problem. Few regular education teachers or administrators have been prepared to work with nontypical children of any type (i.e., those with disabilities or those with special giftedness/talents).

Suggestion. Higher education programs preparing preservice students for teaching all children from infancy to age 8 must include content related to development of all children (including exceptional children), methods of curricular adaptation for these children, and attitudinal perspectives needed for success as a teacher in inclusion settings. There must also be a strong commitment on the part of universities and school systems to sustained in-service initiatives for presently employed regular education teachers and administrators as the inclusion models are implemented.

Problem. Special education teachers have typically not had sufficient preparation in regular education curriculum and methods or in knowing how to serve as consultants and models for regular education teachers.

Suggestion. Higher education preservice and in-service programs in early childhood special education must include regular education knowledge and skill preparation so that special educators will be able to help other teachers integrate developmentally appropriate and individually planned models of instruction. Their preparation must include field experiences in settings where skills needed for consulting and administration roles as well as teaching roles can be practiced, and where special educators model these roles.

Problem. Related services personnel (e.g., speech pathologists, physical therapists) presently have distinctly separate and noncollaborative personnel preparation programs, which has often resulted in their graduates' holding only the perspective of their own professional discipline.

Suggestion. Higher education institutions must chart new ground in providing interdisciplinary programs for preparing professionals whose work roles will require them to be working together. Given the constraints of accrediting agencies, this will not be an easy task; however, some portion of these preparation programs should interface with regular and special education preparation, if inclusive initiatives requiring team approaches are to be most effective.

Problem. Few professionals now in teaching, administration, or related services roles have had systematic training in how to work effectively as part of a team, resulting in ad hoc approaches to teaming and poorly functioning teams whose members lack knowledge and skills about team approaches.

Suggestion. An absolutely essential focus in personnel preparation programs must be on content, including effective team approaches, practice in working in team situations, and observation of varied team interactions. Because few university faculty have engaged in team teaching or other team activity themselves, they also need to develop the ability to model effective team approaches to students, and they will need some assistance in learning how to do this.

Problems and Suggestions Related to Personnel Resources

Problem. Personnel resources of many regular education programs/schools do not permit staffing patterns that can exemplify the team models recommended by inclusion advocates.

Suggestion. Preschools and primary schools must have a sufficient number of adults available (including special educators, related service personnel, teacher aides) to make the inclusion model truly individualized. Regular educators cannot take the responsibility for the learning of all children when the personnel support services that are needed are not in place, especially when they are also being asked to increase children's academic performance. In regular education preschools, which typically have approximately 20 children and at least one aide per class, the need is primarily for adults with special education expertise who can serve in team teaching and consulting roles. In regular kindergarten-primary units, when the size of classes continues to be 25–30 children, the need is for additional personnel (including special educator consultants) and/or smaller class size. In all settings the roles taken by related services personnel must be clarified and methods by which they can best assist the regular teachers should be made explicit.

Problem. The common practice of programs/school districts that encourages regular teacher "volunteers" to take most of the children with disabilities into their classrooms, and which has been questioned on both legal and value grounds (Giangreco, Dennis, Cloninger, Edelman, & Schattman, 1993), results in unequal distribution of such children and greater responsibility for some teachers.

Suggestion. All teachers should be prepared to include children with disabilities in their classrooms and be expected to make their best efforts to adapt instruction, given the appropriate supports they need. Sufficient special educators and related services personnel should be on the school teams so that they can provide individualized support for children in every classroom. Whether children with disabilities should be distributed evenly throughout all classrooms or "clustered" in classrooms when there are insufficient special education personnel to have them actively involved in every classroom has been a matter of debate. Some types of clustering models might be useful. However, this decision should be based on child needs, not on the lack of personnel or the resistance of personnel.

Problem. Special educators have expressed concerns that their expertise is not always considered when the regular educator is not open to a team approach and thus, their role in many inclusion settings becomes marginal.

Suggestion. A focus of team discussions should be on developing teaming approaches that utilize the expertise of all members of the teams and provide the individualized instruction that all children who need learning assistance must have. In such sessions, special educators must address their feeling of loss of control over the children's instruction that the self-contained special education classroom provided them. Both regular and special educators must explore alternative roles and devise methods that enable the special educator to contribute fully in the regular class environment. In early childhood, personnel preparation is increasingly moving to a model that gives teachers both early childhood and special education expertise; thus, there may eventually be teams in which all team members hold both perspectives.

Problem. Because of financial constraints on most programs and school districts, choices about personnel are usually for the least expensive options, which often results in the hiring of untrained aides rather than of behavior specialists or other professional consultants.

Suggestion. Programs/school districts should evaluate the cost-effectiveness of having a number of specialists who can give many teachers assistance in analyzing their environments and choosing methods to accommodate children in the classroom rather than immediately opting for less expensive untrained aides to take care of the "problem" child. These specialists could help teachers to change the environment, adapt curriculum, or learn new management strategies that could be useful for all children.

When aides are definitely needed to work with specific children, they should not be viewed as a means for keeping a "separated service" within the regular classroom for the children. Instead the aides should be given ongoing training and mentoring in order to become effective team members who interact with all children. In this era of cutbacks in education funding, it is necessary for administrators and teachers, working together, to develop creative solutions that make the most of the adult personnel available, incorporate parent and other volunteers, and test alternative staffing patterns that draw on specific team resources, while continuing to promote the "ideal" staff configurations to school boards, parents, and community decision makers. Whether the move to inclusion will result in "cheaper" special education services as regular educators "take over" the teaching of children with disabilities has been a matter of debate. In order to work well, inclusion may require a substantial additional financial commitment. The goal is to have services that are better for both typical and special-needs children because there is general agreement that present practices can be improved.

Problems and Suggestions Related to Organizational Systems and Structures

Problem. Time schedules of schools are not conducive to interdisciplinary team approaches, and when team planning time is provided, effective use of such time is not encouraged or monitored.

Suggestion. Because time for team planning is rarely sufficient in the daily or weekly schedule, creative solutions to enable teachers to have team planning time should be explored. This problem has been increasingly recognized by schools, and many of them are now using a variety of methods to increase the team planning time available. The efficient use of planning time can be addressed by training personnel in teaming strategies, at both the preservice and in-service levels, and developing a planning and reporting system that documents effective use of the time. Many teams need mentoring so that specific planning for integrating curriculum and adapting instruction, rather than just rehashing individual children's problems, is accomplished during the team planning time. Effective use of team planning time is presently one of the greatest in-service needs.

Problem. Administrators lack clear guidelines on assessment and placement policies related to what is the "least restrictive environment" for various children and how can that best be determined, resulting in decisions often being made on parental or teacher/administrator preference rather than on a full ecologically based assessment.

Suggestion. Following Will's (1986) contention that problems may be in environments rather than in children, the preferred model of assessment should include a team assessment conducted within the regular classroom environment, noting what supports can be given or adaptations made by the teacher or other team members to make that experience successful for the child. After this effort has been made, if that environment does not promote a positive learning experience for the child, then alternative settings for some portion of the day (e.g., resource room, self-contained classroom) may be provided or the regular education environment may be revised. This approach begins at the least restrictive end of the continuum and moves to a more restrictive environment, as necessary, but always based on the best needs of the child (not the needs of the parent or teacher or administrator). Likewise, decisions as to whether children with disabilities or with special gifts/talents should be clustered should be based on which type of environment will result in greater learning opportunities for the children.

Problem. A particular concern of inclusive preschool programs is that state funding for typical children at age 3–5 is minimal (and is non-existent for children under 3), thus requiring parents of typical children to pay for the inclusion program while state funding pays for the children with disabilities.

Suggestion. There have been a variety of creative solutions used by early childhood programs to include typical children in their programs and some states (e.g., Ohio) have funded inclusive school district pre-schools. Nevertheless, many programs for children age 3 and 4 do not have funding to provide an inclusive setting with typical children. Until the movement to inclusion is truly inclusive of all preschool children, with a financial commitment to provide the best educational opportunities for all children, not just those with disabilities, the promise of inclusion at the preschool level will be only partially realized.

Problem. With the mandates for academic achievement that schools face, the issue of "fairness" in regard to adaptations of academic work for children with disabilities is problematic.

Suggestion. Because this has been a recurring dilemma of American society, it is not a problem that is easily solved. What is needed, however, is a commitment among all parties to discuss this problem openly, with attention to all perspectives, and to reach a consensus, at least for each program/school district, as to how adaptations and evaluations of performance will be handled for children who have disabilities or are gifted with special talents. Professionals in special education and early childhood special education have a perspective on this issue that should be heard because their philosophy and experience with developmentally appropriate practice and individualization of curriculum can help inform the debate. The dilemma of excellence and equity, however, will continue to be of concern to most educators.

Problem. Research evidence indicates that the mere presence of diverse children in a classroom does not automatically result in an increase in social skills, greater breadth of friendship and social acceptance, or more empathy and tolerance for those different from oneself.

Suggestion. The models of social acceptance provided by teachers and other adults and their facilitative efforts to encourage social skill development are essential for this important goal of inclusion to be achieved. Because lack of social acceptance is something many children face, not only those with disabilities, this social goal must be one that teachers, administrators, and parents actively promote, both within the classroom and in the broader society. Activities that engage children in cooperative learning, assist them in gaining empathy and respect for all people, and allow them to practice social skills on a daily basis must be embedded in the classroom environment if this goal of inclusion (and of our society) is to be realized.

FUTURE OF INCLUSIVE TEACHING AND LEARNING

The fears of those who oppose inclusion (especially full inclusion) are that these models will not result in better educational opportunity, movement to more effective teaching strategies, or increased valuing of diversity in our society. During periods of "educational reform" it is often difficult to predict what the future of the implemented changes will be and whether they will be judged to have resulted in deep or only surface changes in the structures, personnel and resource allocations, values, and learning progress of those involved. At times it appears that these questions were all answered by Dewey (1966), who saw "education for democracy" as the vehicle for change and the provider of opportunities for all children in our democratic society. As the author's experiences can attest, it has always been possible to have inclusive classrooms in early childhood, at least at the preschool level, but these were usually ad hoc efforts without the support services, personnel expertise, and methodological innovations that have been developed in recent years.

Because of the basic agreement between early childhood philosophy and practice and the goals of inclusion, however, it may be that early childhood educators are in the best position to demonstrate that these goals can be substantively and validly demonstrated to be effective. Although the research base is not yet clear on the question of inclusion effectiveness, reports of preschool teachers and parents have generally been very positive. With the models from Head Start, Early Intervention "reverse inclusion," and both public and private preschool inclusion efforts, much is being learned about the practices that work best at the preschool level. It remains to be seen whether the early childhood system of values and methods exemplified at the preschool level can transform present kindergarten and primary schools in ways that make the inclusion goal a reality.

Both regular early childhood and early childhood special education have much to learn from each other but, because they already share many common values and methods, the chances for inclusion to be effective are greatest at this educational age level. Teachers in these areas believe that all children, whatever their disabilities or gifts, must have the opportunity to learn through a range of modalities and have a team of excellently trained educators to assist them. They also believe that, if typical children have the opportunity to play and work with children with disabilities (and vice versa) during their early childhood years, they will carry those experiences with them into their upper age level school experiences and be more accepting of diversity throughout their lives. The dream of a diverse society that includes and values all people and that gives all children the opportunity to learn at their highest potential may rest in the hands of those educators who take responsibility for the learning of all of the children in inclusive environments and demonstrate effective methods of inclusion practice. Ultimately the realization of that dream will be in the hands of the children who experience such optimum learning in an inclusive environment.

REFERENCES

Baker, J. M., & Zigmond, N. (1990). Are regular education classes equipped to accommodate students with learning disabilities? *Exceptional Children,* 56(6), 515–526.

Bergen, D. (1993). Teaching strategies: Facilitating friendship development in inclusion classrooms. *Childhood Education,* 69(4), 234–236.

Bergen, D. (1994a). Teaching strategies: Developing the art and science of team teaching. *Childhood Education,* 70(5), 300–301.

Bergen, D. (1994b). *Assessment methods for infants and toddlers: Transdisciplinary team approaches.* New York: Teachers College Press.

Bergen, D., & Mosley-Howard, S. (1994). Assessment perspectives for culturally diverse young children. In D. Bergen, *Assessment methods for infants and toddlers: Transdisciplinary team approaches* (pp. 190–206). New York: Teachers College Press.

Bricker, D.C. (1989). *Classroom life as civic education: Individual achievement and student cooperation in schools.* New York: Teachers College Press.

Bruner, J. (1983). *In search of mind.* New York: Harper & Row.

Covert, S. (1995). Elementary school inclusion that works. *Counterpoint, 15*(4), 1, 4.

Deno, S., Maruyama, G., Espin, C., & Cohen, C. (1990). Educating students with mild disabilities in general education classrooms: Minnesota alternatives. *Exceptional Children, 57*(2), 150–161.

Dewey, J. (1966). *Democracy and education.* New York: Free Press.

Dickman, G. E. (1994). Inclusion: A storm sometimes brings relief. *Perspectives, 20*(4), 3–6.

Education of All Handicapped Act of 1975 (P.L. 94–142). 89 Stat. 773.

Education of All Handicapped Act Amendments of 1986 (P.L. 99–457). 20 U.S.C. §§1400–1485.

Feinman, S. (1991). Bringing babies back into the social world. In M. Lewis & S. Feinman (Eds.), Genesis of behavior: Vol. 6. *Social influences and socialization in infancy* (pp. 281–326). New York: Plenum Press.

Fuch, S., & Fuch, L. S. (1994). Inclusive schools movement and the radicalization of special education reform. *Exceptional Children, 60*(4), 294–309.

Gartner, A., & Lipsky, D. K. (1987). Beyond special education: Toward a quality system for all students. *Harvard Educational Review, 57*(4), 367–395.

Giangreco, M. F., Dennis, R., Cloninger, C., Edelman, S., & Schattman, R. (1993). "I've counted Jon": Transformational experiences of teachers educating students with disabilities. *Exceptional Children, 59*(4), 359–372.

Hamre-Nietupski, S., Hendrickson, J., Nietupski, J., & Sasso, G. (1993). Perceptions of teachers of students with moderate, severe, or profound disabilities on facilitating friendships with nondisabled peers. *Education and Training in Mental Retardation, 28*(2), 111–127.

Individuals with Disabilities Education Act of 1990, PL. 101–476. *Federal Register, 57*(189), 44794–44852.

Jenkins, J. R., Pious, C. G., & Jewell, M. (1990). Special education and the regular education initiative: Basic assumptions. *Exceptional Children, 56*(6), 479–491.

Mather, N., & Roberts, R. (1994, Fall). The return of students with learning disabilities to regular classrooms. *Perspectives on Inclusion,* pp. 6–12.

Peck, C. A., Carlson, P., & Helmstetter, E. (1992). Parent and teacher perceptions of outcomes for typically developing children enrolled in integrated early childhood programs: A statewide survey. *Journal of Early Intervention, 16*(1), 53–63.

Perske, R. (1988). *Circles of friends.* Nashville, TN: Abingdon Press.

Raver, C. C., & Zigler, E. F. (1991). Three steps forward, two steps back: Head Start and the measurement of social competence. *Young Children, 46*(4), 3–8.

Reynolds, M. C., Wang, M. C., & Walberg, H. J. (1987). The necessary restructuring of special and regular education. *Exceptional Children, 53*(5), 391–398.

Roberts, C., Pratt, C., & Leach, D. (1991). Classroom and playground interaction of students with and without disabilities. *Exceptional Children, 57*(3), 212–224.

Sabornie, E. J., Marshall, K. J., & Ellis, E. S. (1990). Restructuring of mainstream sociometry with learning disabled and nonhandicapped students. *Exceptional Children, 56*(4), 314–323.

Semmel, M. I., Abernathy, T. V., Butera, G., & Lesar, S. (1991). Teachers' perceptions of the regular education initiative. *Exceptional Children, 58*(1), 9–24.

Shanker, A. (1994, February 6). Where we stand: Inclusion and ideology. *The New York Times*, E-7.

Shapiro, J. P., Loeb, P., & Bowermaster, D. (1993, December 13). Separate and unequal. *U.S. News and World Report*, pp. 46–60.

Stainback, S., & Stainback, W. (Eds.) (1991). *Curriculum considerations in inclusive classrooms: Facilitating learning for all students*. Baltimore: Paul H. Brookes.

Stainback, S., & Stainback, W. (1992). Schools as inclusive communities. In W. Stainback & S. Stainback (Eds.), *Controversial issues confronting special education* (pp. 29–43). Needham Heights, MA: Allyn & Bacon.

Van Dyke, R., Stallings, M. A., & Colley, K. (1995, February). How to build an inclusive school community: A success story. *Phi Delta Kappan*, pp. 475–479.

Will, M. C. (1986). *Educating children with learning problems: A shared responsibility*. Washington, DC: Office of Special Education and Rehabilitative Services, U.S. Department of Education.

Wolery, M., Martin, C. G., Schroeder, C., Huffman, K., Venn, M. L., Holcombe, A., Brookfield, J., & Fleming, L. A. (1994). Employment of educators in preschool mainstreaming: A survey of general early educators. *Journal of Early Intervention, 18*(1), 64–77.

Zigmond, N., Jenkins, J., Fuch, L. S., Deno, S., Fuchs, D., Baker, J. M., Jenkins, L., & Couthino, M. (1995, March). Special education in restructured schools: Finding from three multi-year studies. *Phi Delta Kappan*, pp. 531–540.

Chapter 10

Early Childhood Programs: International Perspectives

Mary Renck Jalongo
James L. Hoot
with Jyotsna Pattnaik
Weiwei Cai
Sunhee Park

An international group of educators gathered to share their countries' progress in developing policies and programs for young children. During the discussion, an American member of the audience turned to her friend and was overheard saying, "When it comes to educating children, the United States is a third-world country." As this candid remark points out, there is much to be learned from international collaboration on behalf of young children.

We set two major goals for this chapter on international early childhood education. First, to make certain our analysis of international programs for young children was more than the fleeting perceptions of tourists, we collaborated with three teacher educators and former doctoral advisees from other countries. Second, we wanted to identify emerging themes in international education as well as develop specific proposals for promoting international collaboration in the field of early childhood education.

WHY STUDY EARLY CHILDHOOD EDUCATION IN OTHER COUNTRIES?

Although progress has been made in arriving at international consensus concerning the rights and needs of children (United Nations, 1989), the early childhood field has much work to do with regard to improving educational programs for children worldwide. This will require an open, honest dialogue that engages all countries in assessing their successes as well as their shortcomings in providing quality programs for the very young. Thus, the first reason for studying early childhood education in other countries is to get a sense of the struggles and achievements of our global neighbors and, in light of that knowledge, to examine ways to become advocates for young children, both at home and abroad.

A second reason for examining early childhood education from an international perspective is that recent technological advances and economic forces have driven nations into an era of more openness. With this openness comes public scrutiny of the treatment of young children, such as the deplorable situation in Romanian orphanages. Membership in a global community also brings about inevitable comparisons between and among the ways that various nations meet young children's needs.

Although each country has its unique characteristics, early childhood educators worldwide share some similar concerns. Most of us encounter conflict between what we believe is best for young children and what is dictated or expected by some traditions, parents, administrators, and/or colleagues. Thus, a third advantage of studying other countries is to discover common challenges that unify early childhood educators as they strive to put the world's best educational theories and research into daily practice.

A final reason for exploring a global perspective is to help educators more clearly articulate overarching goals for the field. Although we share a commitment to educate the very young, we still live in a world where children's simplest and most basic needs (e.g., the need to have caring parents, adequate nutrition, and basic health care, the need to be a child, have a home, play) are frequently neglected or denied. For all of these reasons, an international perspective on early childhood education can make a significant contribution to the field.

A FRAMEWORK FOR EXPLORING GLOBAL ISSUES

To guide readers in exploring international perspectives on early childhood education, we have adapted the following list of questions to stimulate reflection as we focus on particular nations (Kammerman & Kahn, 1994):

- What is the apparent demand for early childhood education in this nation? What percentage of mothers with young children at various ages are employed outside the home?
- What different kinds of programs for young children are offered?

Is there a system of family child care? center-based care? public school? On what hours/schedules/calendars do these programs typically operate? How well do these programs meet the needs of families?

• Who is served by the programs? all children? children who are economically privileged? children at risk? children identified as gifted and talented? What is the basic view of the child?

• How are the programs funded? federal funds? other public sources? parents? some combination of these?

• What other forms of family support are available? family leaves? after-school care? health care? social services? How is the role of parents defined in the programs?

• How is the staff trained? What qualifications are necessary to work in the various programs? What is the status and income level of the profession? What benefits are offered? What is the turnover rate?

• What is the primary focus of the programs? What purposes do they serve? What type of curriculum (e.g., "custodial" or educational) is involved? How is program quality monitored?

• What unique characteristics do the early childhood programs in this country have? How has the culture and the society in which these programs operate influenced standard practices?

Our co-authors from China, India, and Korea were invited to reflect on these questions and develop succinct profiles of early childhood education in their native countries.

EARLY CHILDHOOD EDUCATION IN CHINA

Over three thousand years of Chinese education have been combined with modern Western educational thought to produce contemporary early childhood education. The policy of one child per couple, instituted in densely populated areas of China, has strongly influenced Chinese early childhood education programs. This 1979 policy has dramatically changed the traditional belief in the superiority of male children over female children and has focused greater attention on early childhood education. Moreover, the one-child proviso has created some widespread social, personality, and achievement concerns about Chinese children. Many Chinese parents express concern that their only child will become a self-centered personality who lacks social skills or worry about the child's future success in an increasingly competitive society.

During the last 45 years, the structure of Chinese society has been altered by the high percentage of women employed outside the home. Most Chinese believe that working for the public and making the same amount of money as men is one of the basic avenues by which women gain equal status and contribute to their family's income. Thus, Chinese women not only—as is traditionally believed—"hold up half the sky" at home, but increasingly "hold up half the sky" in the world of work.

Characteristics of Chinese Early Childhood Programs

Education in China has always been viewed as an avenue to train future leaders and citizens as well as to cultivate individual morality. General characteristics of most early childhood programs in China include the following:

- The Chinese government provides free health examinations and free epidemic prevention to all children in the country.
- A minimum of 6 months of paid maternity leave is provided to workers, and Chinese early childhood programs provide services to children from 56 days of age until entrance into first grade.
- Most parents are partially or fully reimbursed by their working unit or place of employment for their child's school tuition and meal costs.
- No child is retained in kindergarten because early childhood education is considered to be a period of preparation for starting regular school.
- All early childhood teachers must have art education training before they can be considered for a teaching position.

Diversity in Chinese Early Childhood Programs

In China there are many different program options for children and families, including:

- *Kindergarten programs supported by the central government.* These educational programs usually serve children of middle-class families, have the best facilities, are often located in a park or other desirable area, and are staffed with teachers who have a bachelor's degree or special training.
- *Programs supported by the local government.* When a residential housing project is first proposed in China, the plan always includes different types of early childhood programs. Cost and quality of these facilities vary depending on the financial situation of the local government, but tuition is generally affordable.
- *Programs supported by working units.* These kindergarten and child care programs are designed for both educational and custodial purposes. They are located within walking distance of the parents' worksite so that parents can visit their children during break time. Since such

programs are open only to employees, the working unit absorbs most of the cost. The quality of the facilities in these programs, however, seldom compares favorably with that of programs supported by the government.

• *Private family care.* This is typically custodial care provided by retired women who provide flexible services at a reasonable cost based on the family's needs.

• *Programs to prepare for elementary school.* Like American kindergarten, this one-year academic program that precedes the primary grades is frequently housed in an elementary school. These preparatory programs ordinarily follow the school year calendar, with both half-day and whole-day sessions.

• *Out-of-school programs.* The children's palace, art schools, and athletic schools are the places for gifted children to develop their special talents (Swartz, 1989). Generally speaking, programs are scheduled after school and on weekends. Children are required to interview before they officially enroll in the programs, and the teachers who work for these schools are professionals in different specialty areas.

• *Private elementary boarding schools.* These schools are funded entirely by fees collected from parents, and these schools are clearly for the affluent, with 1 year's tuition costing as much as an average worker's 2-year salary. Private elementary schools attract high-quality staff. In China, there is considerable debate about the overall effect of these boarding schools on children's growth and on society because of the resulting segregation by economic status.

Education for Children with Special Needs

Traditionally, children with special needs were considered a private family matter and outside interference was not considered desirable. However, with the passage of the Compulsory Education Law in 1986, the Chinese government launched major changes (Mu, Yant, & Armfield, 1993). This law explicitly stated that all children with special needs have a right to education and local governments are responsible for establishing schools with special classes for children who are blind, deaf, or mentally retarded. In 1990, the Protection of Handicapped Persons Law placed mild to moderately handicapped children in mainstream education. Services for special needs children in remote areas, however, continue to be limited due to transportation difficulties.

Development of Schools for Parenting

With two parents and four grandparents lavishing attention on one child (known as "4:2:1"), young children in China are often referred to as "little emperors." Increasingly, parents feel that they have only one chance to be good parents and see their child become educated, well adjusted, and successful in life. During the last 10 years, a number of "Parent Schools" have been established to offer educational programs that deal with the problems of raising only children. Chinese parents regard extensive collaboration with educators as part of responsible parenting.

In summary, early childhood education in China is dedicated to optimizing children's potential in all areas of development and to helping young children mature into qualified citizens.

EARLY CHILDHOOD EDUCATION IN INDIA

Universal early childhood education in India is a relatively recent development. Throughout the history of India, formal education was limited to male members of high-caste groups. Mass illiteracy among children of low-caste families as well as female children has had a cumulative effect of unequal distribution of educational opportunities among the population. Efforts to educate children from all sections of the society began in 1937 with the educational philosophy of Gandhi and were further reinforced by Maria Montessori's 1939 visit to India. In postindependence India, early childhood education has been a constant focus of all major committees and commissions established by the government (Ministry of Human Resource Development, Government of India, 1986, 1993).

Throughout Indian history, children have enjoyed a special status in society. Childhood is considered to be a unique and enjoyable period in an individual's life, so children are pampered by the adults in the family and in the community. Numerous occasions mark the importance of the early years. For example, the whole community celebrates the birth of a child, a child's first intake of solid food, the naming ceremony for a child, and the child's first day of formal education. Informal learning of young children in a natural environment through songs, dance, play, and talk is a regular component of child-rearing responsibilities of adults and older children in India. However, the growing demands of a newly industrialized nation have altered many of the basic child-rearing practices in India. There is a rapidly emerging need for a more comprehensive system of early childhood education.

Need for Early Childhood Education In India

The following three needs have had a major impact on early childhood education in India:

• *The need for child care.* Women of all social-class backgrounds are seeking employment outside the home. In response to the need for child care, various women's groups, labor unions, religious groups, and political parties have influenced the Indian government to support a system of child care. One result of these collaborative efforts is that female employees in India now receive a 3-month maternity leave with full salary.

• *The need for an educated citizenry.* Because older girls frequently function as caregivers, they often drop out of school to care for younger siblings. Early childhood programs, therefore, have the potential to make universal, compulsory primary education in India a reality (Kaul, 1992).

• *The need to support young children's development.* The young child involved in early childhood programs receives improved health care and better nutrition as well as opportunities for social learning and educational enrichment (Kaul, 1992).

Emerging Educational Expansion for High-Risk Groups

In 1993, the Ministry of Human Resource Development in India identified target groups for expansion of early childhood services. These groups include young children who live in poverty in urban communities; who live in economically depressed areas where they are required to participate in agricultural and household chores; who are the offspring of itinerant, seasonal, or construction laborers; who belong to tribal communities or live in remote areas; and who have special needs or physical disabilities. Many innovative research projects have been initiated by major agencies working in India, such as UNICEF, to meet the needs of these young children. The Children's Media Laboratory Project, for example, produces both print and nonprint materials in different languages and distributes them free of charge.

Programs Available in India

There is a variety of federal, voluntary, and private programs serving children from birth through age 8.

• *Programs run by the government.* "Integrated Child Development Services" (ICDS) is India's national program for children between 0 and 6 years that serves more than 8.6 million children in 215,012 centers (Bhavnagri, 1995; Muralidhran, 1992). ICDS was established (1) to provide quality health and nutritional services to pregnant and lactating mothers, (2) to enhance children's physical and social development, (3) to coordinate efforts of various groups and agencies, and (4) to provide health and nutrition education to mothers. ICDS services include supplementary nutrition, immunizations, health checkups, referral services, treatment of minor illnesses, parent education, and preschool education.

• *Programs Run by Voluntary Organizations.* Voluntary organizations assisted by government agencies offer a wide range of special programs designed for specific contexts, such as the mobile creches, which started in 1969 in Delhi to serve the children of migrant laborers.

• *Programs Run by Private Institutions.* Private programs in India include parochial schools, corporate-sponsored preschools, laboratory schools at universities, and so forth. Preprimary schools in private sectors are more academically oriented. The language of instruction in some Indian schools is Hindi (the national language); in others, one of many different state languages; and, in still others, English, with English the popular choice in private schools.

Teacher Training and Program Evaluation

Teacher training institutions in India offer (1) a specialized 2-year course in nursery school teaching, (2) an integrated 2-year program that prepares teachers for preschool, and (3) a primary teacher training program, which prepares teachers for grades 1 through 5. Early childhood education has become an integral component of newly opened education colleges (Bhavnagri, 1995).

All early childhood education programs run by the government are evaluated regularly. For example, the supervisors and project officers conduct on-site evaluations and national agencies conduct program evaluations (National Institute of Public Cooperation and Child Development, 1992).

Current Trends and Future Goals

In spite of the financial constraints and the ever-increasing population it serves, Indian early childhood education has attained the following goals:

1. *Providing developmentally appropriate education in early years.* India's National Policy on Education reflects a strong stand on developmentally appropriate practice and states: "Early Childhood Education and Care will be child-oriented, focused around play and individually oriented. Formal methods and introduction of the 3 R's will be discouraged at this stage. The local community will be fully involved in these programs" (Ministry of Human Resource Development, 1986 p. 10).

2. *Integrating children with special needs in the regular class-*

rooms. India is also an advocate of inclusion. The "Integrated Education" plan for the disabled is designed to integrate children with special needs into regular classrooms. Although institutions for children with special needs have been established at the national level, these facilities and services have not yet reached the rural population.

3. *Combining Western models of early childhood education with indigenous practices.* Although Montessori, Piaget, and Froebel have had a profound influence on early childhood education in India, materials used for early childhood classrooms are indigenously prepared and reflect the cultural values of the populations served. French (1992) reported that Indian educators typically use natural resources, such as leaves and stones, as manipulatives. She also remarked on the overall child-centeredness of the curriculum amidst visible resource constraints.

4. *Encouraging community participation.* The National Institute of Public Cooperation and Child Development (1992) reported that 55% of Indian women, 47% of community leaders, and 33% of adolescent girls were involved in early childhood programs. Qualitative research methods, particularly the case study method, also have been used to evaluate community participation (Nath & Ray, 1993).

5. *Implementing alternative models in early childhood education.* The National Council of Educational Research and Training has successfully implemented some innovative programs, such as the *child-to-child program,* where older children are trained in basic health, nutrition, and child development, then practice these skills with younger siblings at home as well as younger children at school. This role as caretaker of younger children is highly valued by Indian culture. The *school-readiness program* is a 6–8-week program designed for places where preschool facilities are unavailable. It comes in a kit that includes a package of activities to be conducted in the summer before the child starts first grade or at the beginning of first grade. Additionally, *home-based programs* have been developed for urban and tribal children. The objective of these programs is to develop mothers' skills in the care and education of their own children.

The collaboration of state and union governments has brought a noticeable change in planning, monitoring, and funding of the early childhood programs. As a result, contemporary early childhood education in India is child-centered, context-oriented, and responsive to the needs of individuals and groups.

The task before early childhood education in India is threefold: to educate all of the nation's young children, to elevate the professional status of early childhood educators, and to preserve the long-revered cultural tradition of community involvement in children's informal learning. If implemented successfully, these goals will prove to be new milestones in the history of Indian education.

EARLY CHILDHOOD EDUCATION IN KOREA

In ancient times educational opportunities at all levels in Korea were determined by two factors—social class and sex of the child. The long-standing Yi Dynasty (1392–1910), for example, adopted a system whereby all appointments to government posts were based on national examinations (Park & Hoot, 1990). Only aristocratic males, however, were educated enough to take these tests. Children groomed for these positions memorized classics at home under the tutelage of experienced teachers while selected male children of common people went to informal learning houses to master basic skills. The majority of Korean children were educated solely by their family members—parents, grandparents, siblings, or others who could not work in the fields. Female children, irrespective of class, stayed at home and learned rules of etiquette and how to manage household affairs.

Under the period of Japanese imperialism (1910–1945), formal educational institutions were established to educate Japanese children. Similar programs were developed for Korean children by the Japanese, primarily for the purpose of teaching Korean children Japan's customs and language (Lee, 1986).

The first child care center for Korean children was established by a Christian missionary, Brown Lee, in 1914. By 1930, more than 75% of all Korean child care facilities were operated by Christian groups (Lee, 1985). From 1922 until the outbreak of the Korean War, child care facilities declined (Yu, 1990). With the war, concern for protecting children and caring for orphans resulted in renewed expansion of child care programs. Beginning in 1961, day care centers were supervised by the South Korean government.

Emerging Demand for Child Care

Since the 1970s, South Korea has undergone unprecedented industrialization. A shortage of laborers to meet this demand, a decrease in the number of children per family, an increase in women's desire for self-fulfillment, and the rapid increase in the cost of living have brought about greatly expanded participation of women in the workforce. Traditionally, household chores in Korea were relegated solely to women. Thus, when women enter the workforce, they are expected to do this job *in addition to* their household duties. It is little wonder, then, that a recent study found that 93% of working mothers strongly supported an increase in child care services, 34% of unemployed mothers indicated they would use child care facilities if available, and 66% of unemployed mothers said they would seek employment if child care services were provided (Korean Institute for Research in the Behavioral Sciences, 1990).

Now that both parents are working outside the home in many South Korean families, the once active participation of parents in classrooms has declined and communication between teachers and parents is frequently limited to notes or telephone calls.

Teacher Preparation

South Korea has three basic levels of early childhood teachers: associate teachers (high school graduates who have passed the associate teacher examination), second-class certified teachers (students who graduate from 2-year vocational colleges with at least a B average), and first-class certified teachers (graduates of 4-year programs).

The majority of preschool teachers are trained in 2-year colleges, and only about 20% of South Korean preschool teachers graduate from 4-year colleges. In addition, nearly 97% of all preschool teachers are educated in private institutions (Lim, 1987). The general preservice program consists of four parts: general education, pedagogy, the arts, and a teaching practicum consisting of 1 month of experience teaching preschool children. Since 1983, in-service training in early childhood education has been emphasized in South Korea to upgrade the quality of experienced directors, teachers, and school inspectors (Kim, 1983).

Impediments to Progress: Teacher Compensation and Class Size

The salaries of private preschool teachers in South Korea are comparable to those of public servants (e.g., garbage collectors, grocery clerks, fast-food workers). A beginning teacher's salary is approximately one-fifth the salary of a beginning university professor's. Private preschools pay higher salaries than public schools.

A major reason for poor salaries in South Korea is the oversupply of graduates. In 1989, for example, the total number of early childhood teachers in child care was around 18,000. Since early childhood departments were established, approximately 7,500 teachers have been graduating every year (Lim, 1991). Teacher turnover is very low because teachers work hard to avoid being replaced by beginning teachers, who are paid less. With so many unemployed certified teachers, salaries are individually negotiated at the discretion of directors rather than following a set salary schedule. Few men pursue careers in the field because they believe they cannot provide for their families on such low pay.

Although the salaries for early childhood teachers are low, the responsibilities are many. With the help of one assistant teacher or aide, each teacher is, by government guidelines, expected to provide appropriate programs for 40 young children. Such large classes interfere with close relationships and individualized attention. This situation is a major deterrent to progress in South Korean early childhood education.

IMPLICATIONS AND FUTURE DIRECTIONS

As we reflect on the three countries profiled and our other international experiences, we are led to one general observation and four recommendations. The observation is that the status of women and the status of children in each country described are inextricably linked. In China, India, Korea, and indeed in the United States, we have observed four recurrent themes: (1) that women have borne and continue to bear primary responsibility for children, (2) that working outside the home frequently results in women's holding two full-time positions, (3) that early childhood education has been traditionally perceived as more of a nurturing role than an educational one, and (4) that teachers of young children are poorly compensated and overwhelmingly female. Having made this key general observation, we now turn to four recommendations with regard to international perspectives on early childhood education.

1. *Educational policies and programs should be based on children as learners rather than adults as workers.* National policies concerning programs for young children have to be focused on meeting the needs of all young children rather than on economic supply and demand. It is interesting to note that the United States, which now seems so resistant to a national system of early childhood education, quickly launched federally funded programs during World War II when women were needed to work in factories. Because federally supported early childhood programs enable more women to seek employment outside the home, child care may be viewed as an economic liability when unemployment is high.

One major distinction between poor, adequate, and outstanding early childhood programs worldwide is a clear vision of what will optimize the young child's development and education. The schools of Reggio Emilia, Italy, offer an excellent example of how a clear mission and purpose, subsumed in a philosophy, shape early childhood programs (Malaguzzi, 1993; 1994). These schools have deservedly earned international acclaim as models of the best that early childhood education has to offer, particularly in terms of child-centeredness, creative expression, and family involvement (New, 1993). Yet the schools of Reggio Emilia are also well funded, serve rather culturally homogeneous children/families, and are set within the context of a society that truly reveres its children. As a result, the common assumption that the model can be quickly "transplanted" elsewhere is misguided, at best. Without thoughtful consideration of the philosophies, programs, and policies of early childhood programs, progress in offering the very best to young children will be thwarted. Without its philosophical grounding and theoretical bearings, early childhood education can not fulfill its time-honored tradition and future promise of educating the whole child.

2. *Stronger international professional organizations and standards of practice should be developed.* Affiliation with professional organizations is an important deterrent to "compassion fatigue" (Raywid, 1995). Through professional reading and dialogue with teachers from other areas, educators become connected to a network of like-minded professionals that lends emotional support, stimulates ideas, and affirms quality practices—all influences that tend to counteract the dissatisfactions of teaching. Given the high rate of teacher-reported feelings of isolation in Russo's (1995) study of American teachers, one can only speculate on the isolation that teachers feel in rural areas or in countries where opportunities for professional growth are limited. Whereas the American early childhood educator often has to be selective about conferences and learning opportunities because they exist in such abundance, early childhood educators in many other regions of the world are routinely deprived of such experiences.

A number of educational organizations have a long-standing interest in promoting professional development and addressing international issues. Among these are the World Organization for the Education of Preschoolers (OMEP), the Association for Childhood Education International (ACEI), the International Reading Association (IRA), and the National Association of Early Childhood Teacher Educators (NAECTE). These and other professional associations will have to form more meaningful collaborations, inaugurate new projects, and establish worldwide networks on behalf of the very young.

One worthwhile endeavor is an international standards board, which would open dialogue and respect cultural differences, a group that would consult with countries that are striving to improve early childhood education. Eventually, the standards could be used to offer an official type of validation that would support exemplary early childhood practice in all nations, such as the endorsement now offered through the Association for Childhood Education International. These standards could also become the philosophical framework for an international journal that translates the best ideas from various countries into different languages so that messages about high-quality early childhood education can reach a wider audience of professionals.

3. *Developmental continuity in children's transition from preschool to primary education should be addressed worldwide.* One recurring theme in many countries studied is the double standard that exists for preschool and primary grades. In Mexico, for example, the young child is regarded as the most delightful and innocent of human beings, and programs for the preschool age group generally reflect a child-centered, developmentally appropriate perspective. Yet when those children enter the primary grades, the message is loud and clear: "Grow up and get to work!" Primary-age children are generally thrust into crowded classrooms with 35 to 50 students and spend much of their time doing paper-and-pencil tasks. Of course, this problem is not unique to Mexico. It is just as prevalent in other settings, including the U.S. (Barbour & Seefeldt, 1993). Yet, as a profession, we have barely begun to address the culture shock that these young children must feel when their experience of school undergoes such dramatic and inappropriate changes.

4. *Access to technology for young children and their teachers should be promoted in all countries.* When television was first introduced, it was heralded as a window on the world. Today, similar claims are being made for the Internet, but it remains to be seen whether this technology will attain the lofty goals now imagined for it. Technology can have major implications for teachers throughout the world as they use the Internet, World Wide Web, and other programs to develop professional relationships and share pedagogical ideas. Such programs can also be used to link classrooms internationally and give children firsthand knowledge of other cultures. If, however, these forms of communication routinely exclude countries that are economically disadvantaged, limited access to technology will perpetuate elitism in education. Even in a country as wealthy as our own, just 4% of the population is using the Internet. Therefore, increased access to the new technologies is a major issue for international early childhood education.

CONCLUSION

As we reflect on the diversity among programs serving the very young child worldwide as well as the commonalities between and among them, it becomes increasingly evident that there is much to be gained through international collaboration. Contemporary early childhood educators can no longer afford to limit their scope to their particular program or even their country of residence. As a profession, we must abandon these parochial and nationalistic views in favor of an international perspective. Every one of us in the field must be mindful of the fact that when we speak of "education for all," that inclusive "all" must extend beyond ethnic, cultural, and geographic boundaries to embrace every world citizen of tomorrow, that citizen who is now a young child.

REFERENCES

Barbour, N., & Seefeldt, C. (1993). *Developmental continuity across the preschool and primary grades: Implications for teachers.* Wheaton, MD: Association for Childhood Education International.

Bhavnagri, N. P. (1995). An interview with professor Amita Verma: A leader in early childhood education in India. *Childhood Education, 71*(3), 156–160.

Burkhart, R. (1994). Child care in China. *Children Today, 23*(2), 16–20.

Chen, G. (1992). The characteristics of young children and art education. *Preschool Education* (China), *10,* 16–18.

French, S. (1992). A study tour to India. *International Journal of Early Childhood Education, 24*(1), 68–72.

Kammerman, S. B., & Kahn, A. J. (1994). *A welcome for every child: Care, education, and family support for infants and toddlers in Europe.* Arlington, VA: Zero to Three/National Center for Clinical Infant Programs.

Kaul, V. (1992). Early childhood education in India. In G. A. Woodill, J. Bernhard, & L. Prochner (Eds.), *International handbook of early childhood education* (pp. 275–292). New York: Garland Publishing.

Kim, C. M. (1983, April). Republic of Korea. *Bulletin of the UNESCO Regional Office for Education in Asia and the Pacific* (No. 24).

Korean Institute for Research in the Behavioral Sciences. (1990). Study of national demand and parental need of childcare in Korea. *Research in the Behavioral Sciences, 23*(3).

Lee, S. K. (1985). *The process and direction of development of early childhood education.* Paper presented at the annual meeting of the Korean Educational Association, Seoul, Korea.

Lee, S. K. (1986). The process of formation of Korean kindergarten in its early years. *Research in Early Childhood Education in Korea, 6,* 5–21.

Lim, J. T. (1987). *Development of criteria for evaluation of institute of early childhood education.* Seoul: Korean Educational Development Institute.

Lim, J. T. (1991). Real conditions and improvement in early childhood care and education in Korea. *The Pusan Society for the Study of Early Childhood Education, 1,* 7–26.

Lo, L. N. (1989). Arts education in the mass cultural system of China. *Journal of Aesthetic Education, 23*(1), 101–123.

Malaguzzi, L. (1993). For an education based on relationships. *Young Children,* *49*(1), 4–8.

Malaguzzi, L. (1994). Your image of the child: Where teaching begins. *Child Care Information Exchange, 96,* 52–61.

Ministry of Human Resource Development, Government of India. (1986). *National policy on education.* New Delhi: Department of Education.

Ministry of Human Resource Development, Government of India. (1993). *Education for all: The Indian scene.* New Delhi: Department of Education.

Mu, K., Yant, H., & Armfield, A. (1993, April). *China's special education: A comparative analysis.* Paper presented at the annual convention of the Council for Exceptional Children, San Antonio, TX.

Muralidhran, R. (1992). Training of personnel for programs in early childhood care and education in India. *International Journal of Early Childhood Education, 24*(2), 35–40.

Nath, N., & Ray, S. (1993). *Community participation in ICDS: A case study of Garden Reach, Calcutta.* New Delhi, India: National Institute of Public Cooperation and Child Development.

National Institute of Public Cooperation and Child Development. (1992). *National evaluation of "integrated child development services."* New Delhi, India: Author.

New, R. (1993). *Reggio Emilia: Some lessons for U.S. educators from Reggio Emilia, Italy.* (ERIC Document Reproduction Service No. ED 354 988)

Park, S. H., & Hoot, J. (1990). Recent directions in kindergarten teacher education in the republic of Korea. *Journal of Early Childhood Teacher Education 35*(11:2), 14–15.

Podek, B. (1989). Chinese kindergarten education and its reform. *Early Childhood Research Quarterly, 4*(1), 31–50.

Raywid, M. A. (1995). Building a safe community for learning. In W. Ayers (Ed.), *To become a teacher: Making a difference in children's lives* (pp. 78–85). New York: Teachers College Press.

Russo, K. A. (1995). *A study of work motivation in intermediate elementary teachers.* Unpublished doctoral dissertation, State University of New York at Buffalo, Buffalo, NY.

Swartz, L. (1989). "Raising the cultural level" at the Hangzhou Children's Palace. *Journal of Aesthetic Education, 23*(1), 125–139.

United Nations. (1989). *United Nations Convention on the Rights of the Child.* New York: Author.

Vaughan, J. (1993). Early childhood education in China. *Childhood Education, 69*(4), 196–201.

Wei, N. (1992). Child development in China. *Bejing Review, 35*(22), 28–31.

Yu, A. J. (1990). *Early Childhood Education.* Seoul, Korea: Changji Publishing Company.

Chapter 11

The Professional and Social Status of the Early Childhood Educator

DORIS PRONIN FROMBERG

When I began to teach after completing a bachelor of arts degree with a dual major in early childhood education and psychology, my first job was in a New York City public school kindergarten in Bedford-Stuyvesant. My mother-in-law wondered if I would qualify for teaching in a high school after I had gained additional experience. Her view may be close to the way many laypeople view early childhood education. Growing out of the transparent work of women and motherhood as taken-for-granted, unpaid labor, the group care of other peoples' children in exchange for fees is a relatively recent phenomenon. Laypeople, therefore, often find it difficult to locate the specialized mastery of a body of knowledge and skills in the external practice of early childhood education, first, because the most exemplary practice needs to look playful, and second, because most early childhood workers have not received specialized professional preparation. Thus, early childhood education is a public relations nightmare.

During the time that I received my preparation to teach, New York State offered a self-standing teaching certificate, Nursery through Third Grade. The N–3 teacher certification was consistent with the abundant evidence that specially prepared early childhood personnel have a positive educational impact on the experience of young children in group settings (Bredekamp, 1995; National Association of Early Childhood Teacher Educators & National Association of Early Childhood Specialists in State Education Departments, 1993). New York State is one of six states, however, that currently has no provision for the initial certification of early childhood teachers. In the past few years, an "annotation in early childhood" has been passed, which is an add-on to the PreK–6 elementary teacher certification. This means that, when initally certified teachers begin their employment with young children, they usually have had no

188

preparation to work with this age group because most of their field experiences and courses focused on grades 1–6.

It is paradoxical, therefore, that there is often unnecessary regulation of what should be reasonable professional behavior alongside the lack of support for professional standards that can assure a better quality of educational services for young children. The problem inherent in this paradox lies in the absence of a profession of early childhood that regulates itself and that enforces its own standards and code of ethics.

The first two sections of this chapter consider the paradox of professionalism followed by a working definition of professionalism. In turn, there is a look at the historical perspectives and philosophical traditions of the field of early childhood education, then an interpretation of its knowledge base and other ongoing contemporary issues and trends. I conclude with some implications for the future of early childhood teacher education.

THE PARADOX OF PROFESSIONALISM

A professional status for the field of early childhood education does not now exist. The field reflects an outgrowth of "commonsense" approaches that more nearly comprise an occupation than a profession. In addition, a practical distinction exists between professionals who serve individuals, such as physicians and attorneys, and those who engage in a "public service profession," such as teachers and social workers (Howe, 1980). As it relates to the early childhood field, this distinction has its roots in historical events, public ideologies and perceptions, and a myriad of sociopolitical and economic considerations.

In a sense, professionalism that is defined by high standards is not a democratic concept because it limits entry into its ranks. As an exclusive expertise, professional practice separates the professional from ordinary life and ordinary action. The dual systems of public school and nonpublic school forms of early childhood services further compound the dilemma of early childhood education and professionalism. These dualities create a paradoxical credo that lies undigested in the early childhood field, career-ladder initiatives notwithstanding. Early childhood teaching and status, therefore, are in a developmental stage of amateurism when compared with the composite definition of professionalism discussed below.

This chapter takes the position that the difference between a professional person and a technician resides in the confluence of the six factors discussed in the next section. In particular practice, the distinction exists between those personnel who rely on isolated, technical knowledge as compared with those personnel who are able to approach a domain with "pattern sensitivity" (Hofstadter, 1985, p. 42). The professional is an expert who can assess, plan, adapt, and act with flexibility, basing such functioning on access to a broad field of alternatives. The professional early childhood educator flexibly oscillates between specific events and specific practices within the broader context of an ethical commitment to caring and a broad cultural education. In effect, the early childhood professional processes analogies flexibly and can perceive underlying order within the varying surface forms of "disorderly" emergent events. The early childhood professional, therefore, has a high tolerance for ambiguity. A technician/functionary can sometimes develop a repertoire of isolated activities or can verbalize a list of important principles. It is the scope and depth as well as the capacity for juggling and employing pattern flexibility, however, that differentiates the functionary from the professional.

A WORKING DEFINITION OF PROFESSIONALISM

A profession, as distinct from an occupation or amateur practice, connotes six distinct characteristics: (1) ethical performance that is fair and disinterested; (2) a high level of expertise and skill that "must be essential to the functioning of a society, suggesting that the absence of its knowledge and techniques would weaken the society in some way" (Katz, 1987, p. 3); (3) a body of knowledge and skills that laypeople do not possess (Wise & Liebbrand, 1993, p. 135); (4) considerable autonomy in its practice and control of entry into the profession; (5) commensurate compensation; and (6) a professional organization. Each of these characteristics will be discussed in detail.

Ethical Performance

Early childhood education must be a distinctly ethical profession because the clientele are vulnerable and relatively powerless. Young children tend to want to please adults. That they can please adults by conforming to adults' wishes does not mean that they should be expected to conform to those expectations that are not in the best interests of the children or society in the short and long term. Much of existing early childhood education, for example, is organized in ways to which children have to adapt rather than ways that adapt to young children. It is all too common, for example, to find toddlers patiently watching as their teachers shamelessly worship the calendar each day or 5-year-olds engaging in a letter-of-the-week ritual and sitting for long periods of time to be tested in workbooks. Such technical, unreflective practices by adults abuse young children's willingness to please.

Ethical considerations, therefore, must enter into the development of standards for personnel preparation and ongoing practice. In this sense, I contend that it is not enough to promote "child-initiated practice," or "developmentally appropriate practice," or a "child-centered program," or an "inclusionary program." In the service of these terms, children have been treated to the full range of behaviorist, linear practice to socialization-oriented, emergent curricular methods. It is essential to specify the particular philosophical, sociocultural, political, and curricular orientation that underlies the discourse about personnel preparation. To "study child development" simply is inadequate without specifying the knowlededge base—belief systems and philosophical premises—on which the study is based and how that study relates specifically to the involvement of young children in the process of learning. The "inclusionary" model, when including the behaviorist orientation of some special educators, for example, creates a practical conflict within the practice of a non-behaviorist program orientation.

An ethical field of study embraces more than the *Code of Ethical Conduct and Statement of Commitment* (Feeney & Kipnis, 1990) of the National Association for the Education of Young Children (NAEYC). This statement deals with the ways in which personnel interact with their clients, client families, and one another. An ethical field also has to focus on the part of the code that says that no harm will be done to children. Diminished self-esteem is harmful; learning to deny one's feelings is harmful; and wasting time with trivial pursuits is harmful. Ethical practice, for example, assures that each child will

- Experience a sense of success and competence with thoughtful and reasonable challenges and responsibilites
- Function in an authentic human and physical environment in which children's perceptions, concerns, opinions, needs, and capacities contribute to the creation of experiences, procedures, and activities
- Engage in significant and meaningful learning opportunities adapted to the children's personal cultures and bridge collaboratively to the society at large within the context of an ethical vision of society.

High Level of Expertise and Skill

A professional is capable of expert practice that is based on rigorous and protracted preparation. Professional preparation takes place in coherent programs that equip the participants to make professional judgments and adjustments. Professional practice "rests upon some branch of knowledge to which professionals are privy by virtue of long study and by initiation and apprenticeship under masters [who are] already members of the profession" (Ritz & Myers, 1992, cited in Wise & Liebbrand, 1993, p. 135). Art Wise (1989), representing the National Council for the Accreditation of Teacher Education (NCATE), contends that teacher education for professionals should occur in accredited college-level educational programs that include initiation and apprenticeship, leading in turn to licensing and to advanced accreditation.

Some states have increased the regulations and duration of a preservice teacher program while others have limited such baccalaureate preparation outside of the liberal arts to as little as 18 semester hours, as in Texas. A full-time student in such a program is expected to become transformed from a citizen into a teacher, sometimes within a year. Such a transformation is cataclysmic. It is more usual than not that this person may not have any postgraduate contact with university personnel. This is distinctly different from other professions. We know, for example, that medical preparation requires internships and residencies after 4 years of graduate education and that legal preparation requires ongoing staff-development activities after three years of graduate education.

Early childhood teachers with a baccalaureate preparation, whether in the public or the private sector, often find that their principal or director has less background in early childhood than they. Although some states require a master's degree for permanent certification, it need not be in the field of early childhood education. State certification standards for school administrators do not mention preparation in early childhood education, despite a supportive publication of the National Association of Elementary School Principals (1990). It would be difficult to warrant, therefore, that ongoing induction into the field of early childhood was taking place on-the-job.

Within the context of the early childhood field, when "professionalism" defines longer periods of costly preparation, it may disadvantage the already employed, low-income, often minority group child care personnel, most of whom are women. A parallel industry of community-based organizations has grown up to serve this population in the form of isolated workshops and conferences that fulfill fragmented social service or health agency regulations for clock-hour staff-development contacts. Another parallel exists in the Head Start and Child Development Associate (CDA) staff-development offerings, some of which are coordinated within their separate tracks. Very few of these alternative staff-development activities translate into college-level credits leading to state teacher certification. A speaker with 30 years' experience in Head Start commented that if the funds infused into alternative Head Start personnel development workshops had been translated into college teacher education scholarships, the funds might have been returned to Head Start children in the form of a reduced attrition rate for personnel, along with the increased credentialing of the personnel (Waxler, 1993). Regarding these expenditures and practices, there is a need to ask, "Who is served?" Our best answers need to focus on ethical services to young children and their families.

Mastery of Specialized Knowledge and Skills

A third characteristic—a specialized, professional-level body of knowlege, skills, attitudes, and dispositions—is based on a coherent theory that accounts for the need of professionals in early childhood education to know what to do, how to do it, and why they have selected particular strategies and tactics from among the available range of alternatives. Thus, professional practice moves beyond merely replicating personal experience and personal opinions. Beyond knowledge alone, the professional possesses wisdom (Whitehead, 1929), the capacity to *consciously* use knowledge.

To understand worthwhile meanings takes some time for reflection, some acquaintance with various ways of knowing, some sense of how to critically question generally accepted approaches and questions, and the flexibility—which grows through acquaintance with multiple models and systems—that is so essential if one is to thoughtfully appreciate the complexity of human interaction. Then, and only then, is it possible to integrate expertise with the complexities of curriculum design and development rather than to merely consume a teacher's manual that is based on static and fragmented bits of trivial information. Some examples may clarify these contentions.

The various national proposals and standards for preparing entry-level early childhood personnel, for example, pay an enormous amount of attention to safety and health in comparison with the percentage focused on decision making and issues of meaningful curriculum design and environmental design in the service of significant meanings (Council for Early Childhood, 1993; National Association for the Education of Young Children, 1994). The contrast is apparent in the following anecdote:

A young child has taken a chair to the window and is standing on it.

Novice Adult (Assistant, rushes over): Get down. You could hurt yourself.

This adult assesses the physically obvious.

Educationally Oriented Adult (moves quickly beside the child): What are you seeing outside?

This adult assesses the child's focus, values her curiosity and independence, encourages descriptive language and imagery-building, while remaining close enough to provide safety from falling. In effect, the context (background) provides a basis for new text (meanings), rather than becoming the focus and closure. (Personal Communication, B. Nilsen, 1994).

This anecdote parallels the development of aides or beginning student teachers who focus first on how effective they will be in practice by asking, "What can I do?" rather than on the educated and experienced student teacher's focus on "What can the child do? What will be the child's experience/learning in this situation?"

The professional also can move beyond a novice's orientation on skills (in the technical sense of how *I* can make/help children learn) to a professional focus on the learners' experiences (in the expert sense of how *children* can engage in experiences from which they might make new connections that are based on meanings that they can perceive and integrate).

Autonomy in Practice

Autonomy is a fourth characteristic of professionalism. A professional engages in autonomous practices within a profession that maintains the autonomy to set standards for, control entry into, and monitor retention within, the field. In effect, a profession regulates itself through credentials, examinations and other standards, and membership in professional organizations.

There has not been a single professional voice, however, that has loudly countered the acceptance of regulations that are noxious to the learning and general development of young children. In the absence of a true profession, amateurish thinking throttles the practice of quality early childhood education. The medical profession, by way of contrast, offers a more autonomous model. A few physicians who are accorded professional status, for example, do occasionally transgress and are abusive to their patients. Such individuals may be relieved of their license to practice, but the entire profession does not stop ministering to the health needs of their clientele. Part of the tacit understanding that the public does not tamper with medical practice lies in the acceptance that traditionally mainly male physicians have received rigorous preparation and can be trusted to know what they are doing because they are skilled in their work. Exceptions to this particular myth are regarded as aberrations. In contrast, disregard for the qualifications of a mainly female work force in early childhood, coupled with the myth of relatively uncontrollable male sexuality, has nourished the practice of imposing external controls on all early childhood personnel (see Tobin, 1995).

Commensurate Compensation

Early childhood educators are underpaid, particularly those employed outside the public schools. Public school prekindergarten and kindergarten teachers tend to be compensated at the same rate as other teachers with similar credentials that include at least a baccalaureate degree. In nonpublic settings, however, early childhood program directors, with or without a baccalaureate degree, often earn less than the base salary of a new public school teacher. It is not uncommon to find early childhood personnel, often with a high school diploma and sometimes with a 2- or 4-year college degree, employed at or close to the minimum national wage level. The "group caretaker" image has been compensated at so low a rate that a personnel turnover rate between 26% and 41% (compared with a 5.6% public school turnover rate) is typical (Whitebook, Phillips, & Howes, 1993). A great measure of the tension involved in the transformation of early childhood education from a cottage industry to a profession, albeit in the interest of public service, therefore, centers on the economics of the work.

Parents' and policymakers' concern for quality confronts the economic problem of scarce resources in families and the competition for budgetary resources in government. Quality, affordability, and professional compensation often are antagonistic rather than integrated conditions. In a climate of competing resources, early childhood education historically has been cut or, in recent times, merely been maintained rather than improved. The exploitation of uncertified personnel who are low-income, often minority group women, in effect, has been subsidizing child care services in the United States.

Professional Organization

A strong professional organization has the potential to influence autonomous practice. Admission to professional organizations or unions usually is based on professional qualifications. Membership in the American Association of University Professors or the United Federation of Teachers, for example, is open to those who have the required credentials. The democratic scope of the National Association for the Education of Young Children, which includes anyone who works within (or takes an interest in) the broadly defined fields of young children, whether professionally prepared or not, stands in contrast to this practice. The National Association of Early Childhood Teacher Educators exists to further early childhood teacher education and admits to membership all those who are concerned with early childhood teacher education. This descriptive observation of current practice does not mean to imply advocacy for the notion that NAEYC or NAECTE should limit their membership only to persons who hold particular credentials but to highlight the fragmented status of advocacy forums.

Against this backdrop, the leadership of NAEYC in recent years has attempted to develop a career ladder, as well as to participate with NCATE in teacher program accreditation through colleges and universities. NAEYC also has become involved with the National Board for Professional Teaching Standards, which will assess teachers' actual performance as well as their conceptual and technical knowledge. NAEYC and NAECTE have developed position papers advocating the development in each state of a self-standing early childhood teacher certification that includes a minimum of a baccalaureate degree. NAECTE, together with the National Association of Early Childhood Specialists in State Education Departments, advocates that all school building administrators should have had specialized preparation in early childhood curriculum and related supervision. These initiatives begin to point the field in the direction of professionalism. National movements, however, have not yet affected the diversity of teacher certification present across different states.

The National Council for Accreditation of Teacher Education is an attempt to have the general teacher education field regulate itself in a professional manner. NAEYC is the recognized early childhood affiliate organization. Although it appears that all NAECTE members are NAEYC members, NAEYC often appears to be engaged in a balancing act while being tugged by numerous special-interest groups, some of which can prosper only if there is a limited expectation for higher education in preparing early childhood personnel. The status of NAEYC and the fledgling nature of NAECTE undercut the concept, then, of a professional organization that monitors the entry of expertly prepared members into the field.

The next sections consider a few historical and philosophical traditions of the field that have brought us to the present status of the early childhood field, followed by a consideration of the early childhood professional knowledge base and other contemporary issues, closing with a look at possible implications for early childhood teacher education.

HISTORICAL AND PHILOSOPHICAL TRADITIONS OF THE FIELD

When Shirley Morgenthaler's mother finished her first year of college in 1935 and returned to her farm community in the Middle West, she was asked to teach because she was the most educated person in her community (S. Morgenthaler, personal communication, November 1993). If we are to apply this criterion, let us consider what it means to be the most educated person in today's community in light of today's understandings.

The United States moved away from a primarily agrarian to an industrial, and then an informational/communications/services kind of society. The idea of the community offering schooling to its children was rooted in the 17th-century community goal that children needed to learn enough to be able to read the Bible. Schools today continue to remain centered on the isolated, technical teaching of the "basic" three Rs. Motives for changing from this narrow definition of schooling to the development of critical thinkers, connection makers, and responsible employees have grown more recently out of the business community.

In some communities, various forms of literacy qualify one to teach. Historically, and in agricultural societies even today, an apprenticeship system qualified one to teach. Usually, the apprentice would not be expected to learn more than the master but to conserve and replicate the master's practices. It was a finite, skills-based approach to education.

There has been a historical trend, however, for elementary school teachers to function with increasingly more education than one year beyond their students. The requirements developed from completion of a program in a "normal" school/technical teachers' college (still prevalent in England, Australia, and New Zealand), to undergraduate degrees, and finally today to undergraduate degrees plus master's degrees. The following information (Wise, 1989) suggests this trend in the United States:

1935	10% of elementary teachers held the B.A.
1946	15 states required teachers to complete the B.A.
1956	35 states required teachers to complete the B.A.
1955	70% of all elementary teachers had the B.A.
	97% of all high school teachers had the B.A.

All states now require public school teachers to hold a baccalaureate, although "emergency" and "alternate" entries exist for those who have fewer qualifications, often in urban settings. Other professions typically do not accept emergency licenses, although practitioners who are not fully prepared professionals might temporarily "fill in" during an emergency situation.

In general, the historical increase of qualifications for public school teachers has had little impact on nonpublic early childhood personnel. Another consideration is that the historical association of child care with social services to young children and to low-income families compounds the image that "professionals tend to take on the status of their clients" (Howe, 1980, p. 180). Along with the elderly, the very young and low-income populations often are tacitly devalued as inept.

THE ISSUE OF DEFINING KNOWLEDGE BASES

Knowledge in early childhood education and early childhood teacher education is continuously changing. Although the research database in early childhood teacher education is smaller than that for the field of teacher education in general, there are related and parallel findings to consider.

In order to understand the field, it is necessary to consider what understandings we have in common about "knowledge base" as it relates to early childhood education and early childhood teacher education. Awareness of the knowledge base answers this question: What are the assumptions about the image of an effective professional teacher—held in common within an institution—which influence preservice work, preparation and placement for student teaching, and initial supervision and mentoring, as well as transform teaching practice. The early childhood field must disseminate a knowledge base perspective from which professionals can generate multiple coherent models. A shared knowledge base can help unify a teacher education program and professional development in a spiraling fashion.

Knowledge bases should be organically grown rather than artificially cross-bred by state or national regulations. Knowledge bases in this sense reflect the collaborative development by a local community of professionals through ongoing dialogue that is enriched by their infusion of insights. Deliberations concerning shared knowledge bases consider such issues as what is worth knowing, why it is worth knowing, who is served by particular approaches, who is not served, and what teaching and learning alternatives make sense within the shared framework.

A knowledge base for early childhood education is not a "core" body of knowledge that is conceived as a division of competencies set into separate boxes, suitable for deposit as additive informational modules.

Knowledge bases that are interpreted in such static, linear, atomistic terms might relate mainly to technical activity.

The contemporary history of early childhood knowledge bases has evolved from a mixed Freudian-determinism, biological-Gesellian, occasionally Erikson/Isaacs-sort, sometimes Piagetian outlook, with a nod to Dewey. Despite these shifting roots, the pervasive presence of eclectic and behaviorist strategies, such as stars and other extrinsic rewards, continues. These traditions fall mainly within the scope of child development approaches to practice. Thoughtful issues about curriculum take a second place to an isolated study of child development, the study of individual children for the most part. Little attention has been accorded the sociocultural contexts and personal family cultures from which children come to school and which serve as the sources of children's knowledge base.

Teachers today should expect to deal with the realities of predictable unpredictability, which describes the nature of each early childhood group setting that takes an ethical stance in relation to children. Professional teachers, of course, prepare ideas and materials for flexible use with the children based on their assessment/professional judgment of what will have meaning to the children. To work from this perspective, teachers need preparation and encouragement in risk-taking, being comfortable with ambiguity, and connection-making. It makes sense to support such highly skilled and caring early childhood teachers who can provide multiple forms of representation, extended blocks of time, and a reasonable variety of choices. I suspect that the scarcity of a sufficient number of such professionally prepared early childhood teachers suggests that a massive effort of staff development will be needed.

IMPLICATIONS FOR PROFESSIONALIZING EARLY CHILDHOOD TEACHER EDUCATION

Unique forms of early childhood teacher education, distinct from elementary education, would be reflected in the implementation of four interconnecting dimensions of work.

1. *Linking/Bridging—Emphasizing What to Teach.* The early childhood teacher needs to actively integrate a rich background of knowledge and diverse cultural experiences in order to be able to appreciate and adapt to young children's ways of learning. In one way, this dimension is consistent with Dewey's (1916) notion that the teacher's job is to help learners move toward humanity's fund of knowledge. A contemporary egalitarian definition of "humanity's fund" would include consideration of

varied perspectives such as culture, gender, race, variously abled persons, and other orientations. The ways in which prospective teachers have been taught and the ways in which they have learned also form part of the "fund" that they acquire. In another way, the professional teacher focuses strongly on the conditions by which children build their connections to the shared knowledge of their society and supports their sense of wonder, questions, and shared episodic connections to the perspectives of others.

2. *Alternatives—Emphasizing How to Teach.* The early childhood educator needs to acquire a repertoire of alternative strategies and tactics, paying particular attention to the inclusion of play in the educational program. Other interconnected conditions for learning include inductive experiences, cognitive dissonance, social interaction, physical experiences, revisiting, and a sense of competence (Fromberg, 1995). Environmental design is yet another distinctive feature of early childhood teacher education because, for young children, a decentralized physical setting can help to support the seven conditions for learning.

The preservice teacher should be given sufficient opportunities to practice various strategies within an environment that includes a gradual increase of responsibility. In order to develop the power to select from among alternatives, it is useful for preservice teachers to take responsibility for independent planning and working with children, while receiving coaching support. Within these kinds of supportive relationships, they would engage in a series of experiences with the same small group over time and then with groups of increasing size.

3. *Reflecting—Emphasizing Why to Teach.* Reflecting on work with young children by using audiotape, transcripts, and videotape provides an opportunity for teachers to increase their self-awareness and to rehearse alternative ideas as each one replays events. Such critical self-study makes it possible to focus practice in each subsequent encounter with children, thereby building spontaneity and flexibility along with additional insights for future plans. Self-awareness is essential to the work of an ethical professional. The teacher who works in these ways engages in a form of active, participatory curriculum research that blends practice, theory, and research in a recursive process.

4. *Community and Family Involvement—Emphasizing Who Teaches.* Early childhood education has a distinct commitment to working closely with families and communities as part of children's experiencing a caring community inside and outside of school. Teachers need to learn how to welcome family and community involvement through a variety of forms. Practice in articulating the purposes and practices of early childhood education is essential in order to attempt to guarantee accep-

tance of ethical practices. Advocacy is another way to involve family and community in early childhood work. Sharing information concerning local and state early childhood education initiatives, writing to legislators, and explaining program purposes to family and community members as well as other school people are activities in which preservice teachers might engage. Attending teacher conferences, school board meetings, and professional meetings, along with interviewing community members concerning educational and cultural issues, is another activity that can promote advocacy skills.

ADDITIONAL ISSUES AND FUTURE TRENDS

Economic and political as well as sociocultural forces interact to create the issues of staff composition, development, and regulation that affect early childhood education as a profession in the United States. There is, for example, significant underrepresentation of minority group teachers and teachers of color in the population among those who receive bachelor's degrees and become teachers. Among 100,000 minority students who received new bachelor's degrees in 1989, fewer than 10% were in education (Haberman, 1989). The challenge for early childhood education is to increase the number of minority group teachers and teachers of color who hold bachelor's degrees as well as 2-year college degrees. Roughly half of minority students in postsecondary education institutions attend 2-year colleges; about 15% of enrollment in postsecondary schools is minority.

Within the various career-ladder initiatives, therefore, there is a need to engage in a coevolution of 2-year and 4-year college programs based on the collaborative development of knowledge bases shared in common between 2- and 4-year institutions that are located within the same region. At the same time, there is a need to advocate quality 4-year early childhood programs into which recipients of 2-year college early childhood degree programs can transfer. Such collaboration can provide the coherence necessary for quality teacher preparation programs to expand. This informed collaboration is at the heart of the current debate within the field of early childhood education.

In turn, any community-based organizations that offer staff development to early childhood personnel would be doing them a great service by informing them of local 2- and 4-year college programs that they might pursue and working collaboratively with 2-year colleges to create relevant early childhood staff development learnings that can be assured of recognition by, and transfer into, the institution of higher education because they are built on collaboratively developed and shared knowledge bases. To continue to use the time, money, and efforts of early childhood personnel without the prospect of a real career ladder is unethical, self-serving, and exploitive of a significant number of women, minorities, and people of color.

There is also a need to redistribute existing staff-development funds, as well as new funds, in order to provide scholarships and other kinds of support systems for minorities and people of color who are working with young children. One kind of support for such underrepresented persons would be job-sharing, which might provide an additional opportunity to schedule college-level study while employed; colleges might also accommodate course schedules to the typically longer day of child care personnel. There has been a suggestion that funding sources should provide scholarships for minorities who will teach, much as colleges have provided for athletes (Haberman, 1989). All of these considerations are valuable, particularly in light of a significant body of research that supports the notion that qualified minority teachers can improve the quality of education for minority children through modeling and sensitivity to cultural nuances and learning needs (King, 1993). This research is relevant in light of population shifts that produce increasing numbers of young children from minority groups, children of color, and children for whom English is a second language.

Along with these kinds of accommodations, it behooves all states and the federal government to consider early childhood education as a unified function. At present, there are separate and often parallel, nonintegrated regulations concerning standards for early childhood personnel, administered by a variety of state and federal agencies such as departments of social services or health or agriculture or education. A profession would be better served by a single agency for children within each state that deals respectfully with a single association that represents the profession.

If. This chapter began by considering the paradox of professionalism in early childhood education, and it closes with concern that this paradox continues. The state of the field would be very much improved if each state had a self-standing early childhood teacher certificate for initial entry into the field; if each college of education were to qualify for NCATE accreditation; and if each state were in a full partnership arrangement with NCATE. If each policymaker were to imagine the need for each teacher to be good enough for his or her children, grandchildren/future grandchildren, nieces, nephews, and neighbors, perhaps there might be some movement toward a professional ideal.

But. In reality, it is likely that early childhood educators will have to engage in significant advocacy initiatives in order to move toward such an ideal. The reality of affordability may mean that early childhood personnel will need to negotiate differentiated staffing rubrics, based on dynamic knowledge bases that include coherent opportunities for a career ladder. Another reality is that the issues of autonomy versus external regulation of a public service profession; opportunities to assure a high quality of distinct, expert preparation versus a history of voluntarism and commonsense perspectives; and ethical, disinterested fairness versus commensurate compensation will have to reveal over time—with evolving awareness—what sort of self-organizing system we might expect for early childhood education as a profession. On the way, influenced by sensitive dependence on initial conditions, there will be plenty of phase transitions, bifurcations, and very strange attractors in the form of political waves.

REFERENCES

Bredekamp, S. (1995). Early childhood education. In J. Sikula, T. J. Buttery, & E. Guyton (Eds.), *Handbook of research on teacher education,* (pp. 323–347). New York: Macmillan/Assoc. of Teacher Educators.

Council for Early Childhood. (1993). *Child Development Associate credential.* Washington, DC: Author.

Dewey, J. (1916). *Democracy and education.* New York: Macmillan.

Feeney, S., & Kipnis, K. (1990). *Code of ethical conduct and statement of commitment.* Washington, DC: National Association for the Education of Young Children.

Fromberg, D. P. (1995). *The full-day kindergarten: Planning and practicing a dynamic themes curriculum* (2nd ed.). New York: Teachers College Press.

Haberman, M. (1989). More minority teachers. *Phi Delta Kappan, 70*(10), 771–776.

Hofstadter, D. R. (1985). *Metamagical themas.* New York: Basic Books.

Howe, E. (1980). Public professions and the private model of professional professionalism. *Social Work, 25*(3), 179–191.

Katz, L. G. (1987). The nature of professions: Where is early childhood education? In L. G. Katz & K. Steiner (Eds.), *Current topics in early childhood education* (Vol. 7, pp. 1–16). Norwood, NJ: Ablex.

King, S. H. (1993). The limited presence of African-American teachers. *Review of Educational Research, 63*(2), 115–149.

National Association for the Education of Young Children. (1994).

NAEYC position statement: A conceptual framework for early childhood professional development. *Young Children, 49* (3), 68–77.

National Association of Early Childhood Teacher Educators & National Association of Early Childhood Specialists in State Education Departments. (1993). *Early childhood teacher certification: Executive Summary.* New York: Author.

National Association of Elementary School Principals. (1990). *Early childhood education and the elementary school principal.* Alexandria, VA: Author.

Tobin, J. (1995). Post-structural research in early childhood education. In A. Hatch (Ed.), *Qualitative research in early childhood education* (pp. 223–243). Westport, CT: Praeger.

Waxler, T. (1993, June). *Head Start staff development.* Presentation at the NAEYC National Professional Development Institute. Minneapolis, MN.

Whitebook, M., Phillips, D., & Howes, C. (1993). *Four years in the life of center-based child care in America.* Report of the National Child Care Staffing Study Revisited. Oakland, CA: Child Care Employee Project.

Whitehead, A. N. (1929). *The aims of education.* New York: Mentor.

Wise, A. (1989). Graduate teacher education and teacher professionalism. In A. E. Woolfolk (Ed.), *Research perspectives on the graduate preparation of teachers* (pp. 169–178). Englewood Cliffs, NJ: Prentice-Hall.

Wise, A., & Liebbrand, J. (1993). Accreditation and the creation of a profession of teaching. *Phi Delta Kappan, 75*(2), 133–136, 154–157.

In the film *Listening to Children,* psychiatrist and author Robert Coles describes how a chance occurrence inaugurated more than 30 years of research. While on his way to a professional conference in New Orleans, Coles came upon an angry mob that was protesting the desegregation of public schools. The first African-American child to set foot in an all-white school was a diminutive 6-year-old named Ruby Bridges. She emerged from a car, accompanied by two burly marshals, and walked to the school, a scene that has been commemorated in a Norman Rockwell painting of a black girl in a white dress walking past a tomato-stained wall. Coles was inspired to complete a case study of Ruby Bridges, and, at the end of the film, remarks that she has been one of his greatest teachers. He also comments that "in a better America" everyone would know the Ruby Bridges story and honor her.

It is fitting to end this book about early childhood with this story of a young child, partly so that more educators will take this story to heart and partly as a reminder that not only do adults exert a powerful influence on children, but children also have a profound effect on adults. It is also fitting to conclude this book with the Ruby Bridges story because trends, issues, challenges, controversies, and insights are encapsulated in this single, symbolic event that shaped the future of American public education.

As set forth in the introduction, our original goal in writing *Major Trends and Issues in Early Childhood Education: Challenges, Controversies, and Insights* was to give readers the advantage of multiple perspectives on where the early childhood field has been, where it appears to be headed, and why. In this field, early childhood educators have achieved a level of consensus about what young children need in order to thrive. The task before society is to move beyond the democratic ideal of optimizing every child's potential and make it a reality. Ongoing debate about how to attain this worthy goal stems not so much from discrepancies in early childhood educators' collective vision for children but rather from the moral, social, pedagogical, and political challenge of communicating those ideals to various publics, marshaling the necessary resources, and altering society so that children are truly put first.

Returning to the metaphor of the lens that provided a framework for this book, we hope that the multiple perspectives represented here are comparable with yet another sort of lens. If you visit national parks around the

United States you will often come upon a scenic overlook selected so that visitors can "take it all in." Frequently that site will be equipped with a set of powerful lenses mounted in a large metal stand that pivots, swivels, and adjusts the focus to each person's vision, enabling the user to scan the landscape, detect what would be impossible to see with an unaided eye, and focus on significant details. When this looking is combined with what visitors knew or read recently about the site as well as information supplied by tour guides, on a recorded message, or from fellow travelers, the sightseers see more than scenery. They have, to borrow a phrase from Elliot Eisner (1991), an "enlightened eye," one that simultaneously sees things clearly and delves beneath the surface.

The editors and authors of *Major Trends and Issues in Early Childhood* have worked to make the field of early childhood more accessible to our readers just as that special lens supports the goals of sightseers. It will take an enlightened view of early childhood education to do the right things for young children. As professionals in a field dedicated to the care and education of the very young, we need to stand together, join with families, and collaborate with professionals in other fields to improve the quality of life for every young child.

REFERENCES

Eisner, E. W. (1991). *The enlightened eye.* New York: Macmillan.
Squires, B. (Producer/Director). (1995). *Listening to children: A moral journey with Robert Coles.* [Video tape]. (Available from Customer Support Center/PBS Video, 1320 Braddock Place, Alexandria, VA 22314-1698)

About the Editors and Contributors

Joan P. Isenberg is Professor of Education and Coordinator of Early Childhood Programs at George Mason University in Fairfax, Virginia, where, in 1990, she received a distinguished faculty award for teaching excellence. She has taught young children and held administrative positions in both public and private school settings. Among her most recent publications are two co-authored books, *Creative Expression and Play in Early Childhood* (2nd ed.) (Merrill/Prentice-Hall) and *Teachers' Stories: From Personal Narrative to Professional Insight* (Jossey-Bass). She serves on the NCATE Board of Examiners, is President of the National Association of Early Childhood Teacher Educators, and holds leadership roles in the Association for Childhood Education International. Her research interests are in teacher development, teacher narrative, children's self-expression, and early childhood curriculum.

Mary Renck Jalongo is Professor of Education and a graduate coordinator at Indiana University of Pennsylvania, the editor of *Early Childhood Education Journal,* and author or co-author of eight books. She has received four national awards for excellence in writing and was named her university's distinguished professor in 1991–1992. Her major areas of interest include the fine arts and the language arts in early childhood. Current projects are serving as editorial advisor for *Learning Communities Narratives,* a publication sponsored by the Rockefeller Foundation, and publishing three textbooks with Merrill/Prentice-Hall and Allyn & Bacon.

Doris Bergen is Professor and Chair of the Department of Educational Psychology at Miami University in Oxford, Ohio. She has been an early childhood educator in inclusive classrooms at preschool, primary, and university levels. Her research is primarily in the areas of play, social, and humor development of young children, but she has also studied cross-cultural early childhood practices and beliefs, and effects of adult facilitation on play of children with developmental delays. Her writing is also in these areas, with her most recent book being on transdisciplinary approaches to the assessment of infants and toddlers who are at-risk for developmental delay.

David L. Brown is an Associate Professor of Early Childhood Education at East Texas State University in Commerce. He has been a teacher in the Dallas Independent School District and serves on numerous editorial boards. Currently, he serves as the Principal Investigator of the Texas Head Start/Public School Transition Project.

Lisbeth Brown is a Professor of Education at Clarion University of Pennsylvania. With a background of teaching in both elementary and early childhood settings, she teaches undergraduate and graduate courses in early childhood education and instructional strategies. Her research focuses on parental involvement and communication styles. In addition, she has published numerous articles on parent-teacher conferencing and parental involvement.

Nancy Briggs is a Professor of Education at Edinboro University of Pennsylvania. She has taught in New Jersey, Pennsylvania, and Guam and has served as a Certified Family Life Educator in the family services field, designed and operated an infant-toddler-preschool program, and developed a competency-based associate early childhood degree program at Villa Maria College. Her research focuses on emergent and family literacy and parental involvement. She has also established the "Reading Partners" program for children and their families.

Weiwei Cai is a faculty member at West Chester University of Pennsylvania where she teaches methods courses in elementary and early childhood education. Inclusion and multicultural education are two of her areas of interest.

Marilyn Chipman is Professor of Education at Metropolitan State College of Denver and Area Coordinator of the Early Childhood Licensure Program. A recognized consultant in multicultural education, she conducts seminars for urban and rural educators at local, state, national, and international levels. Her research has addressed the impact of the educational experience on students of color from preschool through graduate school. She has taught in public and private schools, has been a nominee for the Teacher of the Year, and serves on many advisory boards and in community endeavors. Dr. Chipman holds the Ph.D. in Education from the University of Denver. She is the the co-author of the college textbook, *Educating Young Children in a Diverse Society* (Allyn & Bacon).

Bernadette C. Davis has been involved in the education of young children for 10 years. She is currently the master teacher for the Technology in Early Childhood (TECH) Project of the University of Delaware.

Doris Pronin Fromberg is Professor and Chairperson of the Department of Curriculum and Teaching at Hofstra University, where she also serves as Director of Early Childhood Teacher Education. She is past president of the National Association of Early Childhood Teacher Educators and is an advocate of high-quality early childhood teacher and administrator education. She has been a teacher and administrator in public and private schools as well as a field-based curriculum and administration consultant to school districts. She also has served as a Teacher Corps director. Her special interests are early childhood curriculum, teacher education, school climate, and classroom organization. Among her publications are *The Full-day Kindergarten: Planning and Practicing a Dynamic Themes Curriculum* (2nd ed.) (Teachers College Press); *The Encyclopedia of Early Childhood Education,* co-edited with Leslie Williams (Garland); and *The Successful Classroom: Management Strategies for Regular Elementary and Special Education Teachers,* with Mary Ann Driscoll (Teachers College Press). She currently is working on a book, *Play from Birth to Twelve: Contexts, Perspectives, and Meanings,* co-edited with Doris Bergen (Garland).

Stacie G. Goffin is a senior program officer at the Ewing Marion Kauffman Foundation. Formerly a faculty member at the University of Missouri–Kansas City, she has written widely in the areas of early childhood advocacy, early childhood education, and early childhood teacher education. A member of numerous national advisory boards, she is actively involved as a change agent in her own community.

Jennifer Hill is an interdisciplinary doctoral student at the University of Missouri–Kansas City, majoring in education, history, and public administration. Currently working at the Kauffman Foundation in the Youth Development Division, she has worked in youth-related advocacy and service programs. Her specific interests are African-American women and children.

James L. Hoot is Director of the Early Childhood Research Center and Coordinator of the Graduate Program in Early Childhood at the State University of New York at Buffalo. He is editor/senior editor of two volumes dealing with computers and young children, editor/senior editor of three theme issues of *Childhood Education,* associate editor of the *Journal of*

Early Childhood Teacher Education, and president-elect of the Association for Childhood Education International. His primary research interest involves early childhood education in our global community.

Stuart McAninch is Associate Professor in the Division of Urban Leadership and Policy Studies in Education at the University of Missouri–Kansas City. He is currently doing research on issues in teaching the Cold War in American high schools and on school desegregation litigation in Kansas City, Missouri.

Patricia Monighan-Nourot whose teaching experience spans preschool child care and the primary grades, is Professor of Education and Coordinator of Early Childhood Education and Graduate Studies in Education at Sonoma State University, Rohnert Park, California. She is co-author of *Looking at Children's Play: A Bridge Between Theory and Practice.*

Sunhee Park is Assistant Professor of Early Childhood Education at Korea National Open University in Seoul, Korea. In addition to her interest in comparative education, she is currently studying the impact of educational computer software on children's thinking processes.

Jyotsna Pattnaik is a faculty member at Central Missouri State University. She has teaching experience in public schools, colleges, and universities in India. In 1990, she received the Junior Research Fellow award in education from the University Grant Commission of India. In India, she was involved in Child-to-Child, a national project to meet the needs of children at-risk, and in designing audiovisual enrichment programs for children. Her specific interests are multicultural education, children's responses to literature, and Indian dance and art activities.

Shirley C. Raines is Dean of the College of Education and Professor of Curriculum and Instruction at the University of Kentucky. She is editor of *Whole Language Across the Curriculum: Grades 1, 2, 3* and with Robert J. Canady is author of *The Whole Language Kindergarten,* both from Teachers College Press. With Rebecca Isbell, she has written *Stories: Children's Literature in Early Education* (Delmar). She is also the author of the *Story S-t-r-e-t-c-h-e-r-s* Series of teacher resource books from Gryphon House. Shirley is a former executive board member of the Association for Childhood Education International and is active in the National Association for the Education of Young Children and various teacher educator professional associations. Her research interests are in developing teaching cases from professional development schools and young children's literature interests.

Daniel D. Shade is the Director of the Technology in Early Childhood (TECH) Program in the Department of Individual and Family Studies at the University of Delaware. He began studying about young children and computers in 1983 with J. Allen Watson at the University of North Carolina. At Southeast Missouri State University, he co-founded the "Kids Interacting with Developmental Software" project with Susan Haugland. He has published numerous articles on technology and young children, and was editor of the *Journal of Computing in Childhood Education*. His most important contributions have been in the areas of developing a theoretical foundation for the use of computers with young children and the application of developmentally appropriate practice to young children's software evaluation

Catherine Wilson has been a teacher at Chapel Hill Early Childhood Center and is a lecturer at Park College and the University of Missouri–Kansas City where she is also a doctoral student. She is a children's librarian at the Kansas City, Missouri, Public Library.

Sue C. Wortham is Professor of Early Childhood and Elementary Education at the University of Texas at San Antonio. She has published two textbooks and numerous articles on the topic of assessment of young children. She served as Fulbright Scholar to Chile in 1992 and is currently president of the Association for Childhood Education International.

Index

213